SCANDALS, SECRETS, AND
SWAN SONGS

T0350609

Also by Boze Hadleigh

Inside the Hollywood Closet
Marilyn—Lost Images
Hollywood Lesbians: From Garbo to Foster
Elvis Through the Ages
Hollywood Gays
Elizabeth Taylor: Tribute to a Legend
An Actor Succeeds
Marilyn Forever

SCANDALS, SECRETS, and
SWAN SONGS

HOW HOLLYWOOD STARS LIVED, WORKED, AND DIED

BOZE HADLEIGH

LYONS
PRESS

Guilford, Connecticut

An imprint of The Rowman & Littlefield Publishing Group, Inc.
4501 Forbes Blvd., Ste. 200
Lanham, MD 20706
www.rowman.com

Distributed by NATIONAL BOOK NETWORK

Copyright © 2021 Boze Hadleigh
All photos courtesy of Photofest

All rights reserved. No part of this book may be reproduced in any form or by any electronic or mechanical means, including information storage and retrieval systems, without written permission from the publisher, except by a reviewer who may quote passages in a review.

British Library Cataloguing in Publication Information available

Library of Congress Cataloging-in-Publication Data

Names: Hadleigh, Boze, author.
Title: Scandals, secrets, and swan songs : how Hollywood stars lived,
  worked, and died / Boze Hadleigh.
Description: Guilford, Connecticut : Lyons Press, 2021. | Summary: "A
  close-up, no-holds-barred look at 101 stars-at their surprising, often
  shocking, sometimes sordid, but always entertaining real selves and
  lives"— Provided by publisher.
Identifiers: LCCN 2021014920 (print) | LCCN 2021014921 (ebook) | ISBN
  9781493060535 (paperback) | ISBN 9781493063444 (epub)
Subjects: LCSH: Motion picture actors and actresses—United
  States—Biography. | Motion picture actors and
  actresses—California—Los Angeles—Biography. | Hollywood (Los Angeles,
  Calif.)—Biography.
Classification: LCC PN1998.A2 H157 2021 (print) | LCC PN1998.A2 (ebook) |
  DDC 791.4302/80922 [B]—dc23
LC record available at https://lccn.loc.gov/2021014920
LC ebook record available at https://lccn.loc.gov/2021014921

♾™ The paper used in this publication meets the minimum requirements of American National Standard for Information Sciences—Permanence of Paper for Printed Library Materials, ANSI/ NISO Z39.48-1992.

To Ronald Boze Stockwell
and
the incomparable Shelley Steward

CONTENTS

INTRODUCTION

It's been said that America's screen stars are its version of royalty. They're also a version of the classical Greek pantheon of gods, who were human-imaged but had their foibles, even peccadilloes. Different stars then and now symbolize archetypes like the love goddess, the man of action, the powerful woman, the naughty boy, the ingénue, the comedian, or the cynic.

It's a given that actors make films, but the lives of these movie stars with feet of clay interest us even more. Especially, let's be honest, their mishaps and tragedies. Including early deaths . . . would Marilyn Monroe and James Dean have had the same impact and deathless legacies if they were now senior citizens?

Scandals are a prime aspect of fans' obsession with movie-star lives. Not just what the scandal was—having a child out of contractual marriage or being gay is minimally scandalous today—but how the "scandal" affected the star. "Mexican Spitfire" Lupe Vélez, rather than give birth to a child without a legal father, took her life at thirty-six. Pre–Winona Ryder, when actress-inventor Hedy Lamarr was arrested for shoplifting (a major disgrace at the time), she denied the fact and sued her accusers . . . and did so a second time, decades later. But by then her remarkable beauty had faded, and the media mostly wasn't interested.

Of course stars' secrets were and remain a gossip staple. "Gossip" may be true or untrue. For decades there were rumors that Abbott and Costello couldn't abide each other, that Frances Farmer had been lobotomized, that Jean Harlow's older husband shot himself because he was impotent (a lie devised by Louis B. Mayer) although his first wife shot him (his marriage to MGM's platinum bombshell was bigamous).

Not to mention—and in print one didn't!—the sexual secrets of a surprising percentage of stars, especially gay or bisexual male stars (then and now). Apart from such natural diversity, there were the secret white husbands of Lena Horne and Dorothy Dandridge, the secret mental illness of Vivien Leigh, and the extreme, mostly hidden drug use of stars such as Elvis Presley, John Belushi, and River Phoenix.

Of course there's the inevitable decline in any performer's looks and career. Very few stars end their careers on top. The "swan songs" in this book's title refer to a performer's final movie, which is invariably more revealing than their first one. Stardom, time, ego, and "becoming" one's public image impact the end of one's career. Western icon John Wayne, dying of cancer, played a western icon dying of cancer in his swan song. Mae West, who believed herself an ageless sex symbol, concluded her big-screen career starring opposite a future James Bond fifty-three years her junior.

Most stars don't star in their final movies. By then most are supporting players. Some unique personalities finally play themselves, like Gloria Swanson in one of the *Airport* movies or Ethel Merman in *Airplane!* Actors rarely enjoy a starring swan song that also proves a hit and delivers an Oscar—like Henry Fonda in *On Golden Pond*. Two actors, Peter Finch and Heath Ledger, included here, were the only performers to win posthumous Academy Awards.

Many of the 101 actors featured in these forty-eight chapters endured fateful lives off the screen, whatever their celluloid personae. Had Lon Chaney, an American, not died prematurely of cancer, our image of Dracula would be vastly different, for he, not Bela Lugosi, would have played the vampire. The erosion of her spectacular looks wasn't all Rita Hayworth had to suffer; Alzheimer's was then a little-understood and "shameful" illness, and its being kept secret allowed the media to report and condemn Rita's presumed bouts of "drunkenness."

How Hollywood stars lived, worked, and died is sometimes more dramatic than their films. Had Elizabeth Taylor not insisted on trying to fix up pal Montgomery Clift with a purportedly gay priest, Monty's face wouldn't have been ruined in a near-fatal car accident that launched a downward spiral into drugs and off the box-office charts. Disappointment over Peg Entwistle's initial screen role being shortened (as was the film itself) led to her jumping to her death from the top of the HOLLYWOOD sign. Leslie Howard, who had to hide being Jewish, was secretly working for the British government against the Nazis, who shot down the plane he was flying in, killing the *Gone with the Wind* star and its other passengers.

So it went and so it goes, with scandals, secrets and swan songs plus the mental and physical tribulations that embody the human condition. In the end, perhaps the best measure of any life, stellar or otherwise, is: Was it enjoyed? By oneself, especially, and by others.

Boze Hadleigh
San Francisco
10/10/20

FRED ASTAIRE AND GINGER ROGERS

It was said of movie dance partners Fred Astaire and Ginger Rogers, "She gave him sex and he gave her class." It was later said of Ginger that she did everything Fred did, matching him while dancing backward and in high heels.

Astaire began his career dancing with his sister Adele, starting in vaudeville and later graduating to Broadway. "After Adele retired the act so she could get married, Fred was disconsolate, practically destroyed," said Hermes Pan, the choreographer and longtime friend of **Fred Astaire** (1899–1987). "They were performance stars of the first order." Others added that the attractive Adele was the act's real draw and that Fred was unlikely ever to find another ideal dancing partner for the stage. He didn't.

Rather, the skinny, balding, non-sexy dancer born Fred Austerlitz sought work in motion picture musicals, a popular and uplifting genre during the Great Depression. He could hardly have imagined in a few years he'd be en route—with the help of an expensive toupee and an ambitious, disciplined blonde dancing partner—to movie stardom.

Fred made his celluloid bow in a 1931 musical short, then went nowhere fast. But in 1933 he was hired for *Dancing Lady*, a Joan Crawford musical—she too began as a dancer. Later that year he was paired with the former Virginia McMath (a cousin of future star Rita Hayworth), who'd appeared in myriad throwaway screen parts as a young blonde (twelve years younger than Fred). Their film, *Flying Down to Rio*, was an exuberantly glamorous musical starring Mexican beauty Dolores Del Rio (whose cousin was silent star Ramon Novarro).

The picture was a hit, and audiences and critics singled out the dancing numbers of Fred Astaire and Ginger Rogers. A dancing team was born. There would be eight more Astaire-Rogers musicals through 1939, the rest centering on Fred and Ginger. Again, it was the female half that broke up the act, but not for marital anonymity—for ambition. Rogers's star would continue to rise after she parted with Astaire. Federico Fellini, who directed the Italian film *Ginger e Fred* (*Ginger and Fred*, 1986), over which Rogers unsuccessfully sued, said, "Until her looks went away, she could continue in the big movie roles.

"The other, he was not in the movies for his looks. What he did was artistry, sadly not usually of much commercial value in the movies." British film historian David Quinlan referred to "the innovative dancing star who made the grinding discipline of constant rehearsal come to the screen as pure poetry."

Post-Rogers, Hollywood fashioned romantic musical plots pairing Astaire with a variety of leading ladies, often too young for him (e.g., Rita Hayworth) and later, way too young (e.g., Audrey Hepburn), until finally, in *Finian's Rainbow* (1968) he played the female lead's (Petula Clark) father.

Fred also appeared in non-musical films but few dramas. His light-weight personality didn't lend itself to heavy emoting or villainy. He received a supporting-Oscar nomination for the all-star *The Towering Inferno* (1974) and in old age slipped comfortably into grandfatherly roles. He won an Emmy for a 1979 TV movie titled *A Family Upside Down.*

The ex-hoofer's final performance was in *Ghost Story* (1981), a film equally costarring Melvyn Douglas, Douglas Fairbanks Jr., and John House-man. Debbie Reynolds, who worked with Astaire in *The Pleasure of His Company* (1961) and owned a dance rehearsal studio, recalled, "I'm glad Mr. Astaire went out in a classy production . . . he was a class act. I'm glad it wasn't a token part in some TV movie or something in a third-rate picture, maybe some horror thing. . . . I don't remember if *Ghost Story* came out at Hallow-een, but I saw it, it was kind of spooky and I relished the chance to see three grand old men of the cinema again." (She didn't refer to former producer John Houseman.)

Reynolds added, "Some people become more likeable with age, less cocky. Mr. Astaire was one. . . . He still moved with grace but he'd long since reconciled, without bitterness, to putting his dancing days behind him."

————

The quote about Astaire giving **Ginger Rogers** class implies she (1911–1995) didn't have that much to begin with. Understandable, in terms of her pre-Astaire characters. Not a natural blonde, Virginia McMath was pushed into show business by her fierce mother Lela Rogers. From the chorus line and movie bit parts, she moved into frequently brassy and/or loudmouthed roles. She got noticed in *42nd Street* (1932) and *Gold Diggers of 1933* but didn't gain serious attention until later that year in *Flying Down to Rio*.

Subsequent teamings with Fred Astaire were popular, but Ginger didn't experience a non-dancing hit until *Stage Door* (1937), top-billing Katharine Hepburn as the rich "girl" sparring with Rogers as a resentful working-class "girl." Ginger was eager to prove herself without Fred. Rumors that they didn't get along weren't yet common and there never was a feud, despite later pictures with other actors portraying dancing partners who couldn't stand each other. But she agreed to costar a tenth and final time in *The Barkleys of Broadway* (1949).

Rogers won an Oscar, which Astaire never did, for a dramatic role in *Kitty Foyle* (1940), and reached her apotheosis in *Lady in the Dark* (1944), a film of the Gertrude Lawrence stage hit. In it, Ginger wore one of the most expensive and publicized costumes yet seen on an actress, its capacious, wide-opening bejeweled skirt entirely lined with mink. Postwar, the actress's features were already hardening and the makeup getting thicker. The process accelerated in the 1950s, with movies that were mostly silly (*Monkey Business*), desperate (*Forever Female*), or saw her actually playing a villain, as in *Black Widow* (1954). In the 1970s Elizabeth Taylor stated that unlike actors, actresses often got cast unsympathetically due to advancing years and diminishing looks.

Carol Channing costarred with Rogers in *The First Traveling Saleslady* (1956). "Well, it was so terribly underappreciated that Ginger Rogers and I were virtually responsible for closing down RKO Studios!" (The cartoonish Carol's somewhat intimidated love interest was a young Clint Eastwood.)

Rogers's final '50s picture was *Oh, Men! Oh, Women!* (1957), oh, brother, after which she was off the screen until 1964 in *The Confession*, not deemed worth releasing overseas (it aired on British TV as *Quick! Let's Get Married*). Ginger's swan song found her portraying the mother of 1930s rival and fellow blonde Jean Harlow in *Harlow* (1965), one of two Harlow biopics that year. The more commercial *Harlow*, released to cinemas, starred Carroll Baker, with Angela Lansbury as the controlling Mama Jean. Rogers's *Harlow*, starring Carol Lynley (born Carolyn Lee) as the original "platinum bombshell," aired on television.

Fred Astaire's acclaim grew over the decades, he didn't have to play villains, and he wasn't exiled from film musicals, but Ginger Rogers's star dimmed. Loyal older fans usually sustained her stardom on the stage, including the musical *Hello, Dolly!*, post-Channing. Rogers's most enduring companion was mother Lela (Ginger's five marriages produced no children).

Agnes Moorehead worked with Rogers during their latter years in an unsuccessful stage production which, however, earned excellent notices for the prominent character actress. She informed writer Doug McClelland, "I don't give in to public negativity towards people I have worked with.... Without naming our collaboration or reviving any sordid details, a few already exposed by the press, I will only affirm that it was one of my least pleasant working experiences.

"Miss Rogers felt everybody else in the show was less than secondary. . . . Had she cooperated with those in charge and in the know, our show could have been quite popular. Unhappily, and I would not describe her as a happy person, she preferred to play the star to the bitter end and take the entire ship down with her."

LUCILLE BALL

Lucille wasn't Lucy. TV's most enduring star was a comedic genius, but Lucy Ricardo and her post–*I Love Lucy* TV incarnations were characters played by an underrated actress. Friend Carol Burnett said the first time she saw **Lucille Ball** (1911–1989) she didn't like her, because she was playing a stinker in a dramatic film titled *The Big Street* (1942) and treating Henry Fonda miserably.

Before she burst onto television in 1951, where she has seemingly remained ever since, Ball had an extensive movie career that dated back to 1933. The Jamestown, New York, native had tried modeling under the name Diane Belmont—advertising hats and cigarettes—and was a Goldwyn Girl with regulation long blonde hair before appearing in a variety of films and genres that included *The Three Musketeers*, Astaire-Rogers musicals, Eddie Cantor comedies, dramas, "women's pictures," film noir, and *Abbott and Costello in Hollywood*.

Just before *I Love Lucy* she'd been reduced to a harem-type role in *The Magic Carpet*. She'd made her mark in comedy, a rare comedienne who happened to be beautiful. But by age forty her big-screen career was virtually over. She'd been doing a radio sitcom titled *My Favorite Husband* that was intended to transfer to television. Instead, Lucille wanted a TV series she could do with her seven-years-younger husband Desi Arnaz so that the bandleader wouldn't have to be on the road so much and she could keep an eye on him (he fooled around, plenty).

The rest is TV history, and in 1954 Lucy and Desi starred in their own big movie hit, the often hilarious *The Long, Long Trailer*. Their next and final vehicle, *Forever Darling* in 1956, was considerably less successful. Lucy then stayed off the big screen until 1960 and 1963, costarring both times with Bob Hope.

After *I Love Lucy* Ball and Arnaz did *The Lucy-Desi Comedy Hour*, then she went solo—that is, minus Ricky but still with sidekick Vivian Vance—in

The Lucy Show, followed by the considerably less amusing *Here's Lucy* (usually costarring her two children). Over the years criticism mounted that as Lucille aged (she'd debuted as Lucy Ricardo at almost forty) she was still enacting an often clueless, childlike character. But lots of people still loved Lucy.

By that time Lucy and Desi had bought RKO, the movie studio that Howard Hughes had acquired and run into the ground. Desilu was a major TV production entity. Most of its shows were hits, and it was Ball who green-lit a then-risky new hour-long sci-fi series titled *Star Trek*. In the 1960s, after her marriage ended (1940–1960) and Lucy was running things on her own, she was the most visible businesswoman in America. She claimed to be uncomfortable in that position.

She'd also starred—despite her non-singing voice—in *Wildcat*, a 1960 Broadway musical, declaring that she didn't feel she'd "truly made it" until she saw her name in lights on Broadway. Ball remarried, to a comedian born Morton Goldapper, renamed Gary Morton, whom she made producer of her shows. They stayed together until her death. (Another Jewish comedian who switched first and last names was Allen Konigsberg, or Woody Allen.)

Those who worked with Lucy learned she took her TV work very seriously and wasn't much inclined toward humor off-camera. She was a tough taskmaster who'd grown used to being boss. Various actors said they disliked working with her, from movie star Danny Kaye to Tom Bosley (*Happy Days*). She cowed comedy great Jack Benny, instructing him on-set how to "be funnier," she reduced guest star Joan Crawford to tears, and clashed with Richard Burton when he and Elizabeth Taylor guested on her show. Johnny Carson called her Lucille Testicle.

After Lucy's back-to-back Bob Hope movies, she did two more pictures during the 1960s: a minor part in *A Guide for the Married Man* (1967) and a comedy with Henry Fonda, a surprise hit titled *Yours, Mine and Ours* (1968) about two middle-aged people who marry despite each having umpteen kids—and one to come(!). That film's success made Lucille Ball a bankable movie star again.

When the decision was made to film the Broadway hit *Mame*, it wasn't assumed that Angela Lansbury, a non–movie star, would reprise the part that took her faltering career to new heights. Even the biggest musical hits typically inherited new stars onscreen, e.g., Rosalind Russell replaced Ethel Merman in *Gypsy*, Marilyn Monroe replaced Carol Channing in *Gentlemen Prefer Blondes*, and Barbra Streisand replaced Channing in *Hello, Dolly!*

There was chagrin over the fact that Lucille Ball's singing would not be dubbed. But the upbeat, kooky personality of Auntie Mame (the pre-musical *Auntie Mame* had starred Rosalind Russell on stage and screen) suited Lucy admirably. Filming got off to a rocky start when Ball disapproved of Madeline Kahn's performance as Agnes Gooch and had her replaced with Jane Connell, the older and less colorful Broadway Gooch. Criticism over the filtered lenses used in many shots of the sixty-plus leading lady was inevitable but became a focus of the needlessly negative movie reviews. Some New York critics were unduly harsh supposedly because they'd strongly favored Lansbury in the role.

The lavish, tuneful, and entertaining *Mame* (1974) was a financial success. Leading man Robert Preston said, "Her singing is better than I thought and she's a knockout in that wardrobe [by Theadora Van Runkle]. Lucy's kept her figure . . . in the big plantation number she kicks higher than chorus girls half her age."

Looking back in 1999, Bea Arthur, who'd also costarred in the Broadway version, said, "The movie got savaged and it devastated Lucy. She didn't deserve that. . . . It was a wonderful vehicle for her to go out on . . . the black-and-white-and-red title number that centered around her is a showstopper by any standard."

In 1985 Lucille Ball returned to dramatic acting in the TV movie *Stone Pillow*, playing a feisty bag lady. The expected Emmy Award nomination didn't materialize. In 1986 she returned to series television as a seventy-five-year-old Lucy incarnation in *Life with Lucy*, costarring her longtime sidekick Gale Gordon. It just didn't work, perhaps less so because of her age than the format (with dull younger costars and extraneous moppets) and poor writing.

Ratings were dismal, and the network pulled the plug after eight episodes, not bothering to air the five remaining completed episodes. Lucille Ball's legendary career was over. In 1989 she appeared as a presenter on the Academy Awards show with Bob Hope and died that same year of a ruptured abdominal aortic aneurysm . . . some said also of boredom, others a broken heart.

GAY ICONS: TALLULAH BANKHEAD, ANTHONY PERKINS, AND DIVINE

What makes a cult figure? Certainly they have to be more than ordinary, must stand out, even be offbeat or unusual. Bizarre is okay too. But it's also about the audience such an individual attracts and the level of devotion they afford her or him. Some superstars have cult followings but because they're major stars they also—like Judy Garland or Barbra Streisand—have mainstream followings.

The following threesome weren't superstars—except to their fans.

———

"Dahling, I forbid you to refer to it like that!" **Tallulah Bankhead** reprimanded a UK reporter interviewing her about her final movie.

The picture, realistically titled *Fanatic* (1964) in Britain but *Die! Die! My Darling* in the United States, had just been referred to as part of the '60s "hag-horror" cycle of shockers starring past-their-prime female stars looking far from their best and best exemplified by *What Ever Happened to Baby Jane?*

Bankhead, eventually known as "the Alabama Foghorn" for her deep, highly imitable voice—although her accent was English, not Southern—had left the United States to extract major success on the London stage in the 1920s. She'd felt somewhat disappointed at not becoming a quick success in her own country. Her grandfather and uncle were US senators and her father a US congressman and later Speaker of the House.

Tallulah's West End stardom and acclaim prompted Hollywood to contract her for a slew of films in the early 1930s with titles like *Tarnished Lady*, *My Sin*, *The Cheat*, and *Faithless*. She was intended to be the new, homegrown Dietrich, a glamorous vamp who lived for love and disdained the consequences. But her vehicles didn't spark at the box office and beginning in 1933 Bankhead would be out of pictures for eleven years.

Bankhead and her fans believed her magic was best practiced on the Broadway stage. A number of her theatrical hits were made into successful movies, but not starring her. For instance her huge hit *The Little Foxes* became another Oscar-nominated role for Bette Davis. When Davis later played a fading, temperamental stage star in *All About Eve*, Bankhead was convinced Davis was caricaturing her.

Tallulah's screen personality had grown with age, as evidenced in Alfred Hitchcock's *Lifeboat* (1943). The notoriously uninhibited bisexual actress—who famously declared, "Daddy warned me about men and alcohol . . . but he never said a thing about women and cocaine!"—created an upset on Hitch's set by refusing to sport underwear. The droll director did nothing about the complaint, explaining that he wouldn't know which department to contact: wardrobe, makeup, or hairdressing.

Bankhead as the sexually adventurous Catherine the Great in director Otto Preminger's poorly scripted *A Royal Scandal* (1945; *Czarina* in Britain) flopped so resoundingly that she didn't get another lead film role, her last, for nineteen years. Before then the flamboyant star's screen opportunities were limited by her reputation for drinking. Jack Warner agreed she might have been ideal in Tennessee Williams's *The Glass Menagerie* (1950). But he'd had enough of alcoholic stars, among them Errol Flynn, and their costly delays. Instead, he hired English actress Gertrude Lawrence to play the former Southern belle.

Tallulah continued on the stage, her glory days behind her. Quality roles for middle-aged actresses were rare and she preferred a starring part in a second-rate play to a better play as a secondary character. The cult figure was usually a box-office draw, with a significant gay following. Even so, she sometimes experienced embarrassing failures like 1963's disastrous *The Milk Train Doesn't Stop Here Anymore* by Tennessee Williams, pairing Bankhead and golden boy Tab Hunter.

Asked if Hunter were gay—he came out much later—Tallulah famously responded, "How should I know, dahling? He never sucked *my* cock." (A disastrous film version of *Milk Train*, retitled *Boom!*, would star a too-young Elizabeth Taylor and a too-old Richard Burton.)

Aware of it or not, Tallulah had long since become camp, a virtual caricature of herself, fun and funny but rarely taken seriously anymore. In the most popular episode of the post–*I Love Lucy* TV series *The Desilu Comedy Hour* Bankhead spoofed herself as "The Celebrity Next Door" (the part was first offered to Bette Davis, who demanded too much money).

By the 1960s camp was "in," including the twice-weekly from-the-comics TV show *Batman*, on which Bankhead was a guest villainess as The Black Widow. Most of her TV appearances were on talk shows, where her wit and outrageousness were eagerly received and often bleeped. There were no movie offers, except finally in England, where her swan song pitted her against Stefanie Powers (TV's *The Girl from U.N.C.L.E.* and later *Hart to Hart*).

Die! Die! My Darling featured a starkly de-glamourized Tallulah, makeup-free in plain black. She played an ultra-orthodox Christian whose late son was engaged to Stefanie (despite little interest in girls), who stops by while in England to say hello to his bereaved mother, who holds her prisoner and demands the young woman cease wearing makeup and the color red. Mrs. Trefoyle plans to dispatch her visitor to the next world, where she can rejoin her "pure" (virginal) son.

The fanatic's secret is she was once a stage actress reveling in the very "sins" she now so vehemently condemns. The future cult film didn't set box offices on either side of the Atlantic on fire. Manhattan friend Douglas Whitney later explained, "It was a sad ending. Miss Bankhead felt she'd done the picture for no good reason. She didn't like how she looked, but if it had made money or gotten her good notices, because she did a fine job portraying somebody so opposite to herself.... Instead, she was dismissed and the picture assailed by critics.

"Also, she suspected the American movie title was meant to make fun of her."

Two years later, the star lent her unique voice to a delightful animated (stop-motion) picture based on Hans Christian Andersen's "The Little Mermaid" called *The Daydreamer* (1966). The starry vocal cast included Boris Karloff, Patty Duke, Burl Ives, and young Hayley Mills as the mermaid, and Tallulah as the Sea Witch. She half-joked, "Stereotyping, dahlings, that's what it is!"

Despite monumental alcohol and drug abuse, Tallulah Bankhead had reached the age of sixty-five when she died in 1968. Comedian Patsy Kelly, who played maids on screen and after hard times became a real-life maid to Tallulah, as well as her sometime stage costar, posthumously announced, "Every time a celebrity dies they always say we'll never see that person's like again. But in Tallulah's case that's the absolute truth."

— ❦ —

"He flirted, and when I flirted back out of courtesy—he was dishy, I admit—he seemed scared. Thereafter we were professionally friendly," recalled Jane

Fonda of **Anthony Perkins**, star of the basketball-themed comedy *Tall Story* (1960), which marked the film debut of Henry Fonda's daughter.

Perkins's father was Osgood Perkins, a character actor whom Tony characterized as "a big Broadway star." The son (1932–1992) was discovered for film by gay director George Cukor, bowing on screen in *The Actress* (1953). During the '50s Tony Perkins was something of a teen pinup, but that would cease with his other 1960 release, the smash hit *Psycho*. From then on, Norman Bates was more or less Perkins's shadow. Toward the end of his career Tony accepted and embraced him, appearing in *Psycho* sequels and directing himself as Norman.

Post-*Psycho*, Perkins moved to Europe for five years. His agent Robert Hussong explained, "He was still a sex symbol there and did some good films. But he didn't make another American film till eight years after *Psycho*." On returning home, the actor was chagrinned to find that Hollywood now preferred to cast him as quirky oddballs or villains. "Word had also gotten out that Tony was into S&M, and that influenced the roles he was offered."

Perkins acted in numerous films he considered unsatisfying but also took to the stage, and in early middle age took a wife, photographer Berry Berenson, sister of actress Marisa Berenson (*Cabaret*). Perkins was homosexual but Berenson's sexuality has been disputed. If gay or bi, she never came out—she also continued to closet Tony after his death (she died in an airplane during the 9/11 terrorist attacks).

Anthony Perkins got considerable publicity via his presumed heterosexuality (his best-known lover had been Tab Hunter). But the new lifestyle neither curtailed his innate sexuality nor changed his image with Hollywood casting directors. For instance, he played tacitly gay Hector McQueen in *Murder on the Orient Express* (1974). Its director, Sidney Lumet, noted, "Tony stuttered when he was very young. It mostly went away but he had a rather hesitant way of speaking that made it seem as if he wasn't necessarily being frank with you.

"With many actors their essence, if you will, becomes more apparent as they grow older and become more themselves."

Perkins had turned down *Some Like It Hot*, afraid to be seen starring in drag in 1959. Ironically, the year before, in *The Matchmaker* (which when musicalized became *Hello, Dolly!*), he did a brief scene with Robert Morse—who eventually came out as bisexual—dancing together in drag to escape their boss's notice. But where Morse looked "cute" in drag, Perkins looked eerie.

"Tony has an alarming quality," said Brian O'Dowd, his dresser and friend. "Now and then he has an expression as if he's been caught at something. It's perfect for what Tony calls the monster roles he gets offered."

Perkins remained married until he died, giving occasional "family values" interviews, but his ongoing promiscuity was well known on both coasts. Actress-writer Jennifer Lee, who'd roomed with Berry, disclosed, "You'd go to parties at their house and Tony would be in the corner with all the gay boys and Berry with all the straight girlfriends, except for the odd bisexual girl. It was strange. They were so gay, which is fine, but it was always weird to think that he was her husband. You were in their house and it was like being in a gay disco."

Perkins had Bell's palsy, a paralysis of the facial nerve frequently caused by the herpes simplex virus, that affected the right side of his mouth. Supposedly he found out he was HIV-positive when he went to a doctor about the palsy and a technician secretly tested him for the AIDS virus, then sold the news to a tabloid.

Tony continued acting for as long as he could. "He's gotten adjusted to roles as villains and also to gay ones," explained O'Dowd. "What's harder to take is when the size of your roles diminishes . . . or nobody wants you." Perkins traveled to Eastern Europe to continue making movies, telling inquiring friends upon his return, "You don't even want to know."

Emaciated and reportedly wearing padded shirts, Anthony Perkins's final roles, in 1992, were in a telefilm and a made-in-Spain feature film. *Naked Target*, a "thriller-comedy," involved a nude New York courier handcuffed to a valuable briefcase that's set to explode, on the run in Madrid where only his Spanish contact has the key, with several figures in pursuit of the briefcase's contents. Tony played a quirky character called El Mecano. In *In the Deep Woods* Rosanna Arquette mourns a murdered friend, the latest victim of a serial killer. Then Paul Miller shows up, offering to find the killer, but he (Perkins) may be a fake detective—possibly the murderer. (Norman, is that you?)

"My parents and I were estranged for what seemed to me, and I hope to them, a real long time," said **Divine** (1945–1988), born Glenn Milstead.

"When your son dresses in women's clothes, even to make a living, I guess that's not unusual. But they were also mortified when my character ate doggie do in *Pink Flamingos*. That was awful but artistically necessary. To believe my character did that, the audience had to see *me* actually *do* it."

Housewife and mother roles weren't what Glenn Milstead, better known as Divine, originally set out to play. But his biggest movie hit, *Hairspray* (1988), cast him as a housewife and mom. Shortly before his death at forty-two, Divine was adding male roles to his repertoire.

Divine was best known for his work with Baltimore filmmaker John Waters, who made him a cult-movie star via *Pink Flamingos* (1972) and other low-budget oddities. Though the actor almost invariably performed in drag, he bristled and bellowed at being called a drag queen and insisted he didn't wear such clothes in everyday life. Divine did relatively few interviews and once warned he had three taboo topics: drag, the doggie-do scene, and his weight.

"I'll bite or eat the finger off the next reporter who asks why I'm fat. People *know* why I'm fat, but the press is so dumb!"

Some costars felt Milstead overate out of loneliness. Tab Hunter contributed, "Food is Divine's love substitute. He told me he's too cranky and heavy to pursue much of a personal life, meaning a romantic one."

Divine's most famous quote was "All my life I wanted to look like Elizabeth Taylor. Now Elizabeth Taylor looks like me."

Charles Pierce, a master impressionist and "male actress," explained that drag artists divide into two categories: those who recreate female icons or those who devise their own female personas. Like Milstead, Pierce—best known for his Bette Davis—essayed some male characters toward the end.

Pierce noted that Divine was unique in not portraying sexy or beautiful or ladylike females. "He prefers to be loud and scary. But then, one pays attention to a 320-pound personality with overly obvious makeup and big hair!"

In 1986 Divine admitted, "If I were a female actress I'd have rejected all those die-of-boredom lady roles with the little white gloves. Hell, I'd have been Bette and Joan and Liz and Stanwyck rolled into one!"

Paul Bartel, who directed Divine and Tab Hunter in the pseudo-western *Lust in the Dust* (1985) said, "Divine wants career longevity . . . and further choices. To get them, he needs to drop the dresses. . . . There's far more male roles anyway." Bartel added ominously, "Longevity also requires a more reasonable weight, not that I'm a beanpole myself."

At forty Divine hinted he might toss the wigs to pass on screen as a fairly ordinary balding, overweight man. After *Hairspray* (1988) became Divine's biggest hit (later remade with John Travolta as the mother), Glenn acknowledged that even so, housewife and mother roles "aren't exactly what I first set out to play." He seriously experimented with a "new male look" after being offered a recurring male role on the TV sitcom *Married with Children*.

Shortly before dying of an enlarged heart, Divine played a male detective in the movie *Out of the Dark*. It was released posthumously, earning him good reviews and praise for his diversity. Said Tab Hunter, "Divine could have pulled off a truly bi-gender career. He could have continued in his original footsteps but alternated with off-the-wall male characters. Either way, he would never be dull!"

DRUGS: JOHN BELUSHI, RIVER PHOENIX, AND CHRIS FARLEY

Drugs and celebrity have never been strangers, but they've never been as closely bound as in recent times. Once upon a time Tallulah Bankhead mock-boasted, "Cocaine is not addictive, dahling—I should know, I've been using it for twenty years." Where she lived to the unripe old age of sixty-five, the following three males died, respectively, at thirty-three, twenty-three, and thirty-three.

John Belushi (1949–1982) was voted "most humorous" of his high school's Class of '67 in Wheaton, Illinois. He later formed an improvisational comedy trio modeled on Chicago's Second City troupe but was already into marijuana and hallucinogens. He avoided the Vietnam War draft by further elevating his blood pressure through eating salt before the physical exam.

In 1971 John joined Second City and was discovering cocaine and the tranquilizer Quaalude. What one critic called his "belligerent humor" got him cast in the off-Broadway musical *National Lampoon's Lemmings* (1973), a Woodstock spoof. "You couldn't help but notice him," said reviewer Dave Gilbert. "He was large and loud and desperate to be funny. He wasn't always . . . sometimes he was unintentionally funny. Sometimes extremely funny."

As a member of the original *Saturday Night Live* team in 1975, Belushi became a household name. His physical style of comedy included characters like the Samurai warrior and a giant killer bee. He also did boldly unflattering imitations of Elizabeth Taylor, Marlon Brando, and other celebs. But his drug use almost got him fired from *SNL* on several occasions.

In 1978 director Jack Nicholson requested John for a small role in his movie *Goin' South*. The two didn't get along, but later that year the comic actor and writer became a movie star playing Bluto in the unexpected sophomoric hit *National Lampoon's Animal House*.

In high school John Belushi was voted "most humorous," and he became an instant comedy star on *Saturday Night Live*. His ensuing movie stardom didn't last, but his drug habit did—and escalated fatally. Had he lived, he'd have costarred in the megahit *Ghostbusters*.

By the time of *The Blues Brothers* (1980), Belushi had quit *SNL* to concentrate on film, but insiders worried that he was abusing everything—food, cigarettes, pot, alcohol, tranquilizers, and above all cocaine. To play a romantic lead in *Continental Divide* (1981) he lost forty pounds. The film wasn't a hit, nor was the 1981 black comedy *Neighbors* with costar and friend Dan Aykroyd.

Fearful of losing his star status, Belushi took a screenplay and rewrote it for himself, intending a successful comedy/crime caper. He titled it *Noble Rot*. Paramount wasn't pleased with the script or the title. John took the criticism very personally. "He was angry and he was afraid," said a mutual friend of Gilda Radner and John. "He never believed he was movie-star material. He just knew he was funny . . . it's how he coped in school, it's how he earned a living."

After the Paramount meeting the fading star chose to hole up at the Chateau Marmont hotel in Hollywood while his wife Judy stayed in New York. Belushi then embarked on a marathon drug binge abetted by Los Angeles drug dealer Cathy Smith, who introduced him to "speedballs," an injection of cocaine and heroin. The two hung out together from March 1 to March 5, 1982. Early on the 5th after an all-night Hollywood "party" they returned to the hotel, and though John felt unwell, he took yet more drugs. Smith gave him one final shot before he showered and went to bed while she drove away to place a bet on a horse.

Hours later, Belushi's fitness trainer arrived to find him nude on the bed in a fetal position, his tongue hanging out. The trainer couldn't revive him. The autopsy found death was due to "acute cocaine and heroin intoxication." The next year Cathy Smith was charged with second-degree murder, then sentenced to three years in prison for involuntary manslaughter, serving only eighteen months.

Had John lived he'd have costarred in the hit *Ghostbusters* (1984), written by Dan Aykroyd and Harold Ramis, in the role inherited by Bill Murray.

Today a speedball is known as a Belushi.

———

Most stars' final films get released with big box-office hopes, like *Giant* (1956) with James Dean, who reaped a posthumous Oscar nomination. Of course it already had giant expectations via Rock Hudson and Elizabeth Taylor.

Occasionally a final movie takes time to reach the screen, as with Bruce Lee, but especially **River Phoenix** (1970–1993). *Dark Blood* wasn't released until 2012, almost two decades after his death at twenty-three. The unfilmed scenes meant to include River were simply given a voiceover narration. It was too long after the star's death to create much of a reaction,

Phoenix played a very young widower named Boy. The film involved nuclear testing and a couple (Judy Davis and Jonathan Pryce) stranded in the desert. The 80-percent-completed movie just sat until 1999, when destruction of the footage was suggested to avoid paying further storage costs. Director George Sluizer got hold of it. Funding and legal delays used up the next thirteen years.

River was named after the River of Life in Herman Hesse's celebrated novel *Siddhartha*. Sister Rain Phoenix later costarred in *Even Cowgirls Get the Blues*. Brother Joaquin Phoenix won a 2020 Oscar for *The Joker*—River was nominated for a supporting Academy Award for *Running on Empty* (1988).

Screenwriter Jeffrey Boam (*Indiana Jones and the Last Crusade*) met River during shooting of that sequel. "What I heard was, after his parents gave their kids all these wonderful names they joined some Christian cult and started moving the family around. . . . At some point, in the Hollywood area at age twelve or so, River became a professional actor.

"He wouldn't say much about his folks, and rarely smiled. . . . He seemed troubled and kept things to himself."

In 1982 River made his TV debut in the series *Seven Brides for Seven Brothers*, which ran for twenty-two episodes. His movie bow was in 1985 in *Explorers* and he broke through the next year in *Stand By Me*, then went on to *The Mosquito Coast*, *Running on Empty*, *Indiana Jones and the Last Crusade*, *Dogfight*, *My Own Private Idaho*, and *Sneakers*. Meanwhile he got hooked on drugs.

In interviews Phoenix stressed his vegetarianism and condemned meat-eating and sometimes drug-taking. But by 1990 or earlier he was experimenting with morphine and heroin and by 1992, the year of *Sneakers* (which he told friends not to see, as he'd only done it for the money), River was considered by several directors "unreliable" to work with.

On recent sets he'd often sat zombie-like between takes, staring into space, not reacting to others. Where once he'd felt "chosen" (his word) to be an actor and communicate "true feelings," he now made efforts for each new film he did to fetch him a bigger salary.

"He pretty much hid his private life. We don't know to what degree it contributed to his ... state of mindlessness and drug-taking," said Boam. "He should have been top-o'-the-world. He'd been acclaimed for his talent, even been compared to ... as the new James Dean. But he wasn't a happy kid."

River Phoenix died from a drug overdose outside the Hollywood nightclub the Viper Room on the Sunset Strip (his brother Joaquin—then known as Leaf—was there) after experiencing an eight-minute seizure, his head jerking and his knuckles banging against the sidewalk. The autopsy labeled it death from "acute multiple drug intoxication."

Like John Belushi, **Chris Farley** (1964–1997) died from drugs at thirty-three and came to fame via television's *Saturday Night Live*. He too joined Chicago's Second City troupe, having long since discovered he could achieve or approximate popularity by making classmates laugh. In Wisconsin he'd been an overweight child who turned boisterous in the spotlight.

Chris Farley's wild-and-crazy persona belied his serious side. He did read books and said, "If you saw me in glasses you'd think maybe I was a porky intellectual." He hoped eventually to transcend heavy comedy and star as disgraced comedian Roscoe "Fatty" Arbuckle.

"I did read books," Farley explained. "I wasn't always cutting up . . . if you saw me in glasses you'd think maybe I was a porky intellectual."

He earned a degree in theatre and communications from Marquette University in Milwaukee. *SNL* producer Lorne Michaels saw Chris perform and was impressed by his physical comedy and lack of inhibition (recall how Farley later threw himself into rounded female impersonations and his Chippendale's male stripper next to far more buffed males like Patrick Swayze). Michaels signed the comedian to the show's 1990 season and Chris stayed for five years.

During his *SNL* tenure Farley often participated in movies starring *SNL* alumnae. His 1990s screen career naturally enough focused on comedy, but he hoped someday to transition into drama via the unfunny story of silent comic star Roscoe "Fatty" Arbuckle, who was unjustly accused of rape and murder and was twice acquitted but nevertheless lost his career and fortune and died prematurely. Chris said, "One reason I want to do Arbuckle's story is that a big part of his becoming a villain in the press was the reaction to his weight.

"One of the worst things I found out researching is he had a movie contract that said he had to weigh a minimum of 250 pounds. Like, never mind about his health or mental well-being, it was like a freak-show thing."

Chris Farley, like several heavy comedic stars, didn't nourish a consistent desire to lose weight, afraid his popularity and earning power were tied to his poundage. His initial movies included *Wayne's World, Coneheads, Wayne's World II, Airheads,* and *Billy Madison*. He became a leading man in *Tommy Boy* (1995), teamed with the slim, fey David Spade. A box-office hit, it led to their reteaming in *Black Sheep* (1996). *Beverly Hills Ninja* followed in 1997.

Farley's swan song was *Almost Heroes* (1998), costarring Matthew Perry and directed by Christopher Guest. Chris deemed it his most enjoyable film. He'd been first choice to star as the manic title character *The Cable Guy* (1996), but his full schedule passed the part on to Jim Carrey. The animated hit *Shrek* had been tailored for Chris, who recorded most of Shrek's dialogue before his death (ultimately it was decided to use a different voice).

An anonymous friend was quoted after Farley's death, "Chris loved having lots of money. But it didn't fill the hole inside him. It's a cliché, but he knew he wasn't respected. Not truly. . . . He was sensitive about the word 'gross.' Some of his comedy was gross but he didn't like it being called that.

"He said by 40 he hoped to change his image. But how? He hardly tried to lose weight . . . and the movies he wanted to do just weren't going to be given to him. In a way he was trapped."

Another source said Chris Farley tried to fill his inner emptiness with an excess of food, alcohol, drugs, and paid sex. The funnyman visited numerous reducing spas and rehab facilities over the years and for one year did attain sobriety, but then fell off the wagon. "He said he admired my losing weight," said comedian Tom Arnold. "I encouraged Chris, but some friends said that between his drugs and the weight issue it was just a matter of time."

The binge habit was hard to break, and Farley's last binge comprised a week of continuous eating, drinking, and snorting cocaine. The last individual to see him alive was a paid stripper in his luxury Chicago apartment after midnight on December 7, 1997. Later that day Chris's brother discovered him dead. The autopsy stated death was from an overdose of cocaine and morphine, combined with coronary artery disease.

SUICIDES: CLARA BLANDICK, PEG ENTWISTLE, AND LUPE VÉLEZ

Reasons for suicide vary widely, as with the following three actresses. One was elderly and finished in movies, but more importantly she lived in pain and feared the onset of blindness. The young actresses had different motives. One, disillusioned by Hollywood, chose a highly symbolic way to end her life and the career she felt was going nowhere. She may have had another personal reason or reasons.

The third's reason was very personal. Though she'd attained stardom and was only thirty-six (not "only" by Hollywood standards), she was pregnant by a man who refused to marry her. Was societally induced shame the whole reason? Only the first suicide in this chapter made perfectly clear why she took the ultimate step.

Virtually everyone's heard of Auntie Em, mother-substitute to Dorothy Gale in *The Wizard of Oz* (1939), the film classic from L. Frank Baum's classic children's book *The Wonderful Wizard of Oz*. (In the book, they're silver shoes, not ruby "slippers.") How many people know the name of Dorothy's uncle? At Forest Lawn Cemetery in Glendale, California, the ashes of "Auntie Em" reside mere yards from the remains of Charley Grapewin, who played . . . Uncle Henry. Oz buffs know that fearless boy-dog Toto was played by a, pardon the expression, bitch named Terry.

It takes a buff to name the actress behind Em: **Clara Blandick** (1876–1962), originally Clara Blanchard Dickey. She was born in Hong Kong aboard an American ship captained by her father. The vessel's name was the *Willard Mudgett* (not far from midget, as in an Oz Munchkin).

Clara made her stage bow in 1901. Decades before becoming a harried farmer she was an attractive and fashionable young woman. Asked about having played the dowdy screen role, she half-joked, "I guess Kansas wore me down." (Vivian Vance of *I Love Lucy* habitually asserted she was from New Mexico until she finally admitted she was a Kansas native. She stated that had she been Dorothy she'd have waited patiently for a tornado to cross her path and carry her far off.)

Like many actors of her era, Blandick seemed to age prematurely and after her looks faded and substantial stage roles dried up she followed the work trail to California and got what film parts she could. Though they were small, sometimes minuscule, the studios churned out so many movies that she was able to survive. After *The Wizard of Oz* she was seen in dozens more pictures, typically as spinsters, disapproving elderly women, and landladies. She did get to play a "cold-blooded murderess" in the mystery caper *Philo Vance Returns* (1947).

Rarely interviewed, for journalists then as now usually sought out stars, Clara informed the press she missed out on the fun and glamour of Oz. "I wasn't in the Technicolor sequences." Seldom if ever asked about "Uncle Henry," her comments about Judy Garland were invariably praiseful of the talented, likeable teen.

Blandick's final two movies were in 1950, as a housekeeper in *Key to the City* and a landlady in *Love That Brute*—sadly, after so many years in Hollywood she went uncredited in her screen swan song.

Clara retired and became reclusive. In 1905 she'd married, then separated in 1910 before divorcing. She had no children. Through the 1950s her eyesight continually deteriorated, and her arthritis became increasingly painful.

On Sunday, April 15, 1962, after returning from Palm Sunday services at her church, the ex-thespian made an acting showcase of her room. She placed mementoes and photographs of herself to best advantage and got out her résumé and stage and movie clippings for display. Her hair already styled, and wearing an "elegant royal blue dressing gown," Clara swallowed a fatal dose of sleeping pills, lay down on her sofa—a plastic bag tied around her head—draped a gold blanket around her shoulders, then waited.

Her body was found by her landlady.

Clara Blandick's suicide note read: "I am now about to make the great adventure. I cannot endure this agonizing pain any longer. It is all over my body. Neither can I face the impending blindness. I pray the Lord my soul to take. Amen."

Virtually forgotten as an acclaimed stage talent who Bette Davis said inspired her to become an actress, **Peg Entwistle** (1908–1932) is instead remembered, alas not by name, for the way she died. She jumped off the H of the HOLLYWOODLAND sign that advertised a nearby housing development (in 1949 the –LAND was removed and the letters shortened from fifty feet to forty-five feet).

Millicent Lillian "Peg" Entwistle was born in Wales to English parents. At what point she and her divorced father, who got custody, arrived in the United States is unclear. But in 1922 he was killed in a hit-and-run accident in New York City at Park Avenue and 72nd Street. Peg was taken in by an uncle.

In 1925 Entwistle made her stage debut and in the same year Bette Davis, also born in 1908, saw the fast-rising seventeen-year-old in Ibsen's *The Wild Duck*. Davis told her mother, "I want to be exactly like Peg Entwistle!" Who knows but that Entwistle might have become another Bette Davis. . . .

By 1926 Peg was a member of the prestigious New York Theatre Guild, with whom she did ten plays, acting opposite current stars like Laurette Taylor and future ones like Robert Cummings.

Peg married actor Robert Keith in 1927 but divorced him in 1929, citing besides the customary mental-cruelty charge the fact that he didn't tell her he'd been previously married and had a six-year-old son—future actor Brian Keith.

The actress continued working and touring, but once the Great Depression hit, roles became more scarce. Though the dramatically oriented Peg sought bigger acting challenges, she often found herself cast in comedies. In 1932 she was in a play that was canceled.

Later that year she was hired for another play, in Los Angeles. It starred Billie Burke, most famous as Glinda the Good Witch in *The Wizard of Oz*. Thereafter, no stage work was in the immediate offing. The Depression was at its height and unemployment was rife in practically every profession.

So Peg turned to movies, at the time considered a strictly-for-the-money comedown for a stage professional. Her first film was her last, *Thirteen Women*. The revenge thriller produced by David O. Selznick, who later oversaw *Gone with the Wind*, had a ludicrous script. It features a Eurasian villain played by Myrna Loy (born Myrna Williams in Helena, Montana, like her contemporary, Gary Cooper). The character, snubbed at school by her all-Caucasian sorority sisters, enlists a "swami" with mysterious "powers" to help her force most of them to kill themselves or each other.

Eventually Loy (given a Chinese-sounding surname, the better to portray stereotypical villains) does in her accomplice by persuading him to fall beneath an oncoming subway train. The film starred Irene Dunne. Its cast included Englishwoman Jill Esmond, at the time better known than her husband Laurence Olivier, whom she would leave for another woman—they reportedly settled in Wimbledon—and Peg Entwistle. Peg's screen time came to about sixteen minutes of the seventy-three-minute picture. Made nervous by preview audiences' poor assessment of the product, its producer cut several scenes, leaving Entwistle with about four minutes on screen.

The cuts were widely cited as a (or the) reason behind the actress's suicide. (The movie's 1935 rerelease clocked in at fifty-nine minutes.) *Thirteen Women*, later described as one of the first "female ensemble" films, opened in New York City in October, after Peg's September suicide, and in Los Angeles in November.

More than reduced screen time in what was only her first picture may have factored in Peg's fatal decision. At the time of her death she was experiencing difficulty finding work. But was that reason enough for self-destruction? Peg was living with her uncle, who'd also moved to the Golden State. After his niece's death he told the police that he'd seen her suffer "intense mental anguish." Whether anyone else ever witnessed it, who knows?

In the 1980s Brian Keith (who took his own life after his daughter Daisy died) wondered "if the situation with her uncle was on the up-and-up . . . I don't know, I was just a kid. But I heard things that adults refused to repeat when I asked what they meant. Or maybe she really was that volatile, I don't know."

On September 16, 1932, the twenty-four-year-old informed her uncle she was going to walk to a drugstore, then visit friends. Two days later a female hiking the southern slope of Mount Lee came upon a purse, a woman's shoe, and a jacket near the HOLLYWOODLAND sign. Inside the purse was a suicide note signed "P.E." The hiker then saw the body below, in a ravine 140 feet beneath the sign, and notified the police. Peg had climbed to the top of the sign's H via a workman's ladder, then leaped to her death, officially caused by "multiple fractures of the pelvis." The body was identified by the uncle. Peg Entwistle's suicide note read: "I am afraid. I am a coward. I am sorry for everything. If I had done this a long time ago, it would have saved a lot of pain. P.E."

Her words could have referred to a number of situations. Peg's unemployment would not have been permanent. Stage-trained actors, celebrated ones even more so, were in demand for Hollywood "talkies." But apart from a not-unusual truncated movie bow and being temporarily out of work, the conditions of Peg Entwistle's life and her emotional state went unexplored.

She was simply categorized as an overly emotional, extremely disappointed female who rashly ended it all.

Over the years, Peg became a symbol of thwarted ambition and of the toll Tinseltown takes on actresses, regardless of talent, looks, or youth. She was held up as a warning to young women not to let short-term acclaim go to their heads.

In one of the interviews that later comprised this author's book *Bette Davis Speaks*, the great star recalled, "When I would start to feel a little too good about a current success my mother Ruthie would say, 'Remember Peg Entwistle.' I knew what she meant, and I would stop, and work even harder. I didn't feel fully secure and successful until I won a second Academy Award.

"Miss Entwistle's death devastated me . . . also many of us who could have been in her place. May she rest in peace."

Almost the emotional opposite of the self-contained, propriety-minded Clara Blandick was volatile **Lupe Vélez** (1908–1944), born Maria Guadalupe Villalobos Vélez in Mexico, where she began a career in vaudeville as a dancer. Partly inspired by the recent Hollywood success of compatriot Dolores Del Rio, Lupe left for California and the big screen.

Bowing on film in 1927, she eventually worked with directors like D. W. Griffith, Cecil B. DeMille, and William Wyler. With time, younger competitors, and a strong accent made obvious by talkies, Lupe's career faltered and she returned to Mexico to make movies. What kept her celebrity alive in Hollywood was her semiprivate life. When new to town, she'd been romantically linked with Charlie Chaplin, Tom Mix, and Clark Gable. Her first long-term relationship was a noisy one with Gary Cooper. Vélez, seldom averse to publicity, often yelled and fought in public.

After concurrently dating Errol Flynn and Johnny Weissmuller, she plumped for "Tarzan" and married him in 1933. There were rumors of physical abuse on both sides, though Lupe was only five feet tall. Twice she filed for divorce, then reconciled, finally divorcing in 1939.

That year, her Hollywood career revived with *The Girl from Mexico*, the first of a string of "Mexican Spitfire" comedies in which she played the tempestuous Carmelita Lindsay, married to Dennis Lindsay (portrayed by various actors). Her costar in each film was Leon Errol, a talented Australian who enacted both her uncle and the wacky Lord Epping (named after a forest in the state of Victoria).

Post-Weissmuller, Lupe had an affair with *All Quiet on the Western Front* author Erich Maria Remarque. She enthused to her secretary, "We have so much in common, including our names!"—Maria. She then took up with Mexican star Arturo De Cordova, who'd signed with Paramount and was the married father of four. Vélez apprised gossip columnist Louella Parsons that she was engaged to him. She soon announced that it was off, since his wife wouldn't give Arturo a divorce.

Lupe's final paramour was a handsome Austrian named Harald Maresch, stage name Harald Ramon, reportedly after the silent era's number two Latin Lover (after Rudolph Valentino), Ramon Novarro. Velez moved Harald into her Beverly Hills home despite friends' warning that the aspiring actor was using her.

The star was earning steadily thanks to the popular movie series that nevertheless stereotyped her. Producers refused to consider her for the dramatic projects she was seeking to prove her talent. The last in her movie series was *The Mexican Spitfire's Blessed Event* (1943), the event referring to Carmelita's cat's kittens. Lupe's final film was a 1944 Spanish-language Mexican version of Emile Zola's classic novel *Nana*, about a nineteenth-century French prostitute.

In September 1944, Velez learned she was pregnant by Ramon. In late November she announced their engagement. On December 10, four days before her death, she declared the engagement terminated, then kicked the actor out of her house. Apparently he'd refused to marry Lupe, and she refused to have an abortion. Out of shame over the social stigma of her situation and no doubt also romantic disappointment, Lupe Vélez at thirty-six (the same age as non-suicide Marilyn Monroe eighteen years later) planned her demise, surrounded by flowers.

Contrary to the rumor printed in Kenneth Anger's *Hollywood Babylon*, she did not end up with her head in the toilet. After ingesting a fatal amount of the barbiturate drug Seconal, she lay down on her bed and remained there.

Lupe Vélez's suicide note read: "To Harald, May God forgive you and forgive me too, but I prefer to take my life away and our baby's before I bring him with shame or killing him. Lupe."

The note's reverse side added, "How could you, Harald, fake such a great love for me and our baby when all the time you didn't want us? I see no other way out for me, so goodbye and good luck to you. Love, Lupe."

BOGART AND BACALL

Lauren Bacall, Humphrey Bogart's fourth and final wife, is basically the only one the public knows of. From their first film together they were touted as a romantic couple, soon to wed and remain married until his death from throat cancer. The twenty-five-years-younger beauty wasn't Bogey's only actress wife—one was Broadway star Helen Mencken, best known for the lesbian-themed 1920s stage hit *The Captive*. His third wife was alcoholic Mayo Methot, eventually a character actress and reportedly a millstone around the actor's neck.

⸺◆⸺

An urban myth says **Humphrey Bogart** (1899–1957) posed as the original Gerber baby. His mother was a successful illustrator, but the Gerber baby wasn't "born" until 1928. Contrary to his screen images, plural, stage actor Bogart often played young men of means, what he called his "Tennis, any-one?" characters.

When he moved into movies in 1930 Bogart didn't set Hollywood on fire. His parts were small and perhaps his late start in pictures and/or his uneven private life influenced his being cast as unhappy or surly characters and eventually a slew of gangsters. He supported Bette Davis in several films, also James Cagney, and even did a horror movie, *The Return of Dr. X* (1939).

For a long time Bogart was best known as a hoodlum in '30s titles like *Dead End*, *Crime School*, *Racket Busters* (nothing to do with tennis), *King of the Underworld*, *You Can't Get Away with Murder*, and *They Drive by Night*. His portrayal of gangster Duke Mantee in *The Petrified Forest* (1936), starring Leslie Howard and Bette Davis, earned Humphrey media praise and atten-tion but didn't change casting directors' minds. In gratitude to Howard, who engineered Bogart's casting in the bigger-than-usual role, the future star's daughter would be named Leslie.

Movie star George Raft was known for playing gangsters and hanging around with them offscreen. Through indolence and lousy judgment, Raft declined various roles that helped make Humphrey Bogart a star. It finally happened for Bogey in 1941 with the latest remake of Dashiell Hammett's *The Maltese Falcon*—the first picture directed by writer John Huston. This time Bogart was on the correct side of the law, and would for the most part remain so for the rest of his career. As has been proved time and again, audiences prefer to see stars in upstanding roles.

Humphrey Bogart went on to gruffly grace several film classics and won an Academy Award for *The African Queen* (1951). Thanks to the popularity of his characters, often diffident and abrasive yet responsible and open-hearted by fadeout, as in *Casablanca* (1942), Bogart remained an above-the-title star until the end. Whether he would have into his sixties and seventies can't be known, but he'd hit on a winning persona as the movies' unobvious hero—or antihero, before that term became widely known. After his death Bogart remained popular and relevant to younger audiences in a way most of his contemporaries did not.

As film critic Gene Siskel put it, "Bogart transcended Hollywood stereotypes and tropes.... He was nowhere as manufactured as most of the men on screen we were supposed to look up to."

In his last picture, *The Harder They Fall* (1956), Bogart starred as Eddie Willis, a sportswriter turned publicist. He witnesses, then opposes the boxing establishment's often ruthless exploitation of hopeful and intellectually challenged fighters who are valued only as money-making merchandise. The film's victim is South American boxer Toro Moreno (Mike Lane), whose final fight breaks his jaw and nets him $49. Although villainous promoter Rod Steiger has sold Moreno's contract—without informing Moreno—Willis puts the homesick boxer on a plane to Argentina and gives him the $26,000 he himself earned from the crooked promoters.

A furious Steiger threatens Willis, who threatens to write a series of articles exposing him and the corrupt practices of his confederates. The film, and Bogart's career, ends with him at the typewriter, preparing to prove that the pen of truth is mightier than the corrupt sword.

Friend and costar Peter Lorre said, "Some famous actors you become friendly with ... not most. Some, or more than a few, you would not want to.... Humphrey Bogart was a mensch, you understand? Down to earth.... He took his performances seriously. But he did not take Hollywood seriously."

Lauren Bacall (1924–2014) was born Betty Perske but like several actresses (Rita Hayworth, Shirley MacLaine) took her mother's surname (Bacal) in a slightly amended form. Her father had left his wife and daughter. The slinky, feline teen took up modeling to support them both and one photograph found its way to director Howard Hawks, who cast "Lauren"— friends always called her Betty—in *To Have and Have Not* (1944), starring Humphrey Bogart.

A star was born, for the stunning nineteen-year-old had personality, a distinctive husky voice, and a straight-ahead directness when making a play for the older Bogart character. Though she came across as confident, even cocky, Bacall later revealed that she kept her head lowered to keep it from shaking. "This was the big leagues. I was nervous as hell." Adding to her anxiety was that anti-Semitic director Hawks might find out she was Jewish. At first she wasn't sure about Bogart either.

They became an item, but he was still married, and Mayo Methot (1904–1951) was known for her temperament. The couple were nicknamed the Battling Bogarts. Their home sometimes resounded to broken crockery and flying pots and pans. Methot threatened Bacall. The young actress at first avoided her married costar but came to realize as their personalities meshed that she wasn't putting asunder something that wasn't already broken.

With little public explanation Humphrey extricated himself from Mayo and wed Betty in 1945. By public demand, the new couple made three more films together but Bacall didn't work that steadily, spending more time with their two children—Bogart had never had any. In the early '50s Lauren took three years off, returning third-billed in *How to Marry a Millionaire* (1953) opposite Marilyn Monroe and Betty Grable (Bacall played "the smart one"). (In some posters and other *Millionaire* advertising, promising box-office contender Monroe was billed first. Sometimes it was box-office veteran Grable. Likewise in Bacall's final film she was sometimes third-billed, after two younger actors, and sometimes billed first—enviable for a star in her mid-eighties.) In her late twenties Lauren was still a knockout but now more a woman than a "girl." As she matured her persona remained glamorous but became more knowing, even cynical.

Post-Bogart she turned more toward the stage. She was engaged to Frank Sinatra, who'd socialized with Bogart and Bacall, whose drinking pals formed the original "Rat Pack." Suddenly he broke it off; Lauren declared, "Frank behaved like a shit." In 1961 she wed hard-drinking actor Jason Robards Jr. (son of an actor), by whom she had a second son. They divorced in 1973. In the '60s Bacall made hardly any films and was locked into supporting roles—even if juicy ones, as in *Murder on the Orient Express* (1974)—until *The Fan* (1981).

In the latter she played a Broadway star stalked by a murderous fan who eventually turns against her. She fatally stabs the young terrorist in an empty theatre. In real life she was filling Broadway theatres in musicals like *Applause* (in the Bette Davis role from *All About Eve*) and *Woman of the Year* (in the Katharine Hepburn role). The Tony winner admitted, "I don't sing or dance like a dream but I'm having the best time. The stage is far more gratifying, there's never a dull moment."

Lauren Bacall looked set to receive an Oscar as costar and director Barbra Streisand's mother in *The Mirror Has Two Faces* (1996). But, unsurprisingly for Academy voters, they gave the award to a much younger female. Journalist Lance Loud clarified, "Yes, the Academy is sexist . . . [but] there's the fact that the longer someone is in that venomous business the more rivals and enemies they acquire, knowingly or not. A newcomer or young performer has fewer adversaries, so fewer voters will vote against her. Or in some cases him."

Bacall, ever classy, slim and yet deeper-voiced, worked as long as she could. "I have to make a living," she said simply. Columnist Liz Smith noted, "She's too special for TV movies and is still sought for features. But Betty Bacall declines to do trash. Some redeeming quality is called for before she signs on the dotted line."

That distinctive voice was heard in various commercials over the years and in 2014 on the animated TV series *Family Guy*. Lauren Bacall's final movie was *The Forger*, completed in 2009 but unreleased until 2012. Also known as *Carmel-by-the-Sea*, it was filmed in the Northern California beauty spot. Bacall played Anne-Marie, a mystery woman with a complicated past— she may or may not be an art forger—who induces the young protagonist to live with her and plans to make herself his legal guardian. Josh Hutcherson stated, "It was an honor working with Ms. Bacall . . . she's the most distinctive star I've met. Even if you didn't know about that long-ago Bogart connection, she's just so impressive."

CENTENARIANS: GEORGE BURNS, BOB HOPE, KIRK DOUGLAS, AND OLIVIA DE HAVILLAND

Until relatively recently one could pretty much count the number of centenarian stars on one hand. Those few were mostly female. British actress Athene Seyler (1889–1990) felt that was because men "fret so much about what not to do." Estelle Winwood (1883–1984), better known in the United States, opined, "It's as much about luck as avoiding most but not every bad habit."

American actor Eddie Albert, queried in the 1960s by *TV Guide* while starring on *Green Acres* what his biggest remaining goal was, replied to live to be one hundred. He "only" made it to ninety-nine. On the other hand he missed experiencing the death the following year of his only son, actor Edward Albert, at fifty-five.

Gruesomely ironic was the case of Joan Davis, who died of a heart attack at fifty-three in 1961. (In 1945 Davis was crowned Queen of Comedy along with Bob Hope as King of Comedy. In the early '50s her sitcom *I Married Joan* was NBC's "answer" to *I Love Lucy* on CBS.) Had Davis lived to fifty-five she would have been a victim of or experienced the fire in her Palm Springs home that killed her mother, daughter, and two grandchildren.

———

George Burns (1896–1996) was an unlikely movie star. He was also an unlikely comedy star. Friendly rival Milton Berle declared, "The first time I met George I saw that he had what it took to become famous: Gracie Allen." The two married in 1926 and performed successfully in radio, films, and television until she retired not long before her death in 1964.

Born Nathan Birnbaum (the surname means pear tree), George said in later years, "I did the most with what I had. If I'd looked like Tyrone Power I'd have gone into the movies, but I had a face made for radio. If I'd had Einstein's brains I'd have gone into . . . I'm not even sure I know what it was he went into."

"I wasn't hilarious. I didn't look funny or talk funny. If not for Gracie I'd probably have become a dull rich producer. Instead I became rich and had a wonderful time doing what we did." Post-Gracie he did produce, on TV and in nightclubs.

Burns's persona included an ever-present cigar (how did he live to one hundred?), rat-a-tat patter, droll yet caustic wit, and bizarre semi-spoken songs. Gracie had a unique comic voice, an ingenuous delivery, and a delightful ditziness. They were an intriguingly mismatched couple and thus a popular one.

George's best friend was solo comedic star Jack Benny. At one point during the long Broadway run of *Hello, Dolly!* after Carol Channing was followed by a parade of Dollys, producer David Merrick (who'd done an all-black *Dolly* with Pearl Bailey) semi-jokingly invited Benny and Burns to do a drag version, with George as the male lead and Jack as Dolly. Benny accepted, for a one-night stand. Merrick regretfully declined, requiring at least a few months' run.

Benny was a major success on radio and television, but his pictures had laid eggs. However he was slated to costar in an almost guaranteed hit via the movie of playwright Neil Simon's hit comedy *The Sunshine Boys*. In 1974 Jack died unexpectedly. George Burns replaced him, costarring with Walter Matthau in the hit 1975 movie and winning a Best Supporting Actor Academy Award.

He marveled, "You spend years of your early life developing an image, a character you think will go over with the public. Then this happens—falls into your lap—and you learn producers and normal people are happy for you to fundamentally just play yourself. Your old, real, aging self. No sweat. I'm happy to be aging, which is another word for still breathing."

Since the demise of Burns and Allen, the comedian had faded from public view. But at almost eighty he was launched on a new film career. His last had been *Two Girls and a Sailor* in 1944, followed by his narration of the 1956 Judy Holliday vehicle *The Solid Gold Cadillac*. After *The Sunshine Boys* he played the title character in *Oh, God!* (1977; also *Oh, God! Book II* in 1980) and went on to starring, costarring, and minor roles in a string of pictures that ceased in 1994 with *Radioland Murders*, a comedy mystery in which he did a cameo as a one-hundred-year-old comedian. "I'm too young for the part but I'm a good enough actor to fake it."

In his nineties George Burns was fond of telling audiences, "I can't die. I'm booked." His most famous quote was about acting: "The most important thing in acting is sincerity. If you can fake that, you've got it made."

—◦◦—

"**Bob Hope** started funny," said comedic actor and coach Dick Schaal, "but became such a self-conscious institution and pillar of the establishment that his final movies are painful to watch. His humor and manner were by then embalmed. Ignore those and watch his early films—see the difference."

Born Leslie Hope (1903–2003) in Britain, Hope was brought to the States as a child. After appearing in several mid-1930s shorts he was more widely seen in *The Big Broadcast of 1938* (1938). It featured W. C. Fields, who prophetically told pal John Barrymore, "The guy's more at home with a microphone than an audience . . . a natural born host," adding that Hope's funniest attributes were his walk and his ski-slope nose. Once the Oscar ceremonies began broadcasting on television, Hope was tapped for hosting duties more often than anyone else.

His big break was the horror spoof *The Cat and the Canary* (1939), and in 1940 he began the Road comedies that teamed him with first-billed singer-actor Bing Crosby. Their friendly rivalry was a staple of each man's persona, but costar Dorothy Lamour later admitted, "It was mostly for show. Their real rivalry was who was wealthier? They didn't socialize."

Hope was considered at his funniest through the 1940s. UK journalist David Quinlan noted his affinity for "roles which highlighted his ability to get into situations which exposed the yellow streak running down his back." He was more of an audience substitute than the smooth, unflappable Crosby. In 1948 Hope was successfully paired with sex symbol Jane Russell in *The Paleface* (and its sequel *Son of Paleface* four years later). He was also effective, if overly domineering, in comedies with Lucille Ball and Phyllis Diller. After the mid-1950s his screen vehicles declined steeply in quality. "In the '60s he was marking time between TV specials," offered Second City alumnus Schaal (also Valerie Harper's first husband and a regular on the *Mary Tyler Moore Show* spin-off *Phyllis*).

Edie Adams costarred in Hope's *Call Me Bwana* (1963). "He was seldom without an entourage . . . mostly his gag writers and yes-men. . . . He didn't really relax or take the time to socialize with the cast." Gina Lollobrigida pronounced Hope's *The Private Navy of Sergeant O'Farrell* (1968) her "worst one of my American motion pictures." *Bwana* (boss in Swahili) elicited some adverse reactions for its racist humor, as did *Cancel My Reservation* (1972) for its Native American stereotypes. In the 1980s Hope had to apologize for his TV "joke" about the Statue of Liberty catching AIDS from the Long Island Ferry.

Over the decades Bob Hope became a fixture on NBC-TV with his specials. He garnered high ratings via his long-standing status and big-name guest stars. He also habitually entertained the troops, particularly during the Vietnam War, invariably resulting in a TV special. It did become known that Hope avoided the "hot spots"—unlike, say, actress Martha Raye or for that matter, during the Korean War, Marilyn Monroe—and had little interaction with the troops themselves.

Jim Henson, the main man behind the Muppets, declared, "It was touching how grateful Bob was to join in [*The Muppet Movie*, 1978]. We were pleased to have him aboard.... But when we got started his concentration was on camera placement. His eyes were dead, very little humor or enthusiasm to speak of, simply peering to make sure he was front and center before the camera."

Hope's big-screen swan song was a cameo playing himself in *Spies Like Us* (1985). Starring Dan Aykroyd and Chevy Chase as inept novice spies, the comedy was something of an homage to the Road pictures. He'd already played himself as Oscar emcee in *The Oscar* (1966). When there were no more movies, Hope did TV guest shots, for instance a voice "appearance" on *The Simpsons* in 1992. His final TV special was the 1996 compilation *Laughing with the Presidents*, which manifested signs of the dementia that in time would envelop him. His final appearance was a 1997 TV ad for K-Mart directed by Penny Marshall.

For a man who wasn't that obviously comedic and once said he'd rather have been a conventional leading man "who actually got the girl," Bob Hope had a run of over sixty years that perhaps has no comic parallel.

Kirk Douglas would have gone on making films had a severe stroke not significantly reduced his screen opportunities. He then turned to books, also to charity. Born Issur Danielovitch (1916–2020), he was a ragman's son, as one of his book titles proclaimed. He wasn't that handsome or likeable, but he was magnetic and compelling, with a dimpled chin, fierce smile, and confidence to spare.

He didn't enter movies till about thirty, having taken acting class with the future Lauren Bacall, who said, "Kirk, as an older student, was impatient. In his approach too . . . when he asked me out.

"He wanted instant intimacy. I said no. He was intimidating although appealing. I liked older men [Douglas was eight years older] and we were both Jewish but I was waiting for someone a bit . . . calmer." Via her first film she connected with Humphrey Bogart, twenty-five years her senior.

Douglas's first two films costarred Lizabeth Scott. "He had all this pent-up energy. I wondered when he would play a really aggressive man."

He did in his third film, the noir classic *Out of the Past* (1947), and in *Champion*, the boxing-themed 1949 picture that made him a star. Myriad hits, classics, and other movies followed, including *Young Man with a Horn* (with Bacall and Doris Day), *The Glass Menagerie, Ace in the Hole, Detective Story, The Bad and the Beautiful, 20,000 Leagues Under the Sea, Lust for Life, Paths of Glory, The Vikings,* and his signature role and film *Spartacus* (1960), which helped break the political blacklist by giving screen credit to its screenwriter, Dalton Trumbo (columnist Hedda Hopper excoriated President Kennedy in print for going to see the film).

Douglas had four sons by two wives, including actor Michael. Youngest son Eric, a sometime actor and stand-up comic, stated, "He wasn't an easy dad. Not just in terms of following in his footsteps, but usually he was away working. When you did see him again he could be scary. He came on strong."

Coworkers sometimes had reservations. Doris Day, who didn't bad-mouth costars, said her one "joyless" moviemaking experience was working with Kirk Douglas. Director Robert Aldrich said of *The Last Sunset* (1961), "Rock Hudson was a hard worker and professional. . . . Kirk was a pain. He wanted to either be the boss or a co-boss. I told him to go direct himself." Douglas later directed two films, neither a success. One actress said she resented the actor trying to give her acting lessons on-set, and more than one said he flirted aggressively.

Kirk Douglas didn't win an Oscar, perhaps partly due to personality, perhaps to not inhabiting a role as emotional as friend Burt Lancaster's in *Elmer Gantry*, and perhaps because though *Spartacus* was probably his best chance, some or many Academy members, especially older ones, disagreed with hiring Dalton Trumbo, one of the Hollywood Ten, who'd been jailed for their political beliefs and refusing to name names before Congress. Besides being a star, Douglas was a producer, his production company Brynna named after his mother.

Kirk Douglas rose from poverty—his first memoir was *The Ragman's Son*—to a major acting career spanning six decades. His biggest professional regret was not starring in the movie *One Flew Over the Cuckoo's Nest*, produced by his actor son Michael Douglas. Kirk lived to 103.

A disappointment for Kirk was not getting to enact the role that later won Jack Nicholson an Oscar in *One Flew Over the Cuckoo's Nest* (1975), produced by son Michael. But although his post-1960s films were generally less popular or worthwhile, Douglas worked steadily until his 1996 stroke (another book was titled *My Stroke of Luck*, about the new avenues it afforded him, including time to rediscover his Jewish heritage).

Kirk Douglas's movie swan song was the independent film *Illusion* (2004), in which the two-time director starred as a film director dying alone, viewing pictures he'd directed. A film editor from his past appears and transports him to an old movie house (reminiscent of the Ghost of Christmas Past in Dickens's *A Christmas Carol*) where he also views the illegitimate son he'd seen only once, now regretting having ejected him from his life.

Douglas's last TV appearance was in a 2008 French mockumentary titled *Empire State Building Murders* costarring Ben Gazzara and Mickey Rooney. He then announced his retirement. The man who survived a helicopter crash in 1991 asseverated, "I come from very strong stock and have always had a very strong will. Bull-headed, my mother used to call me. For better or for worse."

When former movie star Joan Fontaine, immortalized as the nameless heroine of *Rebecca* (1939), died in 2013 at ninety-six, various newspaper obituaries reprinted her famous quote: "I married first, won the Oscar before Olivia and if I die first she'll undoubtedly be livid because I beat her to it!"

Joan's elder, more esteemed sister died in 2020 at 104.

One book biography of the de Havilland siblings was sarcastically titled *Such Devoted Sisters*. After the Englishwomen moved to California with their mother Lilian Fontaine, **Olivia de Havilland** (born 1916) became an actress before her year-younger sister. When the lovelier Joan entered the same business, she had to refrain from using the surname of their father, who in any case had walked out on his wife and toddler daughters.

Olivia's film debut was in no less than Max Reinhardt's classic *A Midsummer Night's Dream* (1935). But as with her friend Bette Davis, De Havilland had to battle the brothers Warner for worthy roles (both actresses eventually sued the studio; Olivia won her case). By contrast, Joan Fontaine found distinction relatively early. In 1939 she had a small part in the all-star hit *The Women*, starring Norma Shearer and Joan Crawford, in 1940 she starred in the classic *Rebecca*, and in 1941 won an Academy Award as Best Actress in *Suspicion*.

For better or worse, dramatically speaking, Olivia avoided unladylike roles most of her career. "I think playing bad girls is a bore." She felt it was harder to make them interesting, preferring "good girl roles because they require more from an actress." However, note that the more celebrated female character in *Gone with the Wind* (1939) is Scarlett rather than Melanie.

In time, de Havilland professionally outstripped her sister, costarring in *Gone with the Wind* and winning two Oscars, for *To Each His Own* (1946) and *The Heiress* (1949). She also continued longer in the business. Post-ingénue, Joan Fontaine developed a slightly brittle edge. Ex-husband Brian Aherne volunteered, "Joan smirks more often than she smiles. Olivia smiles . . . not always sincerely."

The sisters had never gotten along, and their mother encouraged their rivalry. Some insiders said Joan chafed at her elder sister's bossiness; others said Olivia resented her younger sister's looks and less inhibited, more outspoken personality. For a long time both publicly denied any mutual hard feelings. But Joan was a presenter at the Oscar ceremonies the year Olivia was nominated for what would be her first statuette. As de Havilland walked offstage holding her award her sister was backstage and extended her hand in congratulations.

Olivia turned away, but a photographer was there to capture the moment and confirm the absence of sisterly feeling.

The siblings stopped speaking after Lilian's death in 1975. Joan claimed she wasn't invited to the funeral and that Olivia had made key decisions about their mother's health care without consulting Joan. She declared, "I wish I *had* a sister. I've always been the intruder in her life, the interloper." In 1978 Fontaine published her memoirs, *No Bed of Roses*. De Havilland refrained from doing so and declined all requests—and major-money advances—to write a book about the making of *Gone with the Wind*, all of whose performers she outlived.

Olivia lived in Paris from 1953 on (her second and final husband was a Frenchman). The 1960s provided fewer leading-lady roles, so in 1964 she joined the cycle of shocker films featuring older female stars, with *Lady in a Cage* (the cage is an in-home elevator that gets stuck). Unlike *What Ever Happened to Baby Jane?* two years earlier, it wasn't a success.

A planned reteaming of Bette Davis and Joan Crawford fell apart when Joan departed *Hush . . . Hush, Sweet Charlotte* (1964), mostly due to Bette's machinations. Joan was replaced by the less compelling and less competitive Olivia de Havilland. After a press screening of *Charlotte*, Bette advised her costar, "You were very good in it, Olivia. When you weren't in a scene with me, you managed to keep the audience's attention."

At *Charlotte*'s New York premiere Olivia observed, "The fans are so young! Their parents could hardly have been born when Bette started out."

De Havilland then stayed away from the screen until the '70s, when she appeared in *Pope Joan*, about a possible historical female pope (Liv Ullmann), *Airport 1977*, and *The Swarm*, about killer bees, and a few other movies and telefilms. The '80s brought more TV roles, including the Queen Mother in a largely fictional account of Prince Charles and Diana's "royal romance" and Olivia's final acting performance, in *The Woman He Loved* in 1988, about former king Edward VIII and American divorcee Wallis Simpson. De Havilland played Wallis's beloved Aunt Bessie.

She subsequently participated in documentaries on and anniversary celebrations of *Gone with the Wind*, citing her role of Melanie as her favorite.

In 2017 Olivia de Havilland sued Ryan Murphy Productions over its unauthorized and inaccurate depiction of her (via Catherine Zeta-Jones) in the TV miniseries *Feud* about Bette Davis and Joan Crawford. "Olivia" was shown "gossiping" about her costars and referring to Joan Fontaine as "my bitch sister." De Havilland declared she'd never called her sister a bitch, at most referring to her as a "dragon lady." The ladylike star also objected to being depicted as a gossip, asseverating that she never gave an interview in which she dished her fellow actors.

The court went against Olivia, who then appealed to California's Supreme Court, which upheld the decision. A 2019 petition to the US Supreme Court was declined. In any case, the centenarian's suits and the resultant publicity made clear that the TV situation and lines attributed to her were fictitious.

Part of Olivia de Havilland's legacy is the de Havilland Decision, the result of her 1943 lawsuit against Jack Warner and company. Her win meant that studios could no longer add time to the standard seven-year contract whenever a player was suspended for illness or refusing a film they considered injurious to their career. David Niven later wrote, "Players were sometimes trapped for 12 or 15 years working off a seven-year contract."

Bette Davis wrote, "Olivia should be thanked by every actor today. She won the court battle that no contract should ever have to continue more than seven years."

HER GUY: RICHARD BURTON

"Without his looks and charisma, his voice alone would still have made him a star," said costar Lee Remick of **Richard Burton,** "and he was not 'ruined' by Elizabeth Taylor. He'd have become a star without her."

Charles Bronson, who appeared in *The Sandpiper* (1965), a Taylor-Burton vehicle, felt, "As a superstar she was able to pull him up to near her level of fame and super salary. She also dragged him down to a self-indulgent, money-first lifestyle and commercialized a great talent."

Richard Jenkins (1925–1984) was the twelfth of thirteen children. His mother died soon after the last delivery. He escaped the Welsh coal mines through his voice and his interest in poetry and the classics. Toward the end of his life he admitted he'd rather have become a writer. "At times my profession shames me with its false adulation and lack of brain-intensive or back-breaking work."

Today Richard Burton is almost invariably associated in public memory with Elizabeth Taylor. Before Liz he was known in Britain for his voice, his promising future on the stage, and for drink. In Hollywood he was a leading man but not a big star. Burton disliked interviews but was more candid than most stars, as in *People* magazine: "Perhaps most actors are latent homosexuals and we cover it with drink."

He admitted to some past same-sex relationships. The first may have been with instructor Philip Burton, with whom Richard moved in at seventeen. His official studio biography claimed he moved in as a child, to render the situation platonic. Richard and the man whose surname he took remained lifelong friends and Burton (who wound up in Florida) was included in the star's will.

A number of the aspiring actor's mentors were gay men, including Chaucer translator Neville Coghill, who helped Richard develop his feeling for verse, and actor-director Sir John Gielgud. Welsh actor-writer Emlyn Williams gave Burton his first professional stage role, in *The Druid's Rest* in

1943. Richard kept those aspects of his past secret until Elizabeth Taylor encouraged him to talk about them and become comfortable with them.

Gielgud got him into the play *The Lady's Not for Burning*. When it played Broadway Richard's thespic future seemed set. In 1948 he'd screen-debuted in the Welsh-themed *The Last Days of Dolwyn* (US title: *Woman of Dolwyn*), but his British films had minimal US impact.

His Hollywood debut was "electric," said Henry Koster, director of *My Cousin Rachel* (1952), from Daphne du Maurier's novel. It starred Olivia de Havilland, who'd seen Burton in *The Lady's Not for Burning* and offered him $1,000 a week to costar in *Romeo and Juliet*. He turned her down, apparently brusquely.

He believed she took her revenge when they made *My Cousin Rachel* (remade for TV in 1983 with Geraldine Chaplin and as a feature in 2017 with Rachel Weisz). "I was merely a second-class citizen as far as Miss De Havilland was concerned. She refused to allow me to have costarring billing . . . I think Miss de Havilland wanted Gregory Peck for the part. . . . I never warmed to Miss De Havilland."

Known for propositioning actresses, Richard reportedly made a pass at the nine-years-older Olivia, which she rejected. He denied having made a pass. In 2013 de Havilland wrote, "Richard Burton was wildly talented." But he was "a coarse-grained man with a . . . coarse-grained behavior."

Burton received an Oscar nomination for his US debut but, oddly, in the supporting category, despite his being the movie's largest role. Perhaps the film title or its billing influenced the Academy.

The Taylor-Burton affair that began during *Cleopatra* (1963) was the most publicized in movie history. Once they became a couple Richard's salary soared, and even though usually second-billed to Taylor (unless she agreed to a supporting role to boost the project's box-office prospects), he was an international superstar. Film distributor Harry Walders summed up, "Fifty percent of all box-office income in 1966-'67 was made from movies starring one or other or both Elizabeth Taylor and Richard Burton," a record unequaled by any other film duo.

After their critical and commercial triumph in *Who's Afraid of Virginia Woolf?* (1966), the Taylor-Burton collaboration faltered and reviewers often panned their media dominance and reckless spending as well as the screen vehicle in question. (*Woolf* was more of a triumph for Liz—a second Oscar—with yet another non-win nomination for Richard.)

Some Academy voters held his "marrying up" against him. Others looked down on his, and her, commercial choices of vehicle. The actor's handsome but pockmarked face and emotional performances mirrored his personal voyage. Early on, his expressions and characters typically exhibited youthful integrity: later, middle-aged disillusion. Insiders said he resented being passed over for the Oscar, particularly when it went to John Wayne, "a self-repeating type, not an actor."

Eventually and inevitably Taylor-Burton transferred their "act" to TV with the prophetic two-part "programming event" *Divorce His, Divorce Hers* (1973). Post-Liz, Burton's films were less successful, like *Exorcist II: The Heretic*, and—especially the British or European productions—less widely distributed, like *The Assassination of Trotsky, Sutjeska*, and *Massacre in Rome*. Lee Remick, his costar in *The Medusa Touch* (1978), told magazine editor Sarah Petit, "I don't excuse myself, I did that one for a specific monetary reason.

"But Richard Burton, with such talent? Yes, chronically alcoholic but still functioning professionally. . . . What is the point of a film where a man has the power to blow up, for instance, airplanes just by willing it to happen? And *keeps* doing it . . . is that sick or is it entertainment? Why did Richard accept? Just to star in something more? For money? He had more money than I ever dreamed of. . . . Sad."

A big reason for the permanent breakup of Liz-and-Dick was their working together in the theatre, Burton's original and preferred but neglected medium. Noel Coward's *Private Lives* was Taylor's second play ever, in 1983. Because her company was producing it, contractually Richard was Elizabeth's employee. When he asked for time off to go do a movie, she declined, holding him to his legal agreement. Additionally, when he missed an occasional performance it barely affected the box office, but when Elizabeth Taylor didn't show up, mass refunds were in order. He knew she still hoped for a reconciliation after their two marriages and two divorces, so in humiliation and anger he up and wed a younger blonde.

After a tragedy involving his favorite older brother for which Burton felt responsible, he no longer cared to try to stop drinking. He continued working, no longer potent at the box office but still a prestigious name in movies and on TV miniseries like *Wagner*. The blonde marriage didn't work out, so he married a brunette. The drinking binges continued, and he looked wasted but kept on working and earning. Unlike Taylor, he refused to consider putting himself through rehab.

Richard Burton's final movie was *1984* (1984), from George Orwell's dystopian novel. He played the antagonistic O'Brien. Reviewer Ken Ferguson noted, "The Burton voice remains mostly intact . . . the eyes often betray a fed-up lifelessness. . . . Less than a warning against Big Brother, *1984* is dispiritingly grim."

1984 costar John Hurt said, "A cerebral hemorrhage officially caused his death . . . but an actor who knew Richard far better than I did said it was 'bottled disillusionment.' Maybe he wanted too much and then, when he finally got it, it wasn't what he'd hoped for."

FIRST FILM/LAST FILM: TRUMAN CAPOTE, HELEN GAHAGAN, AND JOHNNIE RAY

Why would someone who has a major, even leading, role in a motion picture not make a second movie . . . and another one and another one?

Because the film was a hit but moviemaking bored him, or he was in poor health and substance abuse made memorization and concentration difficult?

Because her starring role was in a flop and she felt embarrassed to have "lowered" herself to movies and ought to have remained in the *theatuh*?

Because the movie was a hit but his role was a little embarrassing and he was hard to cast and maybe drinking made things difficult and he was more comfortable singing?

These aren't the only three whose first was their last, and there are probably as many reasons as there are individuals.

———

"It wasn't hard work at all. It was *boring* work!" exclaimed **Truman Capote** of his first and final movie, Neil Simon's murder-mystery spoof *Murder by Death* (1976). The most famous writer in America basically played himself as one Lionel Twain, who resides at Two-Two Twain (get it?). There he hosts a gaggle of sleuths comically based on the characters Nick and Nora Charles, Sam Spade, Charlie Chan (stereotypically and politically incorrectly played by Peter Sellers), and Agatha Christie's Hercule Poirot and Miss Marple.

Twain offers a large wad of cash to whoever can solve an impending murder which he doesn't survive. Though some moviegoers found the ending maddeningly ambiguous, the all-star comedy was a hit. Yet Capote, who'd crowed loudly and widely about his screen bow, never acted again.

(Rather, there were posthumous movies and a one-man show about him. One of the films featured an Oscar-winning impersonation of Truman by Philip Seymour Hoffman, and the play earned Robert Morse a Tony Award.)

Known as "the Tiny Terror," Truman Capote was a literary giant whose writing career and life were cut short by drugs and alcohol. His busy social life also cut into his work—until he wrote about too many of his friends and they cut him off. His first movie, Neil Simon's detective-mystery spoof *Murder by Death* (1976), was his last movie.

Why didn't the writer continue in pictures, especially as his literary output had been consistently dwindling?

Rival gay author Gore Vidal offered, "How often can he play himself? And what else could he realistically play?" Toward the end of his life, Vidal acted in a handful of motion pictures. None got as much publicity as Truman's turn.

Another reason for cutting his celluloid adventure short may have been Capote's steadily declining physical and mental condition via drugs and alcohol. He appeared on various TV talk shows in obvious states of inebriation and/or other chemical dysfunction. His cure attempts were half-hearted and unsuccessful.

A yet more personal reason wasn't voiced publicly. "Truman was vain to the end and sorely disappointed in his vanity," said a female socialite friend in 1985. "In his youth he'd been cute, even sexy . . . very boyish. He relished being desired and courted. . . . Being short, all the weight he gained looked worse on him, and the chemical dependency bloated his face. . . . Truman hated how his face looked, super-magnified up on the big screen.

"I told him he didn't much care how he looked on television, so why did this bother him? He became upset. Not about my comment, about the comparison. TV is here today, gone in 60 minutes, he said. Movies are forever. Truman had respect for movies, hardly any for television."

Eventually the ex-writer left New York for Los Angeles, purchasing a one-way ticket and settling into the cozy Hollywood Hills home of pal Joanne Carson (talk-show host Johnny Carson's ex-wife). Truman Capote died there, worn out at fifty-nine, in 1984.

* * *

"For the life of me, I can't imagine why *She* flopped," recalled Christopher Lee, who costarred opposite Ursula Andress in the successful 1965 remake. "The 1935 version was closer to the H. Rider Haggard novel. It had excellent production values, I believe by the same team that had recently made *King Kong*. It had mystery, romance, drama, conflict, humor . . . special effects.

"I thought it was marvelous."

Lee's list omitted **Helen Gahagan**, who starred as the two-thousand-year-old Ayesha, known to her subjects as She-who-must-be-obeyed. Some fans of the classic 1887 novel felt the distinguished stage actress didn't register strongly on screen or was too cold and remote. Contrarywise, some critics of Hammer's 1965 *She* considered Andress, a tiger-ish blonde, too voluptuous for the role of a semi-immortal queen. One reviewer dismissed her as "that Bond Girl"—she was the first, Honeychile Rider, in *Dr. No.* (Interestingly, the German-speaking Swiss star's speaking voice was dubbed in both pictures.)

No question Ursula Andress was more beauteous and sexier than Helen Gahagan's imperious, raven-haired Ayesha, who served as a prototype for Walt Disney's wicked queen in *Snow White* two years later.

However, Gahagan, best remembered as a congresswoman (married to two-time Oscar-winning actor Melvyn Douglas), may not have been the reason *She* didn't pack the movie houses. RKO, hoping for another fantasy-adventure hit on the order of *King Kong*, spared no expense filming *She*, whose extended sacrificial-dance sequence is unforgettable. Robert Day, who directed the remake, observed, "The Americans might have taken a bit more care with the cast—not that *King Kong*'s cast was exactly sterling."

Day noted the woodenness of male lead Randolph Scott, who later found his niche in westerns, also the "simpering female second lead . . . and Nigel Bruce trying too hard for humor [and] far preferable as Basil Rathbone's Dr. Watson."

Christopher Lee added that "Miss Andress in the role seemed to relish her absolute power . . . whereas Miss Gahagan seemed bored by her 2,000-year reign. That may have been truer to character but may have bored audiences."

She focuses on Ayesha's discovery of a young man she believes to be a reincarnation of her original love. Not wishing to lose him after a half-century or more of mortal life, she plans to make him immortal like herself. Nor wishing to lose him to the young woman in his party with whom he's falling in love, she plans to kill her rival via ritual sacrifice. Of course *She* is thwarted, and both movie versions' most memorable set piece is the climactic scene in which Ayesha ages acceleratingly and dies at a full two thousand years.

Helen Gahagan Douglas, as she was later known, didn't dwell on her screen debut cum swan song. She theorized that perhaps a story centered on an all-powerful and vengeful female who dies by ageing hideously was too strong for the mid-1930s, when Depression-era audiences generally preferred comedy, romance, and uplift. Melvyn Douglas eventually opined that his late wife (1900–1980), a "lady of charm and wit," may have been too unrelievedly grim in the role.

In 1950 the Democratic ex-actress ran for the Senate. She was the first person to nickname her ambitious opponent Richard Nixon "Tricky Dick." Nixon, who saw his chance during the McCarthy witch-hunt era, resorted to smear tactics, and labeled Helen "the Pink Lady," supposedly "soft on communism." Though his nickname stuck, Nixon won that race and eventually the White House but was the first US president to be forced out of office.

———

"Presley said I was a big influence on him . . . my uninhibited performance style," said **Johnnie Ray** in West Hollywood in 1984.

"When Elvis came along and hit the big-time I didn't begrudge him. I liked him. He was getting to be as big as I was. . . . But you can't see into the future."

In the early 1950s Johnnie Ray (1927–1990) was the most popular singer in America, not just via back-to-back number one hits like "Cry" and "The Little White Cloud That Cried." His openly emotional singing style drew the fascination of that repressed decade's youth but also drew doubts, derision, and damaging but true gossip about his sexuality (he briefly had to marry a nightclub owner's daughter but was arrested more than once on possibly trumped-up "morals" charges; a jealous Frank Sinatra paid to have Johnnie socked in the face and questioned his "sincere manliness").

In some quarters Ray was reviled for "singing like a Negro." No major white male singer had performed so histrionically in concert or actually cried while singing. Johnnie always held that his Detroit arrest was engineered by racist white police who resented his style and his having friends of both races. "Not all of 'em, but most cops really had it in for me . . . I still avoid cops whenever I can."

Still, while he was selling records and selling out nightclub engagements, Johnnie was hot. Darryl Zanuck, head of 20th Century-Fox, signed him, predicting a big movie career. Ray was slotted into the studio's big musical for 1954, *There's No Business Like Show Business*. Its characters, besides Marilyn Monroe as one son's girlfriend (not Johnnie's), comprised a showbiz family: Ethel Merman and Dan Dailey as her too-young husband, with Donald O'Connor, Mitzi Gaynor, and Johnnie as their kids. (Dailey and Ray were eventually rumored to be having an affair.)

Show Business, whose tunes were all by Irving Berlin, attracted publicity and controversy via Marilyn singing "We're Having a Heat Wave" in a skimpy tropical costume that showed her midriff but not her belly button (those were taboo then) and in a too-sexy (for the 1950s) manner. By contrast, Johnnie's character was asexual—the son who becomes a priest. He later explained that he hadn't realized his role was tantamount to "playing gay. Not that all priests are gay, but in that context . . . it was the wrong situation to place me in . . . I did whatever I was told."

The movie was a hit but Ray wasn't rushed into another one. He was hard to cast (as was Liberace the following year in his first and final starring vehicle, *Sincerely Yours*; Sinatra didn't put down the non-singing pianist) and Fox was reportedly waiting for the right sort of lead role following Johnnie's box-office success in support. But as time went by the negative publicity increased and Ray's record sales decreased. His alcohol intake also increased and was reflected in person. Finally he was released from his movie contract.

Between 1953 and 1987 Johnnie Ray appeared on dozens of TV shows, almost always as his upbeat self. With time it became more widely known his drinking was impacting his memory. He stuck to singing until that too was gone.

"One thing you learn, usually too late," Ray concluded, "is strike while that iron is hot, boy. Don't let 'em keep you on ice too long. The public forgets very quickly . . . so do those guys who write and make the movies. . . . Anyway, singing's what I enjoy. Being an actor is more like [being] a puppet. I'd rather pull my own strings."

What Johnnie Ray didn't add or perhaps admit was that in 1968 he got one more movie role, in *Rogue's Gallery*—as a policeman. Its producer, Paramount executive A. C. Lyles, summarized, "We thought Roger Smith might become a big draw like his wife [Ann-Margret]. He played John Rogue. . . . If memory serves, Johnnie Ray was 10th-billed? I'm not sure we spelled his [first] name right. . . . An associate said Ray did it strictly for the dough and later disowned it. I'm not sure I blame him."

SECOND INFANCY: LON CHANEY AND TYRONE POWER

The French, generally less hung-up on sexual taboos and age, have described the forties as "the infancy of old age."

Had the following two actors not died in their forties they'd have starred in many more films. Apart from stardom, they had little in common. The younger was celebrated primarily for his good looks, the elder for his ability to transform his plain looks into a staggering variety of looks and characters.

—•—

Had **Lon Chaney** survived, our image of Dracula would be very different, for he was slated to play the vampire role Bela Lugosi made famous in 1931. Chaney (1883–1930), all of whose films but one were silents, was renowned for his versatility. If ever there was a grim star whose sometimes gruesome movies featured memorably morbid roles, it was "the Man of a Thousand Faces."

For example in *The Unknown* (1927) he was a circus performer with no arms who used his bare foot to throw knives at an unrecognizably young Joan Crawford, with whom he's in love. She likes him partly because she has a phobia about men's arms. Chaney secretly has arms, which he keeps tied behind his back. But he knows he can't woo and win Joan because he has arms. So he finds a surgeon willing to remove them, becomes truly armless . . . and returns to the circus to find Joan has conquered her phobia and is in love with a younger man with arms. The actor powerfully conveys his anguish through his eyes and expressive face.

Chaney played assorted nationalities, he played crooks and heroes, he played variously handicapped characters, and he played the Phantom of the Opera, his most famous role, in 1925. He bowed on screen in 1912 but made his first feature-length movie in 1914. Several of Chaney's films and shorts are lost.

The seldom smiling son of deaf parents, he could transform himself so remarkably that a popular saying warned filmgoers not to step on a spider, as it might turn out to be Lon Chaney! Such was his drawing power that after his premature death his son Creighton Chaney was renamed Lon Chaney Jr. (1906 1973) in hopes of extending his father's box-office potency.

Senior had been a harsh parent to his son, who partly blamed his father for his own alcoholism. Junior did become a horror star, most famously as the Wolf Man and the Mummy (the latter in sequels to the Boris Karloff original), but he wasn't remotely as acclaimed as Lon Chaney. His film career launched the year after his father died and ended in a poorly received offering titled *Dracula Versus Frankenstein* (1971).

Both father and son played vampires, with Jr. as *Son of Dracula*. Sr.'s vampire in *London After Midnight* (1927) did not bode well for his planned turn as the Transylvanian Count Dracula. Photos of Chaney's vampire in the lost film show bizarre yet jokey spiked teeth and eyes rigged shockingly open by wires. Of course the performer (whose makeup box was celebrated) might have chosen an entirely different look as the undead count. Looks apart, *Dracula* would have been a talkie, and Chaney's character transformations didn't extend to foreign accents. Too, the unhandsome actor wasn't notably suave, unlike the star of the stage hit *Dracula*, the Eastern European Bela Lugosi.

Lon Chaney's last film gave him the rare opportunity of remaking one of his silent hits, *The Unholy Three* (1925), as a talkie five years later. His gruff voice suited the crooked character but was suitably disguised when Professor Echo passed for "a little old lady." German midget actor Harry Earles, a fellow crook in the picture who passed convincingly as an infant in a baby carriage, revealed, "Mr. Chaney was very serious about his work . . . proud of his artistry.

"He was not unfriendly but he did make clear that filming was work, not a social occasion." Earles, also known as Harry Doll, later starred in the cult movie *Freaks* and was a member of the Lollipop Guild in *The Wizard of Oz*.

After sound came in, several stars worried whether their careers would survive the transition. Audiences expected voices to match silent actors' images and personas. Even superstars were concerned—Garbo and Chaplin considerably delayed their talkie debuts. Lon Chaney lived to learn that his future in talkies was viable. The sound version of *The Unholy Three* was a hit. He died a month after its release, a victim of lung cancer possibly brought on by the artificial snow used in the pioneering days of moviemaking. Upon news of Chaney's death every Hollywood studio observed two minutes of silence. The MGM flag was lowered by a squad of Marines and above the funeral a plane dropped wreaths of flowers.

Thanks to his renamed son and, eventually, video and DVDs, Lon Chaney's name and startling performances aren't forgotten. He was given the usual overly fictional Hollywood treatment in the 1957 biopic *Man of a Thousand Faces* starring James Cagney. The publicity-shy Chaney had let very little be known about his private life or personality. "Between pictures," he'd informed a curious public, "there is no Lon Chaney."

<hr>

Tyrone Power (1913–1958) looked like a movie star and became a movie star. It helped that his father was an actor, but like his father he died prematurely of a heart attack—in Ty Jr.'s case in Spain after a dueling scene with movie villain George Sanders while playing King Solomon.

Power once described the life of a movie star as "only a gilded cage," understandable for a secretly gay or bisexual star forced to act on and off the screen. Joan Crawford noted that Ty, a 20th Century-Fox star, "wouldn't have been tolerated at Metro" (MGM), run by the especially homophobic Louis B. Mayer.

Tyrone was the love of Cesar Romero's life. A supporting actor rather than a star and heartthrob, Romero—Crawford's public escort for years—never wed, but Power did three times. Star Alice Faye admitted decades after Ty's death that she might have married him except "He was too fond of the boys."

He also came close to wedding Lana Turner, who revealed he'd once proposed a threesome involving a second male, to which she'd reacted furiously. Their breakup came soon after. Romero, who costarred with Power in *Captain from Castile* (1947), told cable-TV talk host Skip E. Lowe, "Women said he was a good lover. Ty didn't dislike sex with women. But no question he preferred men." About their sexual relationship, the Cuban American was very reticent.

"I don't talk about him in an intimate manner because to me that was sacred. To me he was the most beautiful man who ever lived."

Again, male beauty proved something of a handicap for an actor. Clifton Webb, who costarred with Power in *The Razor's Edge* (1946), referred to certain critics' carping about Tyrone's looks thus: "Most criticism, especially that rooted in jealousy, should be ignored. . . . If they didn't think you important, they wouldn't criticize you. It's like a tax on achievement."

Early on, Tyrone Power's looks enchanted most females and the fan magazines, but they sometimes made reviews of films he appeared in harsher. His face in the lavish *Marie Antoinette* (1938) was compared to leading lady Norma Shearer's, at her expense. In *Suez* the same year, more derision. Costar Loretta Young later reminisced, "Ty Power was more beautiful than I ever was." But the hit *Suez*, about the building of the canal, included French import Annabella, whom few would guess to be lesbian (or older). In 1939 the two were married off.

After war service Tyrone's features hardened and he was assigned certain roles he wouldn't have been earlier. Apart from westerns, he played a carnival geek in *Nightmare Alley* (1947), by the end of which he looked awful. Cesar Romero stated, "Ty was proud of his performance in that film. It was wrenching. But the fans wanted him ever handsome."

Power wanted some of the fans. While in England he was booked on the TV chat show of an admirer. Pre-show, the men happened to be in the same restroom, for several minutes. Nothing happened. As the heterosexual host began walking out, Ty said, "You blew it."

The host responded, "That's exactly what I didn't do."

Some insiders said Power had very kinky tastes. Romero declined to discuss sexual specifics. "The category is one thing, individual actions are private." However, Power was known to be moody (not temperamental). Ava Gardner, who costarred with him and Errol Flynn in *The Sun Also Rises* (1957), felt, "Ty was sweet and considerate. . . . Errol was fun company but semi sweet and not at all considerate."

By contrast, Kim Novak offered, "He didn't like me. He was dismissive and resentful that I was so new [in *The Eddy Duchin Story*, 1956]. He only spoke to me in scenes where the camera was rolling. He was ice-cold."

For whatever reason, Tyrone Power aged prematurely. He drank, but nothing like, say, Spencer Tracy or numerous more recent celebrities. Billy Wilder directed Tyrone's last completed film, *Witness for the Prosecution* (1957), from Agatha Christie's play. In the role of a charming cad who turns out to be a murderer, Power looked somewhat haggard. Wilder later opined, "The stress of a double life has to be tiring. . . . For a man in his early forties, Mr. Power looked past 50."

Journalist Lance Loud noted "the irony that in his last role Power played a character living a lie. He pretends to love his older wife who helps him swear he didn't kill the old lady for money. . . . Of course when he gets ready to dump the wife it has to be for a younger woman. Then she kills him."

The star had been lessening his workload but was excited about *Solomon and Sheba* and playing "a hero and towering figure," he told one columnist. The biblical queen of Sheba hailed from the Arabian peninsula, but Hollywood cast Italian sexpot Gina Lollobrigida. Costar George Sanders afterward declared, "Ty was happy to be in an epic and happy to be in Spain. He seemed in fine condition."

The costars' duel included heavy costumes and fifteen-pound swords. Supposedly Sanders asked that their scene be shot eight times. Power, exhausted, threw his sword aside and exclaimed, "If you can't find anything there you can use, just use the closeups of me. I've had it!"

In his dressing room he began shaking violently. A doctor was summoned but there wasn't one on the set. An hour later Tyrone Power died at forty-four from a heart attack. Some insiders believed it was precipitated by a scene in which Ty had to carry Gina Lollobrigida up and down a staircase some forty times.

Yul Brynner, sporting hair for a change, replaced Power as Solomon. Over half the movie had been filmed. Its original star can still be seen in some long shots.

"I grieved for Tyrone Power for years," said Sanders. "His death was so confoundedly unexpected and so unfair. . . . We weren't that close, but most anyone will tell you he made a movie set a friendlier place."

CRASH: MONTGOMERY CLIFT

One of the most praised and still-promising Hollywood careers was almost ended and much affected by a May 12, 1956, car crash. Elizabeth Taylor's publicist John Springer recalled, "On the day of that horrific accident, Liz had to persuade Monty to come over to her and [husband Michael Wilding's] place that night.

"Monty was rather tired [from filming] but Liz tempted him by telling him that another guest would be a hip young priest. And in passing, that somebody thought the priest was gay."

Driving back from Taylor and Wilding's place, down the treacherous curves of Beverly Hills alone in the dark, **Montgomery Clift** (1920–1966), traveling at 40 mph in the fog, smashed into a tree. Actress and friend Nancy Walker (*Rhoda*) explained, "Elizabeth helped save Monty's life after the accident. She scooped out the broken teeth that were plugging his throat and would have choked him. . . . When the press arrived, ready to photograph his bloodied, mangled face, she screamed that if they took one photo of Monty she would never let them photograph her again."

Edward Montgomery Clift, son of a bank vice president, grew up in affluence and traveled, seldom attending school. Rather, he was privately tutored. At eight his "Snow White" face with dark hair and eyebrows was turning heads on the street. His mother enrolled him in a top modeling agency, though Monty disliked posing. He preferred acting and at fourteen was on Broadway, working his way through plays written by Thornton Wilder, Tennessee Williams, and Lillian Hellman. He was in no rush to try motion pictures—as attested by his avoiding them until his late twenties—nor to experience national publicity and scrutiny.

But it was only a matter of time, and in 1949 full-fledged movie stardom was his with his third film, *The Heiress*, following the prior year's *Red River* and *The Search*. Though he played a greedy two-faced suitor to Olivia de Havilland (who won a second Oscar), the actress received hate mail from besotted female fans who thought she was "mean" to him in the film's very apt ending. One of the new star's nicknames was the Dark Adonis. Film writer Caryl Rivers later wrote in the *New York Times* about early Clift, "His face had the perfection of a fragile porcelain vase. His beauty was so sensual and at the same time so vulnerable it was almost blinding."

The mass stardom brought by movies incurred its own set of problems. Director Fred Zinnemann noted that while shooting *The Search* Monty accidentally and innocently called a boy "dear," then insisted on a retake, afraid the word might be misconstrued. Tennessee Williams said Clift didn't like him because he was relatively open about being gay and the actor wasn't.

Rod McKuen, the openly bisexual poet-composer, stated, "I've read that Clift hated his homosexuality. Untrue. He hated that public knowledge of it might so easily end his career. Elizabeth confirms this . . . she cites Oscar Levant [pianist-actor-wit], who when an ignorant interviewer asked if Oscar was an 'unhappy Jew' answered, 'No. But I'm not too happy about anti-Semitism.'"

Monty's fifth movie, *A Place in the Sun* (1951), rock-solidified his star status and iconic sex appeal. It also gave him a lifelong friend in costar Elizabeth Taylor. Anne Revere played Clift's mother. "Miss Taylor had a crush on Montgomery Clift. I think everyone's heard that he was the unrequited love of her life. She evidently accepted the reality and, being a good friend, tried to introduce Monty to nice men who weren't necessarily showbiz types." Due to the era's political witch hunts, most of the scenes involving Anne, a blacklisted descendant of Paul Revere, were cut.

During filming, Taylor, twelve years younger than Clift, wrote him mushy love letters which he gave his boyfriend. To boost the picture and deflect rumors of Monty's gayness the studio announced "Clift and Taylor to Wed!" without consulting either party. Director George Stevens approved the publicity.

Monty nearly didn't get to appear in his seventh film, the hit *From Here to Eternity* (1953). Columbia studio chief Harry Cohn didn't want him playing Private Prewitt. "He's no soldier, no boxer and probably a homosexual." Austrian director Fred Zinnemann declined to helm the film of James Jones's bestselling novel without Clift, so Cohn backed down. After Monty's impressive performance Jones asked a mutual friend whether Clift was gay. He then confided, "I would have had an affair with him, but he never asked me."

Montgomery Clift has been called the first modern leading man, a male star whose onscreen sensitivity and realism influenced Marlon Brando, James Dean, and a generation of actors. His looks, career, and life were severely impacted by a terrible 1956 car crash. He died ten years later at forty-five.

Monty reportedly coached Frank Sinatra in the supporting role that would earn him an Oscar. Sinatra was friendly toward Clift until he saw him flirt with another man at a party and had his bodyguards escort him out.

While filming *Stazione termini* (1954; UK title *Indiscretion*, US title *Indiscretion of an American Wife*) in Italy, Jennifer Jones developed a crush on Monty. Screenwriter Truman Capote declared that when the shocked Jones found out "he really liked fellows" she went into her "dressing room and stuffed a mink jacket down the portable toilet."

After the Italian film Monty was off the screen until *Raintree County* (1957), costarring Elizabeth Taylor and Eva Marie Saint. It was during shooting that his car crash occurred, jeopardizing the picture. After its eventual completion it became secretly popular to differentiate Clift's scenes before and after the accident.

Clift had been damaged once before. In 1928 his mother Sunny had taken her three children to Europe on the Ile de France. In the ship's pool an aggressive boy held Monty underwater until he nearly drowned. Trying to catch his breath, he burst a gland in his neck and developed a temperature of 104 degrees and an abscessed ear. Sunny rushed her son to Munich, where he was operated on by a specialist who'd treated the kaiser. The operation was successful but left the long scar visible on the right side of the actor's neck on screen.

Clift completed *Raintree County* before he was fully healed. He spent part of the next year in a third-floor suite at the Chateau Marmont hotel in Hollywood. Virtually hibernating, he removed most of the mirrors and covered others with towels. The left side of his face appeared paralyzed, his nose and mouth were temporarily misshapen, and his eyebrows were bushier and blacker than before. The very few friends he allowed to see him claimed he had a wild-eyed look and reported on the myriad pills and liquor in evidence.

Elizabeth Taylor was of the opinion that Monty's looks hadn't suffered that much, that his features had simply lost their youthful "delicacy."

But virtually overnight he went from star to supporting actor, first in *The Young Lions* (1958) with Marlon Brando—who was said to look up to Monty and look down on James Dean—and Dean Martin, then in 1959 in *Suddenly, Last Summer* with Elizabeth Taylor and Katharine Hepburn. The hit film's producer, Sam Spiegel, was known for not casting gay actors in leading roles; a few years later, Monty repeatedly tried to bypass Spiegel via director David Lean for the lead in *Lawrence of Arabia* (T. E. Lawrence was homosexual). But in vain.

In The *Misfits* (1961), the film finale of Clark Gable and Marilyn Monroe's last completed film, Montgomery Clift was third-billed. The macho Gable sometimes treated Monty sarcastically, one day greeting him with, "If it isn't the little shepherd of kingdom come." Monty and Marilyn bonded. "I look at him and see the brother I never had and feel braver and get protective." She told journalist W. J. Weatherby, who sat on the quote for a long time, "People who aren't fit to open the door for him sneer at his homosexuality. What do they know about it?"

In the all-star *Judgment at Nuremberg* (1961), Clift had a very minor role as a mentally challenged victim of Nazi persecution. His reviews were excellent, but his Oscar advertising may have cost him the award. The ads not only exaggerated his role but capitalized on his ill and battered appearance. The implication was, This is your last chance to vote for him. Not enough did—Best Supporting Actor went to later-openly-gay George Chakiris for *West Side Story*.

In 1962 Clift, malnourished and drinking too much, was operated on for a hernia and for cataracts; he was terrified of going blind. He hoped to film Carson McCullers's *The Heart Is a Lonely Hunter* but at 5'10" and 135 pounds was informed he was no longer bankable. In '62 he got to star as (Sigmund) *Freud*, directed by John Huston, who'd treated him decently during *The Misfits*, at least partly because he had his hands full with Marilyn Monroe, whose husband had written the script. But with *Freud* the homophobic Huston turned on Monty. Nearly everything that went wrong during production he blamed on Clift, ignoring his lead's bouts of pain and recurring health issues.

Monty "was giving of his very best," said former costar Lee Remick. "He was starring for the first time in years. He knew how much depended on his professional behavior and *Freud*'s success." Perhaps the early '60s were too soon for popular interest in the father of psychoanalysis. The film flopped.

In a 1982 TV documentary *Freud* costar Susannah York called Huston "very hard . . . and cruel" to Clift. Brother Brooks Clift asserted that Monty died because of an unfair and vindictive lawsuit brought against him by Huston after *Freud* that Monty eventually won but which kept him out of work for the next four years.

After four years Clift's unintended swan song was a European production, *L'espion* (French for The Spy), also known as *The Defector*. A German critic called it "a forgettable Cold War story . . . an insignificant role for an actor who deserves better material." *The Defector* barely received a US release. Monty did it to prove he was fit to undertake a lead opposite Elizabeth

Taylor in the upcoming *Reflections in a Golden Eye*, from a Carson McCullers novella. When insurance was denied Clift, Taylor offered to put up her million-plus salary as a guarantee and a possible forfeit to allow him to play her gay military husband.

Before shooting commenced Montgomery Clift died from a heart attack at forty-five. (Marlon Brando took his role in the 1967 film.)

Upon Monty's death Elizabeth said, "I am so shocked I can barely accept it. I loved him. He was my dearest friend. He was my brother."

Playwright Robert Patrick (*Kennedy's Children*) noted, "Monty Clift and James Dean managed to let their gayness show. But they were playing straight roles—we could identify with them, not with their roles." *Defector* costar and former roommate Roddy McDowall stated, "He helped modernize Hollywood acting . . . yet he lived too early to be allowed true personal happiness."

Costar and friend Myrna Loy felt, "The loss of his facial beauty was a tragedy. But the greater tragedy was the loss of his health and the need for pills, drugs, alcohol and constant emotional reinforcement."

FUNNYMEN: LOU COSTELLO AND DUDLEY MOORE

Some comedians can be funny on their own, while others only reach their peak when teamed with the right partner. Sometimes a comic pair splits up, sometimes not. Abbott and Costello were a long-running, big box-office duo that didn't get along as well as, say, Laurel and Hardy and finally broke up. Britain's Peter Cook and Dudley Moore got along, but Hollywood came along and Dudley got more money and fame on his own in Tinseltown and didn't go back. Both funnymen died prematurely.

————

He was born Louis Cristillo (1906–1959) to an Irish mother and an Italian father. The comic became known as **Lou Costello**, an Irish name (stress on the first syllable, not the second). His idol was Charlie Chaplin, but in New Jersey he boxed, gaining audience sympathy by withstanding—not always standing—severe poundings.

Tired of the grueling routine, he hitched a ride to Hollywood. Acting was out of reach, so Lou toiled on studio labor crews until he could get stunt work. He was able to double for Dolores Del Rio because he weighed 125 pounds. The work was physically demanding, at times dangerous. Disappointed, he left Los Angeles and joined a traveling burlesque show.

Lou toured the country, performing low comedy as a confused Dutch immigrant. Ethnic humor was still big; for instance Chico Marx of the Marx Brothers always performed with an Italian accent. Also on the bill in Brooklyn in 1935 was Bud Abbott, a former race car driver and lion tamer (who'd have guessed). Offstage the men devised sketches for two. (Their partnership would span over two decades and almost three dozen movies.) Writer John Grant helped them develop classic sketches like "Who's On First?" and steered them away from the risqué material for which burlesque was known, enabling "the boys" to work on radio and Broadway.

By 1940 Abbott and Costello were signed to Universal, a second-tier studio known for its horror movies. They debuted that year in supporting roles in a B-musical, *One Night in the Tropics*. It was their starring debut, the boot-camp comedy *Buck Privates* (1941), that made them stars. Filmed for $90,000, it grossed $10 million. Another hit that year, *In the Navy*, consolidated their box-office pull.

By then Lou had developed his roly-poly figure. His other non-performing interest was gambling. Money was a prerequisite for the habit. Initially the duo's split was 60/40, favoring the taller, slimmer, and nonethnic Abbott. Costello, who took the hard knocks, resented the arrangement. He also came to feel that his name should come first, but Universal refused to consider Costello and Abbott.

Lou once admitted that a good straight man was hard to find, but he grew resentful over several aspects of their act, including the perception that he was the dumb one. Lou was eleven years younger than Bud, who the public didn't know was epileptic. Costello wanted to work nightclubs, and often, for extra money. Abbott feared an epileptic seizure in public.

Clearly Lou Costello was the funnier of the pair. Bud Abbott solo was almost inconceivable, while Lou as a comedic actor was a possibility he increasingly considered. Certain relatives and associates reportedly encouraged the notion, declaring that Bud was the fast-talking but phlegmatic partner who basically never did anything but get Costello's character into trouble.

In time the 60/40 financial split favored Lou. With time their movies became less popular (the routines were at times undeniably repetitious). But in 1948 Universal, which had basically run out of monsters to team in sequels featuring Dracula, the Frankenstein monster, and the Wolf Man, cleverly combined comedy and horror in the surprise hit—their biggest in years—*Abbott and Costello Meet Frankenstein*. It gave the boys' screen career a new lease on life, as they went on to Meet everyone from the Invisible Man and Captain Kidd (Charles Laughton, perhaps temporarily desperate) to the Keystone Kops and the Killer, Boris Karloff.

Additionally, in 1952 the pair got their own television show. But all wasn't laughs in Lou's life, for in 1943 Lou Costello Jr., a toddler, drowned in his parents' swimming pool, leading to wife Anne's drinking problem. On Bud Abbott's side, he'd become an alcoholic, adding to Lou's resentment. The boys' final Meet movie was *Abbott and Costello Meet the Mummy* (1955), a worthwhile capper, even if the Mummy "costume's" decline from careful layering in the 1940s to the tacky '55 zipper version reflected poorly—and cheaply—on the studio.

The duo's swan song was a weak comedy titled *Dance with Me, Henry* (1956) that stirred almost no interest. One critic said the boys had been around so long they were an institution and institutions weren't that funny. Lou, turning fifty, believed he had decades of comedy ahead of him, while Bud was slowing down, although his drinking wasn't. Costello threw in the towel in 1957 after Abbott showed up drunk at a twentieth-anniversary performance of "Who's On First?" in front of an audience of NBC executives.

Additionally, Bud was suing Lou for $222,000 in earnings he claimed were owed him for their TV show. Lou made a solo comedy film actually titled *The 30 Foot Bride of Candy Rock* (1959) that dashed his hopes of a solo movie career. (Abbott did not do a solo film.)

In 1959 Lou had a heart attack from which he seemingly recovered. Weeks later he had a second attack that proved fatal. He'd spent part of the day with Anne, who died less than a year later from heart failure, and part with his manager. Lou Costello's final words were, "That was the best ice cream soda I ever tasted."

(Bud Abbott unsuccessfully tried out a new partner but Lou was irreplaceable. The date for the pre-trial hearing for Bud's suit against Lou occurred after Lou's death, upon which Abbott declared, "My heart is broken. I've lost the best pal anyone ever had." As with Laurel and Hardy, the older, slimmer partner significantly outlived the younger, heavier partner.)

"Dudley was a perfect other half . . . often hilarious yet insecure enough to often give me the upper hand," said Peter Cook of comedy partner **Dudley Moore** (1935–2002). The 1959 revue *Beyond the Fringe* brought together Cook and Moore, and was also a hit when it reached the States.

The 5'2" Dudley was the reactive half of the duo. Where the 6'4" Cook was acerbic, intellectual, and sometimes deadpan, Moore was credulous, often befuddled, and facially expressive. Although Peter was the mastermind, Dudley was the more appropriate solo act, funny with or without a partner. He was also an accomplished pianist, joking that he'd gone to Oxford on an organ scholarship, then continued on "an extended organ scholarship."

Born with a clubfoot, Moore hadn't imagined "becoming any sort of a leading man . . . I simply liked the sound of laughter and discovered comedy was a wonderful panacea—rather than a Greek goddess." When Dudley did get UK acting offers they were usually as a bumbler hopelessly chasing after a blonde. "Early on, I gave up hopes of performing Shakespeare—in my mother's womb, in fact. . . . My very name destined me for comedy. I mean *Moore* is so mirth-making, isn't it?"

American movies tapped the Brit for a small but hilarious role in *Foul Play* (1978), as a desperate would-be swinger with a yen for Goldie Hawn. The hit would have placed Dudley on Hollywood's slate of sought-after comedy supporting actors. But fortune intervened to up his status when star George Segal walked off director Blake Edwards's comedy *10* (1979), charging Edwards with riding on his box-office coattails to revive the career of wife Julie Andrews.

At his psychiatrist's office Blake bumped into and was charmed by the English actor and decided to take a big chance by casting him as the shnook who chases Bo Derek on her honeymoon. "Blake very sweetly told me that the plot and the sexy, voyeuristic comedy would carry the picture even if I didn't," recalled Dudley. "Besides, it had Julie Andrews and a promising new—all right, temporary—star named Bo Derek, but also a bang-up supporting cast."

10 was a hit and Moore was a new leading man, at times carefully posed and shot to conceal the clubfoot about which he remained self-conscious. "What I cannot believe is being some sort of actual romantic figure. Comedic of course, but now I actually get the girl.

"Well, I didn't get Bo Derek but, better, I had and didn't lose Julie."

His next hit, *Arthur* (1981), was successful enough to yield a sequel and cemented Moore's Hollywood stardom. The touching comedy costarred Liza Minnelli and Sir John Gielgud in an Oscar-winning turn as a sassy butler (*Arthur*'s theme song also won an Oscar). Dudley portrayed a love-starved, over-imbibing multimillionaire. Some British reviewers noted that his funny, erratic walking in drunk scenes cleverly camouflaged traces of a clubfooted gait.

Subsequent movies weren't as popular, including *Six Weeks*, mismatching Moore with a perhaps too serious Mary Tyler Moore in a story of terminal illness and motherhood. Dudley later revealed, "It's a fluke when one reaches the top . . . a fabulous, unbelievable time. Staying up there is a near-impossibility. You have to watch your castle crumble bit by bit.

"Mustn't complain . . . much. One remains more or less—appreciably less—sought after . . . one is still overpaid when hired."

Misfortune intervened in the form of a rare and eventually terminal debilitating degenerative neurological disease. The effects of progressive supranuclear palsy were evident when Dudley repeatedly flubbed his lines on the first day of shooting his supporting role in director Barbra Streisand's *The Mirror Has Two Faces* (1996). Ironically, he was replaced by ex-star George Segal.

As the disease progressed Dudley was forced to work less and came to rely on a printed page before him rather than on memory. The brilliant funnyman's last movie performance was reading/voicing a movie director in *The Mighty Kong* (1998), an animated feature about the oversized ape.

Peter Cook, who didn't outlive Dudley Moore, confessed, "His success over there took me completely by surprise. Naturally I was envious. But I couldn't achieve what he did. For one thing, I'm not lovable. He is."

Julie Andrews concluded, "The very private tragedy of Dudley Moore's long physical and mental degeneration was a tragedy for us all."

NOT THE GIRL NEXT DOOR: JOAN CRAWFORD

Joan Crawford boasted one of the longest, most stellar Hollywood careers. She was often held up as *the* example of what a movie star should be. She famously asseverated, "If you want to see the girl next door, go next door."

Crawford believed that dressing up when leaving one's house was simply good manners. It was said she had a separate outfit for answering fan mail, which she did devotedly. She seemingly prized her fans—whom she credited with her stardom and its duration—above her four adopted children. Friend and escort Cesar Romero said, "Joan was very fond of symmetry. She had four husbands and I believe each marriage lasted four years."

Via studio influence Joan was named Mother of the Year, already widely admired for adopting unwanted children (as with Tallulah Bankhead and other sexually active actresses, Crawford probably couldn't have children due to illegal abortions). Small wonder when eldest adoptee Christina—whom Joan almost named Joan Crawford Jr.—revealed that the star was an aloof and sometimes sadistic mother, her fans protested vociferously.

It was a fan who renamed Lucille LeSueur (probably born in 1904) via a contest sponsored by MGM, where she debuted in 1925. Lucille initially disliked "Joan Crawford." She thought the winning surname sounded like "crayfish." Originally from Texas, Lucille had moved to New York and become a chorine and dancer, possibly engaging in occasional prostitution, as have many actresses and actors—among the scarce few to admit it: British actor-director Rupert Everett. For decades it was rumored the young Crawford had appeared in a "stag" or porno film, as a young Sylvester Stallone actually did. But no such film ever turned up.

Joan's rise was slow. It accelerated with talkies and films that foregrounded her as a "modern" and a dancer. By the early 1930s she was a star, and through most of that decade was MGM's most popular actress with the public, even though third-place in prestige after "the divine Garbo" and Norma Shearer, wife of Irving Thalberg, MGM's number two executive.

World War II introduced changes and new faces and Joan Crawford vehicles lost money, partly because they were so lavish. The star was horrified to be labeled box office poison in a trade journal. MGM let her go. Warners snapped her up but had trouble casting her in the right comeback picture. For one thing, first pick of scripts went to Bette Davis, sometimes known as the fifth Warner Brother and a box-office queen at the time.

Crawford swallowed her pride to play a mother—to an awful daughter—in *Mildred Pierce* (1945). It won her the Oscar. In the late 1940s while Davis's career was slipping, Crawford's was on an upswing. The 1950s were difficult times for both middle-aged actresses, although the fussy Joan could be her own worst enemy, as when she departed the prestige film and future hit *From Here to Eternity* (1953) because she disapproved of her wardrobe.

In the '50s blonde actresses, more buxom than ever, became the rage. When Marilyn Monroe attended a class at the Actors Studio in Manhattan without wearing a girdle, Crawford lambasted her in the press. She also fumed against Elizabeth Taylor, declaring that the public liked sexy actresses but expected them to be ladies. Joan relievedly announced her retirement from acting when she married Pepsi Cola honcho Alfred Steele.

But he died prematurely and acting as Pepsi's globetrotting ambassador wasn't enough for Joan, who had to take a supporting role in *The Best of Everything* (1959), centering on three young women. Crawford played an older embittered female executive. When she returned to the screen in 1962, her name was above the title although after Bette Davis's. The surprise hit *What Ever Happened to Baby Jane?* put Davis and Crawford back in the spotlight—with another Oscar nomination for Bette, who had two statuettes, but not for Joan who'd spent hours mastering her character's wheelchair.

At the award ceremonies Davis confidently expected to win a third Oscar but it was Joan who was photographed with each winner and who accepted the statuette on behalf of Anne Bancroft for *The Miracle Worker*. Crawford had contacted the other Best Actress nominees, offering to accept on their behalf should they be unable to attend—i.e., performing on Broadway.

Bette was outraged and got Joan disinvited from the Cannes Film Festival, where both stars were to have publicized *Baby Jane*. Davis went on condition that Crawford not go. Asked by the French press where her costar was, Bette replied, "Joan is a busy, busy woman." Years later the snub came to light, as did Crawford's threat to sue Davis and director-producer Robert Aldrich. A planned reteaming of the legendary ladies, with Crawford first-billed, didn't happen thanks mostly to Bette Davis's machinations. She got her less showy friend Olivia de Havilland to costar, second-billed. (The long-running feud's details are in the "Dueling Divas" chapter of this author's *Celebrity Feuds!*)

Post-*Jane* Joan had a hard time of it. She had to do more television work, and sooner, than Bette, the more talented actress. She did the entertaining but tacky *Strait-Jacket* (1964) for schlockmeister William Castle, sometimes got smaller roles in features than Davis did, and had to go to England to make her final two starring pictures. In *Berserk!* (1967) she ran and emceed a circus, showed off her still shapely legs, and romanced a hunk twenty-six years her junior. As in *Strait-Jacket* the villain turns out to be a wayward daughter. (Producer Herman Cohen had proposed casting Christina Crawford as Joan's daughter, but Mommie vetoed the idea; young Englishwoman Judy Geeson played the murderess.)

Crawford's swan song was *Trog* (1970), in which she played a scientist (with a nice daughter) who discovers a "missing link" in an English cave and seeks to study and educate him in the face of opposition from local bigots and religious fanatics. "It was important that Joan continue in leading, authoritative roles," offered her friend Debbie Reynolds. "She always thought of herself as a star."

As movies were running out Joan Crawford did some TV roles, usually in a macabre vein. Steven Spielberg's first directorial effort was a 1969 *Night Gallery* episode in which a blind millionairess finds a man willing to sell her his eyes so she can see, even if only for minutes. The operation is successful but when Joan opens her eyes all is still dark, for the New York City blackout has just occurred.

Where Bette Davis never cared overmuch about hair, fashion, and looks, Crawford—who reportedly had two facelifts—was very image-conscious. It was a highly unflattering photograph taken at a public appearance that caused her to retire not just from acting but from public view. Joan Crawford, star, became a recluse in her spic-and-span Manhattan apartment and in 1977 reportedly died from a heart attack, although some friends like Debbie Reynolds believed she thought it was time to end her life.

SHE DID IT THE HARD WAY: BETTE DAVIS

"I always admired **Bette Davis**. She made such wonderful roles . . . so varied. If I was her age I would be insanely jealous!" Thirty-seven-years-younger Barbara Carrera was a standout villainess in *Never Say Never Again* (1983), Sean Connery's final stint as James Bond. But overall the Nicaraguan was caught in the Hollywood stereo-trap of tempestuous Latin American beauties.

"How could I imagine I would inherit Bette Davis's final role, to actually play her part? But the movies are magic, and that movie is a fairy tale!"

Many fairy tales include a wicked stepmother or a character temporarily changed into an animal. *The Wicked Stepmother* (1989) features both and was a peculiar and sad ending to one of the silver screen's greatest careers.

Ruth Elizabeth Davis (1908–1989), a New Englander born and bred, was nicknamed Bette by her mother, after the title character in the Balzac novel *Cousin Bette*. The name was meant to be pronounced "bet," and in the middle third of the twentieth century many moviegoers pronounced the name as Bet Davis. (Singer-actress Bette Midler was named after Davis by her movie-fan mother, unaware that most people pronounced the star's first name "Betty.")

Bette Davis, like most actors at the time, trained on the stage. She soon gained the attention of Hollywood, where her first picture was *The Bad Sister* (1931). She later declared, "Surprisingly enough, I played the good sister." Universal dyed her hair blonde but dropped her after the boss's son decided Bette lacked sex appeal (not impossible—shades of #MeToo—that the actress had rejected the bigwig's advances). Warner Bros. then contracted Davis but the roles assigned her were stereotypically passive and dull . . . until she fought to accept an unsympathetic role that several star actresses had turned down.

Bette broke through as Mildred the mean-mouthed waitress in *Of Human Bondage* (1934) opposite Leslie Howard. Hollywood and filmgoers sat up and took notice. The new star didn't receive an Oscar nomination because Jack Warner wouldn't campaign for her, since he'd loaned her out to RKO. Producers routinely made big profits loaning out their stars, their rising performers, even directors like Alfred Hitchcock. Say a contractee earned $1,000 a week; if a producer loaned her or him out for, say, eight weeks for $20,000, he made a profit of $12,000.

(Bette Davis was credited with nicknaming the Academy Award "Oscar" by comparing the statuette's flattish backside to her husband Oscar's—she totaled four husbands and until Meryl Streep was the most Oscar-nominated actor, unafraid to play villains or older than her age or look as plain as her character required. Davis was also the first female president of the Academy, but resigned soon after discovering she was merely a figurehead.)

Even after her breakthrough and an Oscar as an alcoholic actress in Warners' *Dangerous* (1935), Davis had to fight the brothers for roles of substance, even going to court in the process. Because she didn't get the plum role of Scarlett O'Hara in *Gone with the Wind* (1939), the studio fashioned a Southern epic for Bette titled *Jezebel* that earned her a second Academy Award.

The first half of the 1940s were her glory years. Davis became known as the fifth Warner Brother and delivered hit after hit, whether playing "good" or "bad." Her latest was sometimes advertised as "No one's as good as Bette when she's bad!" Advancing age and receding profitability led Warners to drop Davis when her vehicle *Beyond the Forest* (1949) proved a financial and critical disaster.

Luck was on Bette's side when Claudette Colbert injured her back and was unable to go onscreen as stage diva Margo Channing in the classic-to-be *All About Eve* (1950), which garnered more Oscar nominations than any previous picture, including of course Best Actress. Davis later advised friends she'd felt certain of a third win except for Gloria Swanson's stiff competition in her big comeback, *Sunset Boulevard*. The award went to blonde newcomer Judy Holliday in *Born Yesterday*. Though the delightful comedienne was deserving, the mostly male Academy voters then as now evinced a bias toward younger females.

Put another way, the demanding Bette Davis—like Barbra Streisand later—eventually made too many non-friends to fulfill her goal of being the first actress to win three Oscars (the first to do so was the less risk-taking Katharine Hepburn, in a tie with Streisand in her movie debut).

The remaining '50s were not kind to workaholic Bette, who worked when she could, earning another Oscar nomination for *The Star* (1952), a less gothic portrait of a former star than *Sunset Boulevard*. Davis finally returned

to the stage. Film-wise she looked middle-aged and was confined to character parts, unlike Joan Crawford, four years her senior, who'd carefully maintained her looks and was still performing romantic leads (with younger men).

Crawford had long hoped to team with Davis, whom she both admired
and resented. A novel she happened on about two sisters became their
surprise-hit comeback, *What Ever Happened to Baby Jane?* (1962), earning Oscar nominations for Bette and, in support, newcomer Victor Buono,
whose excess weight would lead to a premature death.

Bette Davis continued working through the '60s, '70s, and '80s on big-
and little-screen projects of varying quality (she won a lead Emmy for one
of her telefilms). She was said to have enjoyed the posthumous publication
of *Mommie Dearest* by one of Crawford's four adopted children (Joan died
in 1977). A harried but non-sadistic mother to her own daughter (Bette also
adopted a son and a mentally challenged daughter), Davis was heartbroken
when "B.D." published her attempt at an I-dismember-Mama memoir during Bette's lifetime.

At roughly the same time, the star suffered a massive stroke and
endured a mastectomy and a hip operation. She described her daughter's
book as worse than the lot. After Davis battled back to working condition, she did more television and the motion picture *The Whales of August*
(1987), her last completed film. The supporting cast included Ann Sothern (Oscar-nominated) and Vincent Price. Bette's costar was silent-screen
icon Lillian Gish. They played cohabiting sisters, with Davis as the blind
and crabby one.

"In *The Wicked Stepmother* Bette Davis does me the honor of hypnotizing
me into marriage," explained Lionel Stander from TV's *Hart to Hart*. "I'm a
man of means, my daughter's away, Miranda [Davis] has magic powers, my
daughter comes home, boom, Miranda's running things. . . . Like Miss Davis
herself said, the script could have been better." Shooting began and ended
badly, with Bette plagued by painful denture problems and clashing with her
young director.

The star had looked gaunt in *The Whales of August*. In *The Wicked Stepmother* she wore snappy outfits and a chic pageboy wig but appeared shockingly emaciated. "She was still fiery, she never stopped being Bette Davis,"
said Stander. "But her face . . . ravaged, up on the big screen. . . . you felt sorry
for her."

The proud, unhappy star abandoned the project, aware that in doing so she would never be hired for another film. The moviemakers' solution: Miranda later morphs into Barbara Carrera and, what else, a black cat.

Bette Davis died in Spain at the San Sebastian Film Festival, where she was receiving yet another lifetime achievement award. Despite being the movies' most famous and frequent cigarette smoker, she survived to eighty-one. Her body was flown back to the States and she was buried in the prepared site where her mother and younger sister already lay, at Forest Lawn Hollywood Hills, overlooking Warner Bros. in Burbank. The legend on Bette Davis's monument reads "She did it the hard way."

FATAL OBESITY: LAIRD CREGAR, VICTOR BUONO, AND JOHN CANDY

Fat and movie stardom seldom went together and still don't. The first of this trio wished to become a leading man instead of a villainous though praised supporting actor. He enjoyed villainous leads in his final two films but went on a crash diet and didn't come back. He died at thirty-one.

The second actor, an Oscar nominee for his first picture, was happy enough with supporting roles and his looks but feared an early death. He died at forty-three.

The third, more recently, was a leading man who eschewed weight loss, which he felt would cost him his career. He also died at forty-three.

—◆—

Laird Cregar (1913–1944) is best remembered for his last two pictures, in which he played variations on Jack the Ripper. His film career spanned 1940 to 1945 but most anyone who's seen Cregar remembers him, not just because he was 6'3" and three hundred pounds. In 1942 the highly esteemed John Barrymore called him "the one truly great young actor of the last ten years."

The Philadelphian went west in the mid-1930s to study acting at the Pasadena Community Playhouse. He made a name for himself playing Oscar Wilde on stage. Once in the movies he was lucky to appear in hits like *Blood and Sand*, the early noir classic *I Wake Up Screaming*, *This Gun for Hire*, and *Heaven Can Wait*.

Perhaps praise for his subtle acting went to his head, for Cregar imagined he could transition to romantic leads. A gay man, he developed crushes on handsome costars like Tyrone Power and Alan Ladd and eventually had plastic surgery on his face. It may have softened his intense features, but he was still heavy. His weight also caused him to be cast as characters well older than himself.

Laird achieved star billing in his penultimate film *The Lodger* (1944) as the mysterious Mr. Slade, who rents a room in a London house and goes out nights to do heaven knows what and falls in love with Merle Oberon. Playing a lead thoroughly gratified Cregar, whose swan song was the eerily similar *Hangover Square* (1945), as a mysterious lodger, a musician named George Harvey Bone (in love with Linda Darnell) who, again, may or may not be the Ripper.

It's unlikely that these two nefarious leads could have led to romantic leads. Even so, Laird was determined to try. In 1944 he checked into a Los Angeles hospital for a new procedure, stomach-bypass surgery. Between the operation and months of severe dieting, he lost about one hundred pounds but then suffered two massive coronaries and died in December at thirty-one.

Had he lived, Laird Cregar could have become a major character actor with a long career, perhaps losing weight gradually. "His goal of being a romantic figure," said Linda Darnell, "was understandable in a way but not very realistic." Vincent Price, who delivered Cregar's eulogy, later stated, "He had a big heart, big talent and big dreams. He just went too fast."

***

Victor Buono's first movie was *What Ever Happened to Baby Jane?* (1962). He was nominated for a Best Supporting Actor Oscar as a young musician hired by the ex Baby Jane Hudson (Bette Davis). Two years later in *Hush . . . Hush, Sweet Charlotte* he played Bette's father although thirty years her junior.

"I don't care what they cast me as. You see, I am an actor. . . . Is the picture good? Is the part interesting? Monetary arrangements I leave to my agent."

Buono (1938–1982), from San Diego, had an ex-vaudevillian grand-mother who admired his diction and encouraged him to recite, eventually on radio. After joining the local Globe Theatre he was spotted by a talent scout for Warner Bros. who was "looking for a good heavy." That led to TV appearances on series like *77 Sunset Strip* before Victor was tagged for movies.

His size consigned him to looming characters, often villainous, sometimes psychopathic as in *The Strangler*. One reviewer felt Buono could have been another Sydney Greenstreet after seeing him in the TV movie *Goodnight, My Love* as a white-suited gourmet villain. The actor's diverse films included *Four for Texas*, *Robin and the Seven Hoods*, *Young Dillinger*, *Beneath the Planet of the Apes*, and *The Man with Bogart's Face*. In the latter he played Commodore Anastas. "The older I get, the more foreign or ruthless they want me to play." In the mid-1960s TV series *Batman* he was the memorable villain called King Tut.

In the early 1970s Buono made some pictures in Europe and began acting in several TV movies. Asked his ideal role, he admitted, "I hope for another Edwin Flagg [in *Baby Jane*], someone flawed but not a villain . . . someone arrogant but vulnerable, scared, greedy, ambitious . . . in other words, human." Asked about romantic roles Victor demurred with "I'm not the type."

Broadway and movie actor James Coco, interviewed by this author in *Hollywood Gays*, explained, "I'm the so-called jolly type . . . often cast in comedy. The other hefty type is scary or threatening—remember Sydney Greenstreet?"

Coco, who sometimes lunched with Victor Buono in Manhattan, pointed out that obesity can be a gay teen's way of coping with sexuality. "If you're heavy they don't put you on the spot about why you're not dating girls." Asked if interviewers now and then brought up his sexuality, Coco said it was often assumed because of his excess weight that he had none.

Unlike the sociable Laird Cregar, Buono kept more to himself and wasn't "out" to his colleagues. "One reason I became an actor is shyness. . . . Temporarily becoming another being is simultaneously interesting and cathartic. In character I can be very not shy. Which helps somewhat in real life."

Victor Buono's swan song was an animated feature, *The Flight of Dragons* (1982, also known as *The Flight of the Dragon*). The starring voice belonged to John Ritter (TV's *Three's Company*), with Buono voicing a wolf named Aragh. "Nothing surprises me anymore. . . . The only thing I'm not cast as is a pushover."

Prophetically, Victor said in 1979, "With aging, most everyone has to eat less to weigh the same. I do watch my calories but even not overeating I gain. It creeps up on me. . . . It would be useful to know how long one's going to live. I'm just afraid I won't get to exit middle age." He died of a heart attack at forty-three.

———

John Candy (1950–1994) didn't play villains. He was likeable, somewhat introverted, and a bit melancholic, one of a wave of comedic Canadian actors that included Dan Aykroyd, Mike Myers, Eugene Levy, Martin Short, and Jim Carrey. Candy, whose father died of a heart attack at thirty-five, was heavy as a child and weighed three hundred pounds or more all his adult life.

Besides working in Toronto's Second City troupe and on *SCTV*, John acted in several Canadian films. Moving to Hollywood he had small parts in *1941* (1979), *The Blues Brothers* (1980), and *Stripes* (1981). *Saturday Night Live* tried more than once to sign him but Candy stayed loyal to *SCTV*. However, he costarred in ten movies with *SNL* alumni. "I'm not much for regrets . . . my one really bodacious booboo was turning down [the Rick Moranis role] in *Ghostbusters*."

Some critics and fans felt John was best suited to strong supporting roles in films like *National Lampoon's Vacation*, *Splash*, and *Little Shop of Horrors*. Bigger roles were often embedded in poorly written movies like *Summer Rental*, *The Great Outdoors*, and *Who's Harry Crumb?* An exception was the funny and touching hit *Planes, Trains and Automobiles* (1987) with Steve Martin.

Like most comedians Candy eventually yearned for the greater respect accorded dramatic performances. *Only the Lonely* (1991), as a disconsolate policeman living with his mother (Maureen O'Hara in a movie comeback), was a rare non-comedic lead. John had varied parts in *Home Alone*, *JFK*, and *Rookie of the Year* before scoring a substantial hit with *Cool Runnings* (1993).

A proud Canadian, Candy was ironically buoyant in *Canadian Bacon* (made in 1993 but released in 1995), about a US president (Alan Alda) aiming to boost his popularity by vilifying his northern neighbor. John played a stereotypical American sheriff named Bud Boomer. In his final picture Candy was a guide named James Harlow hired by a small group out west who'd rather return to their eastern hometowns. On location for *Wagons East* (1994), the actor suffered a fatal heart attack at forty-three.

Doctors had warned John Candy he was genetically vulnerable to heart disease, and his wife and children urged him to at least lose some weight, but he remained convinced his girth got him roles. "Movies are a physically-oriented business. You have to have something that's different.

"Even if it's not something terribly positive, you can't just blend in. There must be something special."

Many agreed that his personality was special. Comedian Dick Schaal commented, "He was talented enough he could have made it in character roles without so much weight. Good leading roles for fat men are rare as hen's teeth.

"Character roles are often better anyway. . . . It's too bad when a body type pigeonholes someone. It's also too bad when that same body type cuts short a full lifespan."

DORIS DAY AND ROCK HUDSON

A frustrated Rock Hudson once emphasized that he did three, "only three," movies with Doris Day. The two were good friends but with time popular imagination assigned him a whole slew of Day vehicles and conjoined her name more often with his than his with hers.

The main reason is more of her films have stood the test of time. In several comedies and musicals and a few dramas, Doris Day played feisty characters ahead of their time. Most of Rock Hudson's early movies had him playing improbable ethnicities or bore titles like *I Was a Shoplifter*, *Double Crossbones*, *Tomahawk*, *Iron Man*, *The Fat Man*, *Here Come the Nelsons* (about Ozzie and Harriet and sons), and *Taza, Son of Cochise* (Rock was Taza).

Several of his subsequent films bore schmaltzy, old-fashioned plots, while the '60s teamings with female stars other than Doris Day often seem forced and lack chemistry. Some later films like *The Undefeated* with John Wayne and the all-male *Ice Station Zebra* (Howard Hughes's favorite film, which he saw over and over and over, maybe instead of a sleeping pill) lacked much interest.

A shame the oft-discussed but never acted-on *Pillow Talk* sequel failed to materialize.

～～

Doris Day's film career only ran from 1948 to 1968, yet she was the most successful box-office actress of them all. For a record four years she was the world's top-ranked movie star of either gender, in 1960, 1962, 1963, and 1964 (in 1961 she was only number three). Yet the non-bottle blonde born Doris von Kappelhoff in Cincinnati (1922–2019) wasn't anywhere as hard-driving as a Bette Davis nor as publicized for her private life as an Elizabeth Taylor.

Doris had wanted to be a dancer, but a car accident put in doubt her future ability to walk. While recuperating in bed for several months she listened to and often sang along with music on the radio. Her voice wasn't

Doris Day and Rock Hudson were box-office titans, and she was the most popular movie actress ever. They made three films together. Both eventually turned to television, though Rock continued working in increasingly mediocre films, while Doris quit acting and founded the Doris Day Animal League. She lived to ninety-seven.

merely pleasant; she made lyrics come emotionally alive. A singing career was indicated. As with numerous actresses (including Davis), Doris's father had left his wife and offspring behind. Doris, an only child, wanted to ease her mother's financial burden.

Performing on radio and touring as a band singer, her stage name was changed via the song "Day by Day"—Doris disliked it, thought it sounded "like a stripper." One song hit followed another, most notably the nostalgic World War II ballad "Sentimental Journey." Postwar, Hollywood studios were casting about for newer, more homespun actresses. Foreign accents were out and blondes were in bigger demand than dark-tressed glamour girls—except in film noir, which hadn't been named yet.

Warner Bros. screen-tested Doris for a youthful, peppy role in *Romance on the High Seas*, starring Janis Paige, Jack Carson, and Oscar Levant, who years later would quip, "I knew Doris Day before she was a virgin."

The film was a hit, as was its closing song "It's Magic" (the picture's UK title was *It's Magic*). A star was born, and Day's status at Warners rose steadily as that of older, less sunny contractees like Bette Davis and Joan Crawford diminished. Doris's homey musicals and ebullient personality brightened hit after hit, but eventually her range and talent were evident in vehicles like *Calamity Jane*, *The Pajama Game*, *Love Me or Leave Me*, *Julie*, *Please Don't Eat the Daisies*, and *The Man Who Knew Too Much*, which yielded her signature song, "Que Sera Sera." Doris could portray dead-serious and terrified or enact the idealized girl next door. She sang many of her movies' theme songs and continued her recording career.

In 1959 she and Rock Hudson underwent a change of image and a big box-office boost via the "bedroom comedy" *Pillow Talk*. Hudson wasn't a typical screen partner for Day, several of whose costars were tough rather than smooth (Kirk Douglas, James Cagney) or plain-looking (Richard Widmark, Jack Lemmon) or plain comedians (Jack Carson, Ray Bolger). Rock was handsome, debonair, and previously non-comedic. *Pillow Talk* debuted a more sophisticated and elegantly garbed Doris Day.

The picture, a huge hit, led to two more teamings: *Lover Come Back* (1961), again as initially sparring partners (another "career girl" role), and *Send Me No Flowers* (1964), with Doris as a housewife married to hypochondriac Rock. The tamer third film was less successful.

For the rest of her movie career Day's focus was comedy after comedy, excepting the harrowing *Midnight Lace*, the James Bond–inspired *Caprice*, and the semi-feminist western *The Ballad of Josie*. Most were unchallenging but profitable, although decreasingly so. Several were produced by husband-manager Martin Melcher, who used the star as a moneymaking machine. He wasn't her only dud husband. The first, father of her only child, Terry (who predeceased his long-lived mother and was an intended murder target of Charles Manson), was a sadist who violently abused Doris during her pregnancy.

Doris didn't care to work so hard and sometimes questioned Melcher's choices but avoided confrontations and usually did as he asked. Some of Day's assigned comedies were crowd pleasers, like *The Thrill of It All* and *The Glass Bottom Boat*, while others tanked, like *Do Not Disturb* and *Where Were You When the Lights Went Out?*, set during New York City's blackout.

One comedy that succeeded against expectations was *Move Over, Darling* (1963), the retitled and re-tailored—to Doris's less sexual image—resurrection of *Something's Got to Give*, Marilyn Monroe's uncompleted final film. It costarred James Garner instead of Dean Martin, and also

Polly Bergen, Chuck Connors, and Don Knotts in place of Cyd Charisse, Tom Tryon, and Wally Cox. It was a funnier, more convincing remake of *My Favorite Wife* (1940) with Cary Grant, Irene Dunne, and Randolph Scott.

Day's final film was the comedy *With Six You Get Eggroll*, blending her and her three sons with new husband Brian Keith and his possessive daughter to make an ultimately harmonious family of six. *Eggroll* was enjoyable enough, if not a particularly apt swan song for Doris Day's very big-screen career.

"Doris was lucky Marty Melcher died when he did," asserted two-time costar James Garner. "Not just he was a two-faced crook, he was running her career into the ground and paying himself big bucks as a producer. . . . He wasn't in it for Doris or the long-term . . . just take the money and run."

Day might have extended her career had she accepted the part offered in the hit-to-be *The Graduate*. But she felt the character of Mrs. Robinson, a married woman having an affair with her daughter's boyfriend, was distasteful. Years later Doris Day was first choice to play amateur sleuth Jessica Fletcher in the TV series *Murder, She Wrote* (*All in the Family's* Jean Stapleton was second choice). Instead, Anne Bancroft and Angela Lansbury reaped those roles' rewards.

After Melcher's death Doris found out he and his business partner had lost over $20 million of her money. She sued to try to recover some of her fortune and also learned that Melcher had signed her, without her knowledge, to do a TV sitcom titled *The Doris Day Show*. Practically broke, Day undertook the show to rebuild her finances and so as not to abrogate the contract, since she'd long before granted her husband power of attorney.

The CBS series ran for five years. Additionally, Doris did some TV specials and a short-lived cable-TV series about pets. It was on the latter that Rock Hudson, visibly ravaged by AIDS, made his final public appearance.

In the decades remaining to her, the star, busily and firmly retired from show business, devoted herself to pet and animal charities (she also owned a pet-friendly hotel in Carmel, to which she'd moved from Beverly Hills). She founded two animal charities, including the Doris Day Animal League, which grew to become a major activist entity for the rights and welfare of animals.

Doris often repeated that her entertainment career had been only a prelude to the real work and reward of her life, living with and acting on behalf of animals, for "We are their voice."

Starting in the mid-1950s **Rock Hudson** was a, or perhaps the, major factor in Universal's ascent to a first-tier movie studio. After being signed thanks to agent Henry Willson. who changed his name from Roy Fitzgerald (1925–1985), Rock became a star within three years. By the early '60s, with and without Doris Day, he was one of the world's top movie stars.

After high school Roy had enlisted in the Navy. In Hollywood he drove a truck for a produce firm. Later, as a mailman, one of his recipients was Willson, who had a crush on him and found out Roy had been in school plays and didn't like being a mailman. Henry began introducing the would-be actor to the right people, including directors and studio executives.

For some time, Rock Hudson was deemed unpromising: untalented eye candy who often flubbed his lines. Plus that obviously made-up name . . . TV's *The Beverly Hillbillies* later spoofed it via a movie star called Dash Riprock. Willson named his client and early lover (as were most of his clients) after the Rock of Gibraltar and the Hudson River. But Roy/Rock was a fast learner and ambitious.

His roles grew, but meanwhile his looks and physique gained him coverage. The shirtless wonder was nicknamed the Baron of Beefcake. After myriad turns as everything from an Arabian to Native Americans, soldiers, frontiersmen, and other men of action, stardom arrived in a more romantic vein with *Magnificent Obsession* (1954), starring Jane Wyman. It was a remake of the picture that made a star of (also closeted) Robert Taylor in 1935.

The improbable story, which benefited from its hardworking male star's sincerity, features a playboy whose reckless driving causes an accident that blinds a woman. Desperately repentant, he becomes a doctor, finds a cure, and operates on her—of course they've fallen in love—and restores her eyesight. Plots like that could still go over in more gullible decades.

Universal, where Rock spent seventeen years, realized it would be smarter to place the tall, handsome star in love stories that appealed to the female audience, and the next year reteamed Rock and Jane in *All That Heaven Allows*, about a forbidden love: younger man and older woman (Wyman was eleven years Hudson's senior).

In 1956 Hudson costarred in the hit *Written On the Wind*, which won Dorothy Malone (pining for Rock) a supporting Oscar, and was first-billed in *Giant* with Elizabeth Taylor and James Dean, who died before its release.

Giant brought Rock his sole Oscar nomination—and one for Dean, thus the two likely canceled each other out (Yul Brynner won for *The King and I*).

In 1957 David O. Selznick's much ballyhooed made-in-Italy remake of *A Farewell to Arms* starring wife Jennifer Jones and Hudson was a major flop. By then Willson had married off his biggest client to his lesbian secretary Phyllis Gates to keep audiences from getting the right idea and get tell-all *Confidential* magazine off his back. A number of articles and books have incorrectly stated that Universal sacrificed lesser gay star George Nader to *Confidential* in place of Rock.

The myth may have been bolstered by Hudson eventually bequeathing most of his estate to Nader and his life partner Mark Miller, Rock's former secretary. But it was another Willson client, Rory Calhoun (born Francis Durgin), who was sacrificed, not via his sexuality but his string of robberies and reform-school background that ended at twenty-one. The article did almost no harm to Calhoun's career.

On location in Italy the discontent between Rock and wife escalated into a physical fight due to his looking up a former male lover. After the contractual marriage ended in divorce, leaving Hudson nearly broke, Gates blackmailed him for the rest of his life. Columnist Liz Smith pointed out that although Rock could have blackmailed Phyllis back, she had little to lose, whereas he was Rock Hudson.

One genre the star had barely touched was comedy. Along came a comedy script provocatively titled *Pillow Talk*. The producers wished to pair Rock and Doris Day, who had comedy experience but not in a racy comedy where she tries to seduce the supposedly reluctant protagonist. It was a smash hit (yielding Doris her sole Oscar nomination) and provided a new lease on life for both their careers. For eight years Rock Hudson was one of the top five box-office stars.

The star never wed again and the press didn't print rumors, true or false, but Hollywood and the media knew the truth. In 1962 Hudson was in Dallas to promote his movie *The Spiral Road* at a lunch interview attended by Dallas and Fort Worth reporters. A journalist raised his hand. "I've got a very personal question for you. I hope it's not too embarrassing, and you may not want to answer it . . . I've heard these rumors for years, but there's no way to know for sure unless I ask you." The tension in the room was palpable.

"Is it true that your teeth are capped?"

An eruption of relieved laughter.

In 1966 Rock tried to upgrade his thespic credentials with his most challenging role yet, in *Seconds*, about an older man swapping his body, wife,
everything, by means of a new body—Rock Hudson's. The star was very
pleased with his work and *Seconds* has since become a cult film. But at the
time, almost no one was interested and the praise was faint.

Hudson continued in mostly mediocre films but developed another new
lease on his career through television. He did the '70s series *McMillan and
Wife*, followed by the short-lived *McMillan*, as well as successful miniseries
like *The Martian Chronicles* and an '80s series, *The Devlin Connection*, followed by the notorious but harmless 1984 kiss on *Dynasty* bestowed upon
Linda Evans. Rock's feature films were less and less successful. In his last, the
Israeli-made *The Ambassador* (1984), he had lesser billing and a considerably
smaller role than Robert Mitchum in the convoluted plot of a film that had
a bare-bones release in the United States.

Rock Hudson's final appearance was on Doris Day's pet-themed TV
show. His shockingly wasted appearance translated to photos reproduced
around the world. Ironically, the show aired on the homophobic Christian
Broadcasting Network. On the other hand, in 1977 when Hudson was asked
his opinion of antigay activist Anita Bryant, he copped out with "I don't take
a stand on anything."

In 1980 the actor, known for cruising gay sex spots on both coasts,
informed the press, "I know lots of gays in Hollywood, and most of them are
nice guys. Some have tried it on with me, but I've said, 'Come on, now. You've
got the wrong guy.'" In ancient Greece the word for actor was the same as
for liar.

Rock Hudson didn't come out of the closet voluntarily and hadn't contributed to any AIDS charities. A portion of the profits from his "autobiography"—with which the bedridden actor may or may not have actually
cooperated—went to AIDS. His death put a face to the illness, enabling most
people to say they knew *of* someone who'd died of AIDS. *People* magazine's
Rock Hudson AIDS cover was its biggest seller ever, with over thirty million
copies sold.

Hudson's death caused ex-actor and president Ronald Reagan to finally
utter the word "AIDS" in public, after more than twenty thousand people had
died of the disease.

MENTAL: FRANCES FARMER AND RITA HAYWORTH

Hollywood's sexual double standard has been especially evident due to its performers' visibility. An actor expressing a strong political opinion might be applauded, excused, or ignored. An actress would more likely be censured, labeled, or shunned. An actor exhibiting public drunkenness might be criticized or pitied or joked about, not to mention excused. An actress disembarking an airplane in a disoriented manner, hair uncombed, unsure where to go would be very disappointing and disapproved of by her industry and the media—even if she weren't actually drunk.

Women have always been more vulnerable to mental labeling, even incarceration in mental institutions, their behavior more susceptible to incorrect—or deliberately wrong—diagnosis. The ancient Greeks believed hysteria was a strictly female trait. It derives from their word for womb, as in *hysterectomy*.

<hr>

Most anyone who's seen the biopic *Frances* (1982) with Jessica Lange as **Frances Farmer** hasn't forgotten it. The beautiful blonde Seattle native (1910–1970) went from "the screen's outstanding find" of 1936 to a movie star washed up by 1942 to an inmate wrongfully held in various mental hospitals to a possible lobotomy victim to a dull and broken shadow of her former vibrant, rebellious self.

Frances's biggest liability wasn't her outspokenness or sense of social injustice. It was her mother, who tried to control her like a pretty puppet. Father Ernest was a lawyer who sympathized with labor. Lillian's politics began and ended with rabid anti-communism and set her against her liberal daughter. Frances aimed to work in the theatre or in journalism and when she reached New York hoped to join the Group Theatre, whose blend of art and egalitarian politics she admired.

Instead she was offered a screen test, which she passed, moving to Hollywood with a seven-year contract at Paramount. Her breakout film was *Come and Get It* (1936), in which she played dual roles as a mother and daughter. Columnist Louella Parsons gushingly predicted that Farmer would be greater than Greta Garbo, and director Howard Hawks later declared that she "had more talent than anyone I ever worked with."

Frances didn't want to play the Hollywood-actress game. She disliked trivial interviews and declined to pose for cheesecake. She studied acting to improve her performances and spoke up for unions, workers' rights, and other causes stars, especially female ones, weren't supposed to touch on. She thus became known as "difficult" and a "pinko" and acquired enemies inside and outside the picture business.

Her studio punished her by relegating her to B-movies. Ex-admirer Parsons gloated, "The highbrow Frances Farmer who found Hollywood so beneath her a few years ago is playing, of all things, Calamity Jane."

Disappointed and depressed, Frances started drinking. To keep her weight down she used amphetamines—eventually it was found they could induce symptoms of schizophrenia. In October 1942 the fading star was taken in by apparently vengeful police for drunk driving. She resisted arrest and in January 1943 was hauled off to jail kicking, screaming, and furious. Photographers had been alerted and took pictures that depicted her as violent and vicious.

She was denied a lawyer and sentenced to 180 days at a sanitarium where with her mother's consent she received daily insulin shock treatment. Lillian was convinced her daughter was mentally ill because she'd given up stardom (and its requirements). Frances returned to Seattle to become a writer but she and her mother couldn't coexist. Lillian got the help of an ultra-right-wing doctor who believed all "radicals" were insane to get the ex-actress committed.

At Steilacoom, known to be an abusive mental hospital, Frances was disciplined with assorted "treatments"—e.g., experimental drugs, extreme hydrotherapy, electroshock treatment—and she was allegedly tortured and raped. She may have been unwillingly subjected to a lobotomy, a since-discredited procedure basically designed to boost the egos of quack doctors who could "design a new personality."

Frances was in and out of hospitals until 1949 when she was freed, a shell of her former self. Records of her treatment and abuse and of illegal lobotomies later became unavailable. In any case, Frances Farmer had stopped asking questions. Where once she'd had no use for organized religion, she now converted to Catholicism. She settled for hosting a talk show in Indianapolis but in 1958 appeared on national TV in an episode of *Playhouse 90* titled "Reunion."

Her swan song was a 1958 feature film, *The Party Crashers*, about a teenage gang that crashes "square" teens' parties. Frances played a middle-aged matron named Mrs. Bickford. Her 1958 comeback on little and big screen paid no dividends. The remaining dozen years of the ex-star's life passed in relative anonymity.

Actor Melvyn Douglas remarked, "Hollywood has rewarded many undeserving personalities and been ungenerous to many innocent people. It and the overall system have robbed numerous people on both sides of the camera of their careers and even self-respect. But probably the worst example of collusion to rob somebody of her spirit, her very soul, was Frances Farmer."

At fifty-nine she died of throat cancer, traceable to the toxic drugs "experts" had forced on her.

⌣

Rita Hayworth's mother, Volga Haworth [*sic*], was Irish. But her three given names all came from her Spanish-born father: Margarita Carmen Cansino (1918–1987). Eduardo Cansino was one of The Dancing Cansinos, which included his sister and brother and previously his father. In the United States Eduardo removed Margarita, fourteen, from school so she could dance as his partner. There's been much speculation as to whether he sexually abused her.

In the mid-1930s she appeared as Rita Cansino, when billed, in a number of B-movies, including *Charlie Chan in Egypt* (1935). In 1937 she was signed to Columbia, not a top studio yet, but the one that promoted her to a top star. As Rita Hayworth she had her hair dyed red and her hairline heightened, with an attractive widow's peak, via electrolysis. A poised beauty with a soft, cultured voice, she danced in several musicals but proved adept at drama too.

Her popularity grew quickly and in the 1940s she was known as "the Love Goddess" and was a top World War II pinup. Her apotheosis was the film noir classic *Gilda* (1946). Multiplying her public allure was her romance with and marriage to Aly Khan, by whom she had a daughter, Princess Yasmin. Another marriage was to Orson Welles, who did the unthinkable—and infuriated Columbia boss Harry Cohn—by chopping off Rita's auburn locks and dyeing them blonde for *The Lady from Shanghai* (1948), which Welles

Rita Hayworth began as a dancer, working alongside her Spanish father. Her birth name was Margarita Cansino. In the late 1930s she transitioned to a redheaded movie star, adapting her Irish mother's surname Haworth to Hayworth. Known in the '40s as "the Love Goddess," her later life devolved into the hazy sadness of Alzheimer's disease.

costarred in and directed. When the movie, later a noir classic, wasn't a big hit, Cohn became a lifelong enemy of Welles.

Despite her excellent looks, upon reaching forty Rita Hayworth's roles suddenly went middle-aged and public interest all but vanished. She worked less often and in less mainstream pictures. Her swan song was the Mexican-made western *The Wrath of God* (1972) starring Robert Mitchum. Hayworth didn't have many lines or much screen time but got in a climactic piece of action by fatally shooting the villain (Frank Langella), who happens to be her son, in a church.

Rita's last fifteen years were spent in an increasing fog of premature senility. Alzheimer's was finally diagnosed but not made public. The disease was little known by the public and an embarrassment to its victim. So was media coverage of Hayworth's confusion in airplanes and other public places. Her alarmed behavior, occasional brief hysteria, and disheveled appearance were ascribed to public drunkenness, ruining any chance of future work in film or TV and casting aspersions on her character.

The star's two daughters included one by Orson Welles. It was Yasmin who took care of and shielded her mother who, eventually unable to look after herself, basically sat out the rest of her life in unaware seclusion. When her condition was made public, her daughter helped pioneer public understanding of Alzheimer's and was active in raising funds to combat it.

This author was in Spain when Rita Hayworth died. The country mourned and overnight a profusion of tributes and photos appeared of one of the most beautiful and captivating movie stars ever.

(Tragically, Yasmin's son Andrew Ali Agha Khan Embiricos, who was HIV-positive, died by suicide in 2012 at age twenty-five.)

PLAYING THEMSELVES: W. C. FIELDS, GLORIA SWANSON, ETHEL MERMAN, AND DAVID BOWIE

Writer-critic Quentin Crisp once said that when actors are young they're interested in exploring a variety of characters. When older, stars prefer to explore their own. Some performers, especially of the past, were such characters that they virtually played themselves no matter the role.

Mae West, Groucho Marx, Carmen Miranda, W. C. Fields—their characters' names might change, but the performer and performance remained reliably unchanged. Why tamper with a winning formula?

A fan supposedly got to meet Dame Maggie Smith and gushed, "Oh, Miss Smith, I've seen and enjoyed all your performances."

"Really. Which one did you enjoy most?"

Flummoxed, the forthright fan said, "But I don't need to differentiate, do I? Even if I could...."

The following quartet ended their movie careers playing their favorite characters.

———

"When I was but an impressionable lad," recalled **W. C. Fields**, "my relatives called me a character ... *not* intended as a compliment." It meant the budding comedian (1880–1946) was unusual and should conform.

With time he became more of a one-of-a-kind, especially after the ex-juggler, vaudevillian, and star of silent shorts and pictures debuted his non-pareil voice and delivery in talkies. In 1932 he abandoned his fake mustache and really shone in a delightful and distinctive collection of comedy vehicles that ended in 1941 with *Never Give a Sucker an Even Break*.

Before that, he bequeathed comedy fans such gems as *The Bank Dick*, *It's a Gift*, *You're Telling Me!*, *Poppy*, *You Can't Cheat an Honest Man*, and *My Little Chickadee* (1940), in which he took second billing to Mae West, whose contract reportedly stipulated that she could have him removed from the set if he showed up to work drunk.

Like only a handful of sui generis stars, Fields seemed to inhabit his own little celluloid universe. Alas his real world was overdependent on alcohol, and with time his bulbous nose acquired more than a few unphotogenic gin blossoms. By World War II the entertainer born William Claude Dukenfield was mostly considered an old-fashioned curiosity. His brand of comedy was considered passé, star vehicles were things of the past, and even small roles were rare.

In 1942 he was in *Tales of Manhattan*. And then he wasn't. His scenes were deleted before release of the story about a formal tailcoat that passes from owner to owner in the movie's different segments.

There were no more pictures until 1944. Uniquely, W. C. played himself in his final three appearances. All were brief, virtually guest shots. *Follow the Boys* was apparently shot before Fields was paid $15,000 to record one of his acts for the camera—he'd been a top star with the Ziegfeld Follies and had a fund of skits and "trivialities"—which explains why in some cast lists for the film his name isn't mentioned. *Follow the Boys* may have been released last of Fields's last three efforts.

Song of the Open Road includes singer-actress Jane Powell's screen debut. In it, W. C. juggles. The revue-themed *Sensations of 1945* (released in 1944) is generally considered the star's swan song. One reviewer wrote, "Mr. Fields, not notably musical . . . reverts to one of his Follies sketches." Another said the sketch, about vacating a railway compartment, was "astonishingly unfunny" and that Fields was "visibly ailing." Sadly, W. C. Fields succumbed in 1946 to assorted conditions, including an abused liver and heart failure.

"I usually find movies set aboard an airplane realistic, don't you?" queried **Gloria Swanson**. "That's what brings in the crowds . . . on solid ground they get to watch what they hope never happens to them up in the air."

She added, "That's why I'm playing myself. It's reality-based. . . . Darling, who else should I play? I've done it all, played all the characters I care to . . . and I've been flying for longer than I care to remember."

In *Airport 1975* (1974) the real-life movie-star (1899–1983), still looking great, happens to be traveling with an overnight case stuffed with her jewelry collection—not that she seems an avid collector. She refers to her rocks in a cavalier fashion and when, inevitably, it looks like the airplane is about to crash, she's ready to jettison the jewels in favor of the far more valuable, to her, tapes onto which she's been dictating her memoirs. She's traveling with those too.

Swanson, most famous as deluded ex-silent-movie star Norma Desmond in *Sunset Boulevard* (1950), was actually a star—one of the biggest—during the silent era. Known then and after as a fashion plate (she also designed dress patterns for sewing pattern company Butterick), she appears in her screen swan song sheathed from hood to toe in a dramatic black-with-white-trim creation that on her somehow doesn't seem inappropriate for a transoceanic airplane trip.

After all, she is Gloria Swanson. Nor does the philosophic character or the ageless star seem perturbed by the prospect of crashing to death—*Airport 1975* was lampooned as the sequel where "The stewardess is flying the plane!!" The serene Swanson has already lived at least a few lifetimes and knows she will be remembered.

Ethel Merman (1908–1984) was Broadway's biggest star, during the decades when Broadway stardom meant national stardom. She went from stenographer to Broadway star almost overnight via the 1930 musical *Girl Crazy*. Composers quipped that lyricists had to be on their toes for an Ethel Merman musical, since audiences, to the very back row, would hear every word.

"The Merm" was loud, brassy, and confident. Asked if she got nervous before a performance she replied no, she knew how good she was—otherwise she'd be in the audience. Originally surnamed Zimmerman, the star was often stereotypically assumed to be two things she wasn't: lesbian and Jewish. When she married actor Ernest Borgnine—the split started on the honeymoon—one columnist termed them "the most macho couple since the Lone Ranger and Tonto."

Merman, like fellow stage star Carol Channing, was too *big* for movies. (*Hello, Dolly!* was written for Ethel but Carol inherited it when Merman decided to retire; post-Carol and other stars who played Dolly, Ethel agreed to star in and close the long-running show.) Starting in 1930 Merman appeared on screen but lost out on films of several of her musical hits, including *Annie Get Your Gun* and *Gypsy*.

Stage and screen director Joshua Logan opined, "A few minutes of her on a movie screen is like an hour of someone else. She's overpowering."

As she grew older, Merman was no longer cast on film or TV as brassy dames but as loudmouthed harridans. "I've never been the demure type, so big deal!" Post-musicals, Ethel Merman gave concerts, did TV talk and game shows, and appeared at charity fundraisers—but only under first-class conditions. When one talk host remarked that Broadway had been very good to her, Ethel shot back, "Yeah, and I've been very good to Broadway!"

Her final movie appearance was a unique cameo in the comedy hit *Airplane!* (1980). Ethel Merman played Lieutenant Hurwitz, an officer so shellshocked he thinks he's Ethel Merman. And belts a Merman song to prove it!

Like rival and former friend Mick Jagger, **David Bowie** (1947–2016) appeared in several films but was too "special" to attain movie stardom. The androgynous Bowie remained best known for music and his range of looks, styles, and images. His varied motion pictures include *The Man Who Fell to Earth*, *The Hunger*, *Labyrinth*, and *Merry Christmas, Mr. Lawrence*. (Bowie's son is noted movie director Duncan Jones.) In the 1980s Bowie, who'd met his wife while each was having an affair with the same man, went back in the closet, attempting to widen his fan base.

He tried a variety of film genres, but whether his role was large, medium, or small, there were no hits. He theorized to magazine editor Ingrid Sischy, "On a stage I stand out and can feel my personal power. . . . It's different within the confines of a [movie] studio, where I'm one of a team of people either side of the camera. It makes me feel more a cog in a machine, less of an individual.

"I'd need a super-flashy, stand-out role for true impact. When you're past 30 and not part of the Hollywood set-up that's unlikely to occur."

David was sorely disappointed by the poor reception of *Just a Gigolo* (1978), in which he played the title role. Set in pre-Hitler Germany, the film is most notable as the legendary Marlene Dietrich's swan song. She came out of retirement to briefly enact an aristocratic madam in charge of a stable of high-toned male escorts. Her scenes involved Bowie but they didn't work together, as her role was filmed in Paris, where she lived and would die at age ninety.

Actor turned director David Hemmings later commented, "Bowie, a sour personality, soured unfairly on our film. Because it fared poorly in English-speaking countries he savaged it. Europeans liked it, even loved it. But eventually Mr. Bowie compared it to the more popular *American Gigolo*—negatively, although I thought *that* was a terrible movie."

The singer, who didn't get to perform "Just a Gigolo" (Marlene Dietrich sang it), compared the film to Elvis Presley's cinematic output, opining that *Just a Gigolo* was as bad as Presley's thirty-one pictures combined.

David was offered just a pre-fadeout cameo in the musical American romantic comedy-drama *Bandslam*, aka *High School Rock* (2009). However, the cameo would present him as David Bowie, the rock idol of the film's protagonist who keeps sending him e-mails. Bowie was guardedly flattered. "It's not like I need another film credit or reaffirming my appeal to younger generations that include a high percentage of certifiable cases.

"But playing oneself is a giggle. . . . If nobody sees the picture at least I'll have enacted and viewed my own personal creation." Bowie as Bowie was the singer-actor's swan song.

AND THE LATE WINNER IS: PETER FINCH AND HEATH LEDGER

Two actors have won posthumous Academy Awards. Both grew up in Australia and each portrayed a colorful, highly emotional character.

"There's the sad-glad double edge to a rare posthumous award," noted casting director Renee Valente. "The recipient doesn't know what they accomplished [and] perhaps how highly they're esteemed. Yet that person has been remembered and honored and their talent has been burnished for posterity."

(As of early 2021 Chadwick Boseman, nominated for *Ma Rainey's Black Bottom*, seemed a likely third posthumous Oscar winner.)

———

"I'm mad as hell, and I'm not going to take it anymore!" Howard Beale, the mad broadcaster in *Network* (1976), urged viewers to get up, go to their windows, open them, and yell out that rousing, once quite famous challenge.

Beale was indelibly enacted by London-born **Peter Finch**, whose parents divorced when he was a child. He began his screen career in his late teens as Prince Charming in an Aussie short (now a lost film) about Cinderella titled *The Magic Shoes* (1935). After becoming a national radio and stage star, he pondered the natural move of so many or too many Down Under successes: moving to England. When Laurence Olivier and Vivien Leigh toured Australia in 1948, Olivier took "Finchie" under his wing, and that year Peter left Australia permanently.

"I look back on some of my early film work and cringe," he confessed. "It ranges from adequate to rather good. I always aimed to be better *now*, not someday. Being Buddhist, I live in the moment. Actors can't plan the future. . . . I never aimed at stardom. But once I got a taste of stardom I was surprised, pleased, disappointed and amused—sometimes all at once."

Not showy and not particularly handsome, Finch sometimes supported star actresses like Susan Hayward and Sophia Loren. With age he grew more distinguished and developed gravitas. "Hollywood wasn't certain where I fit in. They hear an English 'accent' and . . . whad do we do with 'im?"

Peter thrived in the UK, eventually winning five BAFTA ("the British Oscar") Awards, two of them for then-daring roles: in *The Trials of Oscar Wilde* (1960) as the persecuted gay writer and *Sunday, Bloody Sunday* (1970) as a Jewish doctor in love with a bisexual man who's also in love with Glenda Jackson. Hollywood Oscar-nominated him for the latter.

Upon reading Paddy Chayefsky's *Network* screenplay Finch was impressed but somewhat daunted, noting the strong temptation to overact a mentally unbalanced character. "Most of the men I play are very grounded. This marks a change." He chose to play Howard Beale simply and directly, as a man who believes he's making perfect sense.

Chayefsky, who would win an Oscar for his screenplay, had written for television during its heyday. "Television is voracious . . . a monster. It can reflect the worst of what we are and is all too ready to lower its compromised standards in the race for ratings. . . . Anyone who thinks *Network* is sheer fabrication isn't paying attention to what's happening on the smaller screen."

Peter Finch had one other role in 1976, the year of his surprising death at the Beverly Hills Hotel from a heart attack at sixty. In the true-story telefilm *Raid on Entebbe*, Finch played Israeli leader Yitzhak Rabin.

To no one's surprise he was nominated for the Best Actor Academy Award in 1977. So was long-ago winner William Holden; same-category competitors from the same picture nearly always cancel each other out (example: Bette Davis and Anne Baxter in *All About Eve*). The remaining nominees were Robert De Niro in *Taxi Driver*, Giancarlo Giannini in *Seven Beauties*, and Sylvester Stallone in *Rocky*. Peter Finch's gold statuette was accepted by his widow. He also won a Golden Globe Award and his fifth BAFTA for Howard Beale.

Network also delivered lead and supporting Oscars to Faye Dunaway as an icily ambitious network executive and William Holden's lover, and Beatrice Straight as Holden's affronted and dignified wife (with about five minutes of screen time).

"The Joker is a dream role," asserted Australian actor **Heath Ledger**. "A couple of friends, when I mentioned it, said the guy in the *Batman* TV series already nailed it. They were being sarcastic. But that [1960s] series was meant to be mass-TV, kid-friendly and campy . . . I think [Cesar Romero] did a terrific job."

When the *Batman* comic strip was resurrected for big-budget movies in the 1980s the arch foe was enacted by Jack Nicholson, billed over the actor playing Bruce Wayne and his alter ego Batman. Nicholson's Joker was manic and threatening; the actor had little to say about his character's psychology.

Some critics felt Nicholson was more interested in grandstanding than revealing what made the Joker tick. UK critic Ken Ferguson predicted, "Surely there's a rivetting backstory behind the Joker. . . . If played by someone less saturated with personality and ego than Mr. Nicholson, we may someday get an in-depth look at the warped personality behind that grinning grimace." In 2019 the Joker did become a lead character, in the controversial *Joker*, which won a 2020 Best Actor Oscar for Joaquin Phoenix in the title role.

Bitten by the acting bug, Ledger left school early to begin work, which would also encompass photography and directing music videos. "Creating and sharing images, things beyond the ordinary, was radically appealing to me." Once he'd scaled the heights in Oz, Heath left for the United States in 1998.

In 2005 Heath played gay opposite Jake Gyllenhaal in one of the year's most publicized films, *Brokeback Mountain*. It marked a commercial and critical breakthrough for Ledger, gaining him the New York Film Critics Circle Award and an Oscar nomination. "It's a story that needed to be told," he explained, "in a genre that needed to be better explored."

Cast in *The Dark Knight* (2008) as a more youthful Joker than the Romero or Nicholson versions, Heath said he hoped to bring the Joker to "deeper life," imbuing what could be a merely mirthful or vicious caricature with "the anguish and hurt that may lurk behind a wide grin or within somebody who chooses to create laughter for a living or as a self-defense."

Starring Christian Bale as Batman, *The Dark Knight* was a critical and popular hit and Ledger's penultimate movie. He moved on to writer-director Terry Gilliam's fantasy *The Imaginarium of Dr. Parnassus* (Christopher Plummer was Dr. P.) but died at twenty-eight from "acute intoxication" via several prescription drugs. It was ruled an accidental overdose. The actor hadn't been close to completing his part as Tony, but because he was popular with his peers the role was completed by Johnny Depp, Colin Farrell, and Jude Law, each depicting a separate transformation of Tony. "The more imaginative the story, the more permutations it can sustain," explained Gilliam.

At the 2009 Academy Awards ceremonies the late Heath Ledger's Best Supporting Actor competition was Josh Brolin in *Milk*, Robert Downey Jr. in *Tropic Thunder*, Philip Seymour Hoffman in *Doubt*, and Michael Shannon in *Revolutionary Road*. Heath's statuette was accepted by his family. Ledger's turn as the Joker also earned him a Golden Globe, the BAFTA, and the Australian Film Institute Award.

CARRIE FISHER AND DEBBIE REYNOLDS

"I didn't know if I wanted Carrie to participate in [*Shampoo*]," said her mother. "Warren Beatty had a very freewheeling reputation and the movie's dialogue was more than racy." But Carrie Fisher made her film debut in the 1975 hit movie.

At the time, **Carrie Fisher** (1956–2016) was just another Tinseltown kid-of, though in her case of two famous parents. She grew up with movie star Debbie Reynolds, who'd been married to singer Eddie Fisher from 1955 to 1959 until he left her for siren star Elizabeth Taylor, causing a national scandal. The perception was that Taylor had enticed him away from his cute, perky wife and their daughter and son.

In fact the couple had discussed divorce at least a year earlier and according to both hadn't had sex since the children's birth. In later years Fisher would claim Debbie was lesbian. Taylor later dumped Fisher for Richard Burton, and Fisher went on to marry actress Connie Stevens and then a Chinese American millionairess in San Francisco, by which time he was long retired.

"Carrie has been able to transform her parental background into something like pop literature," said close friend Penny Marshall. "Her life experiences from childhood on are like grist for her mill."

Fisher came to fame as Princess Leia in *Star Wars* (1977), which broke all box-office records. Interestingly, of its young trio of stars, including Mark Hamill and Harrison Ford, only Ford was able to sustain a major movie career. At forty the self-deprecating actress looked back, "Except to dirty old men, which includes several nameless producers, I didn't have much sex appeal. . . . Someone said the double-bun hairdo they stuck on Leia was a Teutonic turn-off."

But she went on to appear in several movies. *Garbo Talks* (1984) starred Anne Bancroft, with Ron Silver and Carrie. "Annie was fascinated," said Silver, "in how this girl had to grow up in the limelight and

Debbie Reynolds was known as "America's Sweetheart." When singer husband Eddie Fisher left her and their two kids for siren star Elizabeth Taylor, it created a national furor. Initially an actress, Carrie Fisher became a popular author, often writing about her upbringing and struggle with the drugs that later did her in at sixty. Her mother died the day after her, in 2016.

how she could cope with two celebrity parents. . . . Annie was married to Mel Brooks and they had a son. I think she wanted to learn what to avoid as his parents and friends."

Many people were fascinated by Fisher's autobiographical writing when she began putting her life down on paper—enough people to make her a bestselling author and not dependent on acting.

Costar Billy Barty from the comedy *Under the Rainbow* (1981) told the *L.A. Weekly*, "Carrie and I had sort of a heart-to-heart one morning about what makes any actor special and what makes him more or less in demand. . . . Being a dwarf—sorry, little person—I'm head of the list when they want someone shorter than short. Which that's almost never.

"I got a little sentimental about that, but Carrie topped me. She shed a tear or two telling me how it's almost never that a star's daughter has anything like the same special . . . star quality . . . and how a girl in this business will always be compared with her mother."

When Fisher started on the drugs that complicated her personal and professional lives and continued putting pen to paper, the interest in her grew. One critic said of *Postcards from the Edge*, "This drug memoir indicates there is no private corner Ms. Fisher will not explore or exploit. . . . What would she be writing about if she'd had different parents? Or would she be?"

Postcards became a successful 1990 movie that explored, besides drugs, Hollywood and mother-daughter relationships. It starred Meryl Streep as the Carrie character and Shirley MacLaine as the Debbie.

As Fisher got deeper into drugs she aged prematurely and was less in demand even for supporting film roles. She expanded her writing from books to screenplays, theatre, and the Academy Awards telecast. She also wrote a teleplay of *These Old Broads* (2001), which united Elizabeth Taylor, Debbie Reynolds, Shirley MacLaine, and Joan Collins. Carrie also turned to the theatre to perform her own material. "Writing is or gets to be lonely. . . . But when you know you may be performing your words to living, listening people, what a kick in the ass!"

Along the way, Fisher was briefly married to singer Paul Simon, then had a daughter by an openly gay talent agent. In later years she appeared to have no particular romantic interest in her life, socializing most frequently with actor-director Penny Marshall. "Except for helping produce a child, men complicate things."

The *Star Wars* franchise continued, and Princess Leia was promoted to General Leia by episode number eight, *Star Wars: The Last Jedi* (2017), Carrie

Fisher's factual swan song. However, footage of her was key to *Star Wars: The Rise of Skywalker* (2019), in which Leia dies. Purportedly the ninth episode concluded the epic saga.

Fisher died in 2016 from cardiac arrest precipitated by several drugs in her system, including opiates, cocaine, and heroin. Mother Debbie Reynolds, with whom Carrie was close, died the next day.

———

Mary Frances Reynolds (1932–2016) wanted to be a gym teacher. Even after **Debbie Reynolds** made a handful of movies she wasn't sure acting was for her. "Our family moved here from Texas and a few years into my working at the studio I was in *Singing in the Rain* (1952) and some other musicals and, well, by then everyone was so set on me going down that path.

"I enjoyed the work, I liked hard work and steady work. But I didn't see myself as a great dramatic actress or some wonderful singer. . . . In time I settled down to enjoying entertaining people. And of course being a mother.

"Being a wife was no great shakes. Not with the two-faced husbands I seemed to pick. But my family and my work were and are very gratifying."

The modest movie star was an America's-sweetheart type, epitomized in *Tammy and the Bachelor* (1957). She was a pleasant light singer and her song "Tammy" became a huge seller. In the '60s Debbie transitioned to comedy. *Goodbye, Charlie* (1964) was based on a Broadway play starring Lauren Bacall as a sex-mad male chauvinist who dies and comes back as a woman. The film was first offered to Marilyn Monroe, who felt insulted at the idea of playing a man in a woman's body. "I thought it was fun," remarked Reynolds, "but the public didn't."

Debbie lobbied for the title role in *The Unsinkable Molly Brown* (1964), which she was able to snatch from first choice Shirley MacLaine. The musical was based on a tomboy-turned-millionairess survivor of the sinking of the *Titanic*. Her role, played with great gusto, earned Reynolds an Oscar nomination.

Thereafter her movie career declined and besides television comedy Debbie tried treacle with *The Singing Nun* (1966), tried to be hip in *Divorce, American Style* (1967), and tried the *Baby Jane* route with Shelley Winters in *What's the Matter with Helen?* (1971). She also voiced Charlotte the beloved spider in the animated *Charlotte's Web* (1972).

Movies and Debbie seemed to give up on each other, but she kept consistently busy, often performing live with her act—eventually in her own Las Vegas hotel, which she and her son ran. A major movie fan, Reynolds built up a vast collection of golden-era movie costumes and props, intending to start her own museum. Alas, it was a pipe dream, and she wound up having to sell most of her memorabilia. The white halter dress Marilyn Monroe wore in *The Seven Year Itch* (1955) fetched a record amount for a piece of clothing.

Debbie also ran a dance studio in the San Fernando Valley, cowrote two highly entertaining memoirs, did an autobiographical documentary titled *Bright Lights* (2016), and continued to do her act and make personal appearances. "The public and I, we have this thing going. . . ."

The star's most memorable late movie, which would have made an ideal swan song, was *Mother* (1996). The comedy was a rare and delightful look at a mother-son relationship, with writer-director Brooks at his best as Debbie's caring and very shockable son. A Best Actress Oscar nomination ensued.

In her actual swan song, Debbie played the mother of a celebrity, Liberace. "I was given a false nose—you'd better not recognize me!—but I know Frances pretty well. She was a terribly domineering mother, which I gave up trying to be once I learned I couldn't get away with it. Especially not with my daughter."

Behind the Candelabra (2013) was based on the memoir of Scott Thorson, initially Liberace's employee, later his live-in lover—later yet he sued the closeted pianist for palimony. Michael Douglas played "Lee" and Matt Damon was Scott. "Every mother-child relationship is different," surmised Debbie, "and somehow Frances was able to intimidate her children even when they were grown-up. In a way, that's nice. But I do hope they loved her."

HENRY FONDA AND PETER FONDA

Henry Fonda (1905–1982) has been called the American Everyman of movies. His look and voice and level demeanor found him almost invariably playing a role model, whether nationally or an everyday hero. Integrity was perhaps his most salient screen characteristic, and he played a villain probably less than any other star actor. When he finally essayed one it was an event.

Fonda bowed on celluloid in 1935 in *The Farmer Takes a Wife*, billed after star Sylvia Sidney. He wasn't a self-promoter and didn't play at stardom. He was private, shy, and insecure enough that he didn't care to watch himself on screen and sometimes wondered if his latest project might be his last. Hollywood didn't turn his head; unlike most stars he didn't abandon the more grueling, lower-paying stage, which he preferred to movies. Fonda declared that a play's nightly repetition gave him "the chance to try and get it right or at least to keep improving."

In later years he was keenly disappointed not to play the henpecked professor husband on stage in *Who's Afraid of Virginia Woolf?* and furious to lose the male lead in *Never on Sunday* (the low-budget European movie's director had to fill the part). Henry's agent hadn't informed his client about the offer, assuming no major star would accept the minimal salary.

Son Peter Fonda stated, "Dad was down to earth off the screen and on it. At his house, he raised chickens . . . he also painted, he was a good painter. It was a creative outlet. Dad wasn't overly talkative." On screen, Fonda's characters were basic and unpretentious. More than once he played US presidents, including Lincoln. "He was the kind of president you wish would be elected more often," said Peter. "Dad was the opposite of the Ugly American."

Even so, he wed several times and was admittedly and according to his children an emotionally distant and often absent father. "His Nebraskan upbringing," explained Jane Fonda, "instilled a self-repression that lasted all his life. . . . He was warm and caring but had trouble showing it. . . . As I've grown older, I better understand who he was, and I miss him very much."

Jane was responsible for Henry Fonda being one of very few stars who finished his career on top. She'd long since expressed the wish to work with her father, but Hollywood hadn't teamed them. His career eventually languished, with fewer lead roles and fewer roles, period, until he wound up doing TV commercials for GAF cameras. Fonda Sr. good naturedly joked that to an entire generation he was better known as "the father of Jane Fonda," a two-time Oscar winner.

Pre–*Golden Pond*, Peter felt, "It's pretty outrageous Dad never won an Academy Award. He deserved it [and was nominated] for *The Grapes of Wrath* [1941]. Lesser actors than he have won … part of the problem is Dad makes it look so easy. It's not, especially for him. He has to dig deep into himself for the emotion which he then courageously reflects on the screen."

As Jane Fonda went from strength to strength she formed her own production company, IPC—for Indochina Peace Campaign, later International Pictures Corp. IPC's hits included *Nine to Five* and *The China Syndrome*. Ideally, Jane wanted to play her father's daughter, but few projects were written that foregrounded a female protagonist's father. After Jane saw the play *On Golden Pond* she knew she'd found the perfect vehicle in which to work with her father as her father in a story that could yield him an Oscar nomination, at least.

The plot centers on two relationships: a resentful daughter semi-estranged from her uncommunicative father, and an elderly couple whose male half is starting to experience dementia. Virtually every senior star actress in Hollywood coveted the big-screen mother/wife role (Janet Gaynor, the first thespian to win a Best Actress Academy Award, had done it on stage).

Barbara Stanwyck approached coproducer Fonda. The women had long before costarred in *Walk on the Wild Side* (1962), in which Stanwyck played a lesbian madam and Jane a new prostitute named Kitty Twist. Stanwyck twice costarred opposite Henry Fonda during their prime, including *The Lady Eve* (1941).

Instead Jane picked Katharine Hepburn, with whom her father had never worked. An unconfirmed rumor said a deciding factor was politics—Stanwyck was right-wing (she'd opposed Franklin Roosevelt's New Deal policies that helped end the Great Depression), unlike Kate and Jane. The latter felt Hepburn was better suited to the role and a better actress (with three of her four Oscars to her credit at the time).

Hepburn was first-billed, then Henry Fonda, then Jane. The supporting role of Jane's fiancé was played by Dabney Coleman, who'd portrayed the bigoted boss in *Nine to Five*.

On Golden Pond (1981) was a big hit and got Henry Fonda that nomination. Sadly, he was unable to attend the Oscar ceremonies due to prostate cancer and eventually fatal heart disease. Happily, Henry Fonda won the Academy Award, which his daughter accepted on his behalf and took home to him directly after the broadcast.

Peter Fonda (1940–2019), unlike his older sister, never rivaled his father's career. Barely a handful of sons of star fathers have done so, like Michael Douglas and to a lesser extent Douglas Fairbanks Jr. and Lon Chaney Jr.

"I had something of a rebellious or hippie streak," explained Peter about veering away from early films like *Tammy and the Doctor* (1963) that cast him as a generically clean-cut, handsome collegiate type. "Anyone could have played those roles . . . I just sleepwalked through them."

A non-bland role found Peter costarring with Jane Fonda in a portmanteau French film, *Spirits of the Dead* (1969). Its three tales were inspired by Edgar Allan Poe (the French title translated as Extraordinary Tales) and directed by Federico Fellini, Louis Malle, and Fonda's then-husband Roger Vadim, most famous for making an international sex symbol of then-wife Brigitte Bardot. The Fondas' plot, based on "Metzengerstein," involves a medievally costumed Jane and a mysterious horse who may be the reincarnation of her lover, Peter. Lushly photographed by Claude Renoir, the episode and film was little seen in the United States.

Peter hoped to make a picture titled *The Yin and the Yang*, with his sister playing Crass Commercialism. At the same time that Jane was transitioning from sexy roles to more challenging dramatic fare, Peter Fonda was attempting to reflect the changing times in his screen work. He cowrote, produced, and starred in *Easy Rider* (1969), made for under $400,000. When he first showed it to his father, Henry responded that it seemed "pretty thin." The motorcycle-oriented saga of youthful self-discovery was a surprise smash hit and heralded an under-thirty wave of anti-traditional filmmaking. Fonda was Oscar-nominated for the screenplay.

Peter's sole Academy Award nomination for acting was in the dysfunctional-family story *Ulee's Gold* (1998). The titular gold referred to the honey harvested by beekeeper Fonda. He admitted, "The nomination was a joyful surprise . . . much more meaningful than it would have been decades ago. . . . I've enjoyed most of my acting work and not regretted choosing the family profession." (Peter's daughter Bridget Fonda had also become a star, but gave it up in favor of her private life.)

Peter Fonda died of respiratory failure due to lung cancer. He last acted in *The Last Full Measure* (2019), based on a true story that took place during and after the Vietnam War. He played Jimmy Burr, whose life—and that of over sixty others—was saved in 1966 by a helicopter pilot whose well-deserved medal was delayed for thirty-two years due to high-level politicking.

Fonda's opposition to that war was nowhere as well known as that of big sister Jane. He explained, "We, the whole family, felt it was wrong. But Jane got the flak and the attention, because it was so unexpected for a female to openly express a political opinion, and one that disagreed with the government. Jane was never 'anti-American.' She was anti those particular war-minded administrations."

HARD MEN: CLARK GABLE AND RONALD REAGAN

Clark Gable's screen image was tough. In time, likeably tough, but initially hard—at times on the wrong side of the law—a man who got his way and sometimes roughed up women. Back then it wasn't actionable or even very objectionable. It got him attention. It got him fans.

Ronald Reagan didn't reach the same box-office heights. His image was lightweight and generally easygoing. Time hardened his features, and when lead roles dried up he decided to play a villain in hopes of a new career direction.

⌁

Clark Gable (1901–1960) had more than a few secrets. He wasn't the only man who drove a car that accidentally killed a woman, but his studio hushed it up (Hollywood brass and the Los Angeles police department sometimes worked hand in glove). He had what amounted to gigolo relationships with his first two, older wives, who helped him up the celluloid ladder.

Gable wasn't a father in his lifetime—not a publicly acknowledged one. His daughter by married costar Loretta Young, Judy "Lewis," was officially Young's adopted daughter (as a child her protruding ears were surgically pinned back to diminish the resemblance to her father).

For decades Gable was nicknamed "the King," because he'd been crowned box-office king in 1936. Myrna Loy was crowned that year's box-office queen. But no one continued calling her "the Queen." Gable's third wife Carole Lombard joked privately that if Clark had one inch less he'd be "the queen of Hollywood."

The heterosexual Gable's biggest secret was that, like many actors, he'd used the gay casting couch to advance his career. As a recent MGM contractee, he caught the eye of silent-screen star William Haines, who boosted Clark in return for sexual liberties that didn't compromise Gable's basic sexuality.

Producer David Lewis explained, "Gable made it on type, not talent. Handsome, confident . . . he manhandled actresses. . . . When he added a mustache it gave him a vaguely 'foreign,' at that time, air . . . dominant. By pairing Clark with all its top actresses Metro added to his sex appeal and gave him a devoted female audience. He was shaped into a romantic symbol. The man's-man roles came later."

Teamed with Joan Crawford, Greta Garbo, Norma Shearer, Jean Harlow, and other box-office queens, Gable's popularity soared. Teamed with Claudette Colbert he won an Oscar for *It Happened One Night* (1934), as did Colbert and the picture itself—the next time that happened was *Silence of the Lambs* (1991) with Jodie Foster and Anthony Hopkins. By the late '30s Gable was easily the frontrunner to play Rhett Butler in *Gone with the Wind* (1939). One-third of the way through the movie director George Cukor was suddenly fired.

The reason, camouflaged for decades, was Gable's discomfort and anger over Cukor's knowledge of what had passed between him and George's friend Billy Haines (by then a successful interior decorator after his sexuality led to his being blackballed by every film studio). One day an irritated Gable—reportedly aware that newcomer Vivien Leigh was acting circles around him—lost his temper and shouted that he could no longer stand being "directed by a fairy!"

The excuse given to and accepted by the media was that Cukor, stereotypically known as a "women's director," was favoring Leigh and Olivia de Havilland over Gable. In fact Cukor guided more actors than actresses to their Academy Awards, including James Stewart, Ronald Colman, and Rex Harrison.

In 1939 Gable married for the third time—for love, not ambition. But movie star Carole Lombard was killed in a plane crash in 1942, returning from a bond-selling tour to help the war effort. Gable was devastated and joined the Army. He married twice more, and his son was born soon after his death (Gable's grandson, born in 1988, died in 2019 due to drugs; his father refused to pay for his funeral or let him be buried in the Gable family plot at Forest Lawn).

After the war years the star's hits were fewer and most of his pictures less special. Again, he seemed more interesting when paired with significant female leads like Ava Gardner, Susan Hayward, Doris Day, and—in his delightful penultimate movie *It Started in Naples* (1960)—Sophia Loren.

Gable's final leading lady was Marilyn Monroe, who'd sometimes fantasized during childhood that he was her father. His swan song was Marilyn's last completed picture, *The Misfits* (1961). Clark played a cowboy named Gay (for Gaylord) in Nevada where Marilyn goes to get a divorce. Gable and pals round up wild horses for slaughter, which horrifies Monroe. The film was made partly on location in Nevada, where the aging male lead insisted on doing macho stunts in the grueling heat that taxed his health. Shortly after shooting wrapped he died of a heart attack. Marilyn was horrified and saddened when much of the press unfairly blamed Gable's death on her tardiness.

Psychologist Dr. Joyce Brothers pointed out, "Clark Gable was a star for his time. . . . Just as many of today's film stars would not have become stars in his era, it's improbable that today's [2004] audiences would make Gable a prominent film star."

—✦—

For two weeks in 1954 a future US president did song-and-dance routines at Las Vegas's Hotel Last Frontier. **Ronald Reagan** (1911–2004) had starred in B-movies but didn't achieve major stardom, and by then it was too late. He was willing to try assorted avenues that might lead to greater fame and fortune, including live performing, and also TV at a time when it was looked down on by Hollywood.

He'd worked thirteen years at Warner Bros., eclipsed by wife Jane Wyman when she won a Best Actress Academy Award for playing deaf-mute in *Johnny Belinda* (1948). Divorce followed that same year, with Reagan confessing Oscar had come between them. (When the ex-president wrote his memoirs he omitted all mention of movie star Jane Wyman. Reagan's editor Michael Korda had to put his foot down and insist she be included in the book. Wife number one had gone missing thanks to wife number two.)

Besides TV, the actor got involved with the Screen Actors Guild, where his politics favored the producers over the actors. Nancy Kulp of *The Beverly Hillbillies* later said, "It's thanks to Mr. Reagan that we don't get residuals for long-running and constantly rerun TV programs."

Also in 1954 Reagan appeared in *Cattle Queen of Montana*, a B-western starring Barbara Stanwyck, and an early TV movie titled *Beneath These Waters*. Prior to his screen swan song he did two more pictures, *Tennessee's Partner*

(1955) and *Hellcats of the Navy* (1957). The latter was the only time he costarred with wife Nancy Davis, whom he wed in 1952. A combination military suspense picture and love story, neither aspect drew many patrons.

Spring Byington, star of *Louisa* (1950), in which Ron played her restrictive son, later said, "Nancy didn't think acting was a very proper job for a man. I know Ronnie was hoping for a [TV] series of his own. He quite envied Robert Young with *Father Knows Best....* He did become an effective pitchman and paid spokesman. I think Nancy preferred that."

Reagan was also up for narration duties, for instance *The Young Doctors* (1961) and *The Truth about Communism* (1963). One reason acting jobs were scarce was that his features had hardened with age and he'd usually been cast as easygoing young or young-ish characters. "It's one thing to outgrow an image," noted Albert Dekker, who costarred in *The Killers* (1946). "It's another to contradict one's image, facially or otherwise.

"Ingrid Bergman played one good girl after another, then left her husband for an Italian who fathered her baby. That ended her career but fast.... Reagan's face became grim ... he seemed angry. No more nice-guy roles. If he'd had a nice smile he could have played the dad on some family sitcom."

Thespically, what was left except playing a bad guy? Ernest Hemingway's short story "The Killers" had been adapted into a film noir classic that made stars of Burt Lancaster and Ava Gardner in 1946. There were high hopes for the 1964 remake. It starred a pre-stardom Lee Marvin, Angie Dickinson, John Cassavetes, and fourth-billed Ronald Reagan playing a villain for the first time. In one scene he slaps Dickinson very hard. "It hurt," she remembered. "In the film it looks even worse!"

But film noir as a genre was fast declining in the more permissive '60s and noir in color doesn't usually pack the same punch. Albert Dekker commented, "The remake looked cheap, more like made-for-television.... Nobody in it had near the charisma and looks of Gardner or Lancaster."

The picture flopped and Nancy urged her husband further into the public sphere....

JUDY GARLAND

Judy Garland (1922–1969) wasn't the first female Hollywood star who had to go to England to find work. Hollywood prefers them young and problem-free. In her swan song, *I Could Go On Singing* (1962), she played a troubled singing star who at one point near-hysterically rebels against going on stage, insisting she will sing only when and if she wishes, that she's given away too much of herself in performance and needs something of her own to hang on to.

The scene obviously referenced Judy's past, as a child, as a teen and an adult forced to sing for her supper and for those who controlled her. Frances Ethel Gumm was drafted into her two older sisters' singing act, The Gumm Sisters, at age two by her fierce stage mother Ethel, whom Judy later called "the real Wicked Witch of the West." Her solace was her gentle father Frank.

In 1933 the trio's singing and dancing act took them to the Chicago World's Fair, where they became The Garland Sisters. Ethel had put Judy, the act's star, through numerous auditions, and in late 1935 her latest led to a contract with MGM. Sadly, the young teen's beloved father died a month later so she had no buffer between herself and her hard-driving mother.

Judy Garland acquired a second "wicked witch" in the form of MGM chief Louis B. Mayer, who called her his "little hunchback" and belittled her appearance. She was given amphetamines to lose weight and work longer hours. Barbiturates were required to "bring her down." The work pace was tough. Between 1940 and 1942 Garland made seven movies. At nineteen she wed bandleader David Rose. Her pregnancy was terminated by MGM because it didn't conform with a young, carefree image. Her studio engineered Judy's next marriage, to gay Vincente Minnelli, promoted from "race" musicals to big-time Technicolor pictures.

Giving birth to Liza Minnelli in 1946 didn't much lighten Judy's workload. The pace and postpartum depression led to yet more drugs. Garland started filming *Annie Get Your Gun* (from the Broadway hit musical with Ethel Merman) but exhaustion, a nervous breakdown, and hospitalization gave the plum role to Betty Hutton. Judy did one more film for MGM, which unceremoniously terminated her contract after *Summer Stock* (1950; UK title *If You Feel Like Singing*).

The young veteran star was considered washed up in Hollywood. She journeyed to London where her Palladium concerts were so well received she was invited to perform at New York City's Palace Theatre. With producer husband Sid Luft Judy had another daughter and a son and returned to the screen in 1954 in a remake of *A Star Is Born*, directed by George Cukor. The future classic, for Warners, was edited drastically and wasn't the huge, hoped-for hit—neither was *The Wizard of Oz* (1939) at the time. Judy was stung when Academy voters failed to hand her a well-deserved Oscar (for the picture itself or career achievement . . . many awards have been given more for cumulative acting than a particular performance).

She was off the screen until the 1960s. In 1959 Judy almost died from liver failure caused by hepatitis. Again, it was singing, not movies, that propelled her, via her legendary 1961 concerts at Carnegie Hall. The same year, she was Oscar nominated in the supporting category for *Judgment at Nuremberg* and again didn't win. Her marriage to Luft was ending and Garland added Valium and Ritalin to her pharmacological routine. The divorce left her grossly in debt.

In 1962 Judy finished off her screen career. She voiced a Parisian cat named Mewsette in the animated feature *Gay Purr-ee*, worked with developmentally challenged children in *A Child Is Waiting*, costarring Burt Lancaster, and was often mesmerizing in her swan song *I Could Go On Singing* that costarred Dirk Bogarde. The British actor predicted, "She is so wonderful in this picture, it's only the beginning of a marvelous run of Judy Garland vehicles." That was not to be.

In 1964 her acclaimed TV variety show was canceled after just one season. In her last few years Judy undertook two more marriages (another one to a gay man). Concert dates in the States had dried up, so Garland toured the Continent but was increasingly disoriented by drugs and at times unable to perform. In London Judy Garland's fifth husband found her dead in the bathroom. The autopsy stated accidental death via an overdose of the barbiturate Seconal. Friends and relatives scotched rumors of suicide. Though prone to intermittent depression, Judy had a proven ability to bounce back thanks to high spirits and her sense of humor. Besides, she was a devoted mother, even if slightly competitive with her grown daughter.

Judy's body was flown back to Manhattan, where she was mourned by more fans than any star since Rudolph Valentino in 1926. Frank Sinatra said of his generation of singers, "The rest of us will be forgotten. Never Judy."

PLATINUM BOMBSHELL: JEAN HARLOW

She was the original Platinum Blonde and a sex symbol, but **Jean Harlow** (1911–1937) was The Baby to her relatives and to MGM coworkers. Born Harlean—pronounced Harley-Ann—Carpenter, she was renamed after her ambitious mother and was a mama's girl.

Mama Jean has often been blamed for the twenty-six-year-old star's death, partly because she was a Christian Scientist and anti-doctors. (The maternal role was played in two 1965 Harlow biopics by Angela Lansbury and by Ginger Rogers in her movie swan song.) Jean didn't deny The Baby all medical attention, for at fifteen Harlean suffered a severe case of scarlet fever followed by a serious kidney infection. High blood pressure, hypertension, and undiagnosed nephritis ensued over the years. Mama Jean consented to medical procedures when necessary.

At sixteen Harlean fell in love with an affluent orphan. They eloped to Beverly Hills. A girlfriend made a hobby of extra work in films, so one day in 1928 Harlean gave her a ride to Fox Studios (which didn't merge with Twentieth Century until 1935). Harlean was noticed by a casting director who said she could get work if she registered with Central Casting. Mama Jean urged her to follow up (she'd left Kansas City to be with the young couple).

Taking her mother's proffered names, Jean Harlow made her screen debut in 1928 as an unbilled extra in *Moran of the Marines*. She participated in comedies like *Thundering Toupees* and *Double Whoopee*, both for Hal Roach Studios in 1929, the latter starring Laurel and Hardy. Her big break was Howard Hughes's World War I epic *Hell's Angels* (1930), about two flyer brothers, one of whom Jean betrays. Hughes signed her to a contract paying $100 a week, then as her fame grew loaned her out for much more while still paying her $100.

In 1931 she appeared in the gangster hit *The Public Enemy* and costarred in *Platinum Blonde*, top-billing Loretta Young. The picture had been renamed in favor of the rising star whose hair was growing lighter and lighter. Angela

Lansbury later said, "She was the first to be labeled a 'platinum bombshell.' The term was new and had to be explained to [people] who thought it was some kind of a weapon."

Indeed Jean Harlow was viewed by part of the Establishment as a weapon undermining women's virtue and national morality. Her easy onscreen sexuality was attacked by church groups. She and Mae West, an older bottle blonde with a more aggressive sexuality, were in large measure responsible for the stricter censorship code that took effect in 1934 and lasted into the 1960s. The so-called Legion of Decency inveighed against West's and Harlow's screen characters "enjoying sex without shame or embarrassment," though of course sex was never depicted.

Onscreen Jean was noted and notorious for wearing clinging satin gowns and going braless. (Offscreen she favored floppy pants and sportswear.) "Oh, she was slinky," marveled Bette Davis decades later. "But her biggest impact was on all us newcomers who had to be bleached blonde. We had no choice. Every studio wanted its own Jean Harlow after MGM made a fortune off her."

The very fact of Jean having a career, and her escalating fame, ended her first marriage, as it later would Marilyn Monroe's. (Marilyn, whose given names were Norma Jeane, didn't get to fulfill her wish of portraying her muse on screen.) Harlow, like Monroe, loved to read but kept it quiet out of fear of ridicule. Like Marilyn, Jean preferred to socialize with authors rather than actors. She'd had a short story published at school and planned eventually to write a novel. Her Hollywood-themed *Today Is Tonight* wasn't published until 1965, Mama Jean having sold the late Baby's manuscript to MGM while retaining the publishing rights.

Championing the star at MGM was executive and future husband Paul Bern, who'd convinced the prudish Louis B. Mayer to buy out her contract from Howard Hughes. Bern effected Jean's transition from unsympathetic gun molls to likeable vamps, emphasizing her comedic talent as much as her sex appeal. As with Marilyn and playwright Arthur Miller two decades later, Hollywood wondered about the attraction between the blonde and the Jewish intellectual. Bern mentored Harlow, recommending worthwhile books and increasing her confidence in her acting.

Ironically, Jean Harlow's most famous movie scene is the climax of the 1933 classic *Dinner at Eight*. As the moneyed guests saunter in to dine, *grande dame* Marie Dressler does a double take after Harlow's character says she's been reading a book. The tightly gowned blonde calls it "a nutty kind

Jean Harlow's screen characters enjoyed "sex without shame or embarrassment."
Of course sex was never depicted during Hollywood's golden age, but the plati-
num blonde star inadvertently helped usher in stricter movie censorship in 1934.
She died three years later at twenty-six.

of a book." It predicts that someday "Machinery is going to take the place of every profession."

Dressler looks Harlow up and especially down, then reassures her with a pat, "Oh, my dear—that's something you need never worry about."

Two months after her second marriage, Jean was horrified by the death of Paul Bern, which MGM framed to look like a suicide. (She'd been at her other home, where Mama lived and Jean often spent the night.) In fact Paul had long since parted with a mentally unstable actress he'd lived with, unaware that under New York State law she was his common-law wife and thus his marriage to Jean Harlow was invalid. MGM near-panicked, since public knowledge of its sexy star being involved in bigamy would endanger her career and their profits. It was hushed up that Bern's ex had almost certainly shot him.

MGM pushed Harlow to remarry about a year after Bern's death to avoid another scandal. She'd fallen in love with "the Jewish Adonis" Max Baer, a champion boxer (and father of Max Baer Jr., Jethro on TV's *The Beverly Hillbillies*). But Baer was married, and his wife threatened to brand the platinum blonde a homewrecker. Jean agreed to wed MGM cameraman Hal Rosson, about twice her age. Eight months later there was a formal separation.

The three-times-married star continued a box-office winner even after censorship was strengthened. Her looks and humor and down-to-earth personality kept her popular. The public didn't know that since Paul Bern's death Jean's drinking had increased and was affecting her health. Her swan song *Saratoga* (1937) was a routine romance with a racetrack background in which the heroine forgoes wedding the intended rich suitor and falls in love with her earthier leading man, Clark Gable. During shooting Harlow felt fatigued and nauseated. She was misdiagnosed with influenza. When the pain became too great she had to quit the film.

Kidney disease was little understood in 1937. There was no dialysis, no kidney transplants, and antibiotics were generally unavailable. Though Jean was worsening, Mama Jean kept The Baby under her supervision at home rather than in a hospital. After uremic poisoning had spread throughout her body, Jean was admitted to Good Samaritan Hospital, where she died on June 7, 1937, at the age of twenty-six.

MGM writer Harry Ruskin recalled, "The day The Baby died there wasn't one sound in the MGM commissary for three hours . . . not one goddamn sound."

Jean Harlow's unfinished scenes in *Saratoga* (1937) were fulfilled via a double, using longshots and scenes played with the double's back to the audience. Compare to the 2000 *Gladiator*, in which British actor Oliver Reed played Proximo, a slave- and gladiator-owner. After Reed died before completing his part, his voice was digitally reproduced and the rest of him was readily "replaced" by CGI technology.

Soon after Jean's death her mother got a seven-year contract with MGM as a "talent and literary scout and a reader." All told, she would be paid about $50,000, yet the contract stipulated she didn't have to do any work for it. The studio had acquiesced to her demand for remuneration for past "services" on her daughter's behalf, aware she could otherwise unleash a media storm with stories about the maneuverings of the studio that she claimed had worked The Baby to death.

Mama Jean died twenty-one years after her daughter, on the same day and in the same hospital. She was buried next to *the* Jean Harlow at Forest Lawn Cemetery in Glendale, California.

LENA HORNE AND DOROTHY DANDRIDGE

Lena Horne and Dorothy Dandridge were born too soon. Their beauty and talent didn't open the proper Hollywood doors. Lena's looks got her into MGM, but in A-pictures she appeared in minor, even excise-able parts, virtually musical interludes. The younger Dorothy broke through in the 1950s with lead roles and was up for a Best Actress Oscar. Yet as a pioneer and a novelty she enjoyed only fleeting big-time success.

Both women had relationships with white men (their second husbands) that they had to hide. Besides acting, both were nightclub performers. But Lena Horne was a survivor, living to ninety-two, while Dorothy Dandridge, forty-two, was one of Hollywood's tragic casualties.

<hr>

Lena Horne (1917–2010) was Hollywood's first black almost-star. Actually, she was of African, Native American, and European ancestry. The first two precluded her being a romantic lead, so MGM usually positioned her in musical numbers that could be cut from movies exhibited in the Deep South.

Born into a relatively affluent and an educated family, music was her preferred mode of expression. By sixteen she'd joined the chorus of the famed Cotton Club. Lena yearned to sing solo and develop her own style. "In Hollywood they told me not to open my mouth so wide. 'Sing pretty,' they would say." She also felt bound to marry and in 1937 wed Louis Jones, described as a political operative or a political activist. The marriage produced two children and ended in 1944.

Horne started in movies in 1938 in *The Duke Is Tops* (referring to musician "Duke" Ellington). She was the first "colored" performer to be signed to a long-term contract by a major studio. However she was confined to all-black musicals made on the cheap and in black-and-white, and to what amounted to guest appearances in Technicolor A-pictures.

Her best-known vehicle was *Cabin in the Sky* (1943), a "race" musical directed by Vincente Minnelli. "They were unfair to Miss Horne in more than one way," he declared. "She was a very pretty lady but they made no effort to pair her on screen with an attractive colored man."

There was practically no effort made at any studio to find and build up a handsome black or part-black actor into a star. "They thought if her leading man was homely it would add a touch of comedy. . . . In truth, it was less threatening to the status quo." Two attractive non-white leads were presumably too close to the standard Hollywood formula.

By the time Horne began in pictures she was known as a nightclub singer, so MGM pushed her as a singer more than an actress. Her signature song was "Stormy Weather," also one of her film titles (in 1943). Lena sometimes appeared in multi-star extravaganzas celebrating a popular composer. She lobbied for the role of "half-caste" Julie in MGM's big 1951 remake of *Showboat* but the part went to dark-haired Ava Gardner, whose singing then had to be dubbed.

Horne became fed up with Hollywood, where her last film until 1956 was *The Duchess of Idaho* (1950) starring Esther Williams. "The race musicals," explained Minnelli, "went extinct by the '50s. . . . Lena Horne kept waiting to be given her own movie but she was always cast in somebody else's movie."

The chanteuse, who sang and "starred in nightclubs on four continents," re-wed in Paris in 1947. The couple kept their union a secret for three years because bandleader Lennie Hayton was white. In the United States the marriage caused the pair problems for years to come. They remained married until Hayton's death in 1971.

(Marital discrimination also haunted white actresses, for instance Swedish-born Inger Stevens whose friends and fans were amazed to learn after her 1970 suicide that she'd been married to an African American character actor since 1961. However, they were estranged by the time of her death.)

Besides nightclubs, Lena was a recording and a Broadway musical star. "She didn't need Hollywood," observed singer-actress Eartha Kitt. "Not once she began headlining at the top posh spots."

Meet Me in Las Vegas (1956) wasn't touted as a comeback, for it starred Dan Dailey and Cyd Charisse, with Lena Horne way down the cast list. (Its UK title was *Viva Las Vegas*, like the '60s Elvis movie, whose UK title was *Love in Las Vegas*.) The singer-actress was then off the screen until 1969 when she costarred in the non-hit *Death of a Gunfighter* starring Richard

Widmark. Friend Ava Gardner remarked, "Lena's good looks have matured and ripened. . . . She's excellent in the movie. The movie's not that excellent.

"She deserves to finally have a big, starring musical movie showcase." It never happened.

Horne's movie swan song was in an all-black musical. But not a black-and-white cheapie. *The Wiz*, adapted from the hit Broadway musical, was a lavish color production starring Diana Ross as a grown-up Dorothy (in her third and final motion picture). Again, Horne had a stand-out musical number but in somebody else's picture. *The Wiz* was directed by her son-in-law Sidney Lumet. Lena Horne played Glinda the Good, glittering in blue and silver, preparing to send Dorothy back to New York City (not Kansas). Her song, "Believe in Yourself," toward the finale, was perhaps the film's highlight. (Some reviewers said she outshone and looked better than the much younger Diana Ross.) But: a major flop.

Lena appeared as herself in an episode of *The Cosby Show* (1985) and of *A Different World* (1993). She was included in the MGM documentary *That's Entertainment III* (1994), like its predecessors comprised of past musical clips. In 2000 she retired. If anything, Lena Horne's swan song should be considered her multi-award-winning one-woman autobiographical musical show *Lena Horne: The Lady and Her Music*, which opened on Broadway in 1981, where it ran over three hundred performances before going triumphantly on tour.

"My life hasn't always been a song," she recounted, "but I tell the story of my life in songs. . . . Before the critics were used to me it sometimes got remarked how I may rear back during a given song. Then I rear forward. It's simply my deeply feeling that music and that lyric. It takes me aback . . . it pushes me forward. Music has kept me going, kept me pushing through. Music has never let me down."

Dorothy Dandridge (1922–1965) was the first African American to be nominated in a major Academy Award acting category. When she was up for Best Actress for *Carmen Jones* (1954) it was widely assumed the award would go to veteran Judy Garland. Instead it went to young blonde newcomer Grace Kelly.

Along with Lena Horne, Dandridge was one of the first black actresses not to be stuck playing maids. Butterfly McQueen, best known as Prissy in

Gone with the Wind (1939), said in 1965, "To not play a maid you had to be slim and sexy-like and you had to have a certain kind of facial features. But I applaud anybody that's able to throw off the burdens of the entertainment business."

The light-skinned Dorothy Dandridge had her share of burdens. First husband Harold Nicholas of the dancing Nicholas Brothers was an incorrigible womanizer. Their daughter and her only child Harolyn was severely mentally challenged, a fact the rising star had to hide. Nicholas didn't take responsibility after the divorce, so Harolyn was tended by Dandridge's mother Ruby and a female friend until Dorothy placed her in the care of a private nurse (when money eventually ran out she placed the teen, who had a mental age of four, in a state institution). Dorothy also had to hide her post-Nicholas relationships, matrimonial and otherwise, since they were with white men.

A talented singer-dancer, after a few movie bit parts starting in 1937 she became a success in nightclubs in the 1940s. "Miss Dandridge said she preferred singing, also dancing, to most acting," said British actor James Mason. "She felt she could better express herself . . . probably without the confines of a given, perhaps restrictive role. It's a shame she wasn't allowed, as a professional singer, to do her own vocals in *Carmen Jones*."

"Dorothy enjoyed the climb," offered Eartha Kitt, "but when she started climbing the more slippery Hollywood ladder she found it promised more than she would be able to take. . . . I was lucky always to have singing to fall back on, as well as the stage. Movies and the TV, those were occasional gigs."

The '50s would be a breakthrough decade for Dorothy and for racial depictions but as of 1951 she had an "African" role in *Tarzan's Peril* (UK title: *Tarzan and the Jungle Queen*) and appeared in *The Harlem Globetrotters*. When Georges Bizet's nineteenth-century opera *Carmen* was given contemporary American-English lyrics by Oscar Hammerstein II, the iconoclastic film project went to anti-censorship director-producer Otto Preminger, most of whose family had perished in the Holocaust.

Carmen Jones starred singers Harry Belafonte and Dorothy Dandridge, but they were voiced by operatic singers (Marilyn Horne for Dorothy). The all-black musical was a novelty and made its leading lady a star. "She is seductive and wonderfully expressive," noted Preminger, who had a romance with Dorothy. "She is a star of today and tomorrow. I hope to find her another suitable project."

But her next film wasn't until 1957. *Island in the Sun* featured lush Caribbean backgrounds and interracial romances. Besides Dandridge, it starred James Mason, Joan Fontaine, Harry Belafonte, and Joan Collins. Black-and-white romance and yearning was tolerated, kissing and implied sex was not. The daring film was financially successful but Dorothy's subsequent films were mostly unsatisfactory.

"She should have been put up-front," said *Porgy and Bess* costar Sammy Davis Jr. "It was like bad luck. If she was up-front the picture was usually lousy. . . . If it was good she was somewhere back-of-center." Following *Carmen Jones* and *Island in the Sun* the public seemed to lose interest in the pioneering star. Her last worthwhile movie was *Porgy and Bess* (1959) with Sidney Poitier, directed by Preminger.

Hollywood could have continued stirring interest in her with better projects but "the whole Dorothy Dandridge situation was new to us all," said Paramount producer A. C. Lyles. "No one knew what to do with her. Writers weren't creating stories around someone like her."

While waiting for Hollywood to showcase her, Dandridge had to go to Europe to keep working. There, she filmed *The Happy Road* and *Tamango*. But as often happened, a European film, unless it boasted a major star, got minimal US distribution. Rather than becoming more accepted with time, Dorothy remained "exotic" in pictures like *Tamango*, *The Decks Ran Red*, and *Malaga* (1960, UK title: *Moment of Danger*). The latter, about a jewel thief on the run, starred Englishman Trevor Howard. He was quoted, "Miss Dandridge plays the special girlfriend . . . it's not an ideal role or one for a star actress. But most roles aren't, and if Miss Dandridge is hired to add something beyond the usual, what's wrong with that?"

Minimal opportunities and an unsatisfactory, secretive private life, added to guilt over her daughter's situation, led the fading star to depression and prescription drugs. *Malaga* was Dorothy's disappointing movie swan song. A 1962 cheapie flick titled *The Murder Men* would have been her big-screen swan song but instead was later used as an episode of the TV series *Cain's Hundred* and retitled "Blues for a Junkman." Dorothy enacted a nightclub singer and addict newly out of jail. It was released to cinemas in the UK.

Dorothy Dandridge, forty-two, was found dead in her Los Angeles apartment, nude with only a blue scarf around her neck. The autopsy revealed she'd overdosed on her antidepressant, Tofranil. It may have been accidental or suicide. A few months earlier she'd given her manager a note: "In case of

death . . . cremate me right away. If I have anything . . . give it to my mother."
Her bank account totaled $2.14.

"She couldn't cope," felt Sammy Davis Jr. "Hollywood, the big let-down
. . . trying to live like a star, trying to stay up there . . . and Hollywood, man,
they didn't know how to cope with her."

GONE WITH THE WIND: LESLIE HOWARD, HATTIE McDANIEL, AND BUTTERFLY McQUEEN

Much or most of the attention *Gone with the Wind* (1939) still revolves around its two central characters and stars, Scarlett O'Hara (Vivien Leigh) and Rhett Butler (Clark Gable). But the Southern epic includes unforgettable performances by the fascinating performers Leslie Howard, Hattie McDaniel, Butterfly McQueen, and the long-lived Olivia de Havilland (in the "Centenarians" chapter).

———

Most people don't know that **Leslie Howard**, best remembered as Ashley Wilkes in *Gone with the Wind*, was shot down by the Nazis at age fifty. Or that Howard (1893–1943), a top star of the 1930s, was Jewish, of Hungarian origin—birth name: Leslie Howard Stainer—as was Douglas Fairbanks (Douglas Ulman), a leading silent star and cofounder in 1919 of United Artists.

Howard, a tall, blond Englishman with a sensitive, intelligent look, got into acting after experiencing shellshock during World War I. His rehabilitation program suggested a hobby. He chose acting and became a popular stage and screen actor in Britain and the States. His first talkie was his first American movie, *Outward Bound* (1930). He was nominated for a Best Actor Oscar for *Berkeley Square* (1933) and became globally popular in the adventure costume drama *The Scarlet Pimpernel* (1934) with Merle Oberon.

Other '30s hits included *A Free Soul* and *Smilin' Through* (both with Norma Shearer), *Of Human Bondage* and *The Petrified Forest* (both with Bette Davis), and *Intermezzo: A Love Story* (with newcomer Ingrid Bergman), which he also co-produced. He was believable at forty-three in *Romeo and*

Juliet (1936) and was again Oscar-nominated for *Pygmalion* (1938), playing Professor Henry Higgins.

Howard had achieved the coup of persuading fussy, possessive George Bernard Shaw to allow his masterwork *Pygmalion* to be made into a motion picture, which Leslie co-directed. Its success enabled an eventual musical version titled *My Fair Lady*, which won Rex Harrison an Academy Award as Henry Higgins.

In 1941 Leslie directed himself in *Pimpernel Smith*, which marked the debut of his son Ronald Howard (1916–1996), who in the late 1940s gave up his journalism career for acting but never achieved close to his father's fame.

With World War II Howard was back in England, more popular than ever thanks to *Gone with the Wind*, in which he incarnated the gentlemanly Ashley Wilkes. The actor's publicity labeled him "the perfect English gentleman," but although long married he was a frequent if discreet ladies' man.

Ingrid Bergman admitted, "I fell in love with Leslie Howard.... He was sexy in the most understated way. It was said to be the secret of his success with women."

The British public and government appreciated Howard's doing the opposite of numerous actors, directors, and writers who fled their homeland for the United States when Hitler's bombs started falling.

"In his late forties," said Ronald Howard, "my father was still a leading man. But he felt it wise to move further into directing. After we worked together, he directed and co-directed his last two pictures." Leslie Howard's final starring effort was a romantic comedy-drama war film titled *The Gentle Sex* (1943).

The same year, he produced but didn't appear in *The Lamp Still Burns*. The title referenced nursing pioneer Florence Nightingale, known as "the lady with the lamp." The movie concerned an architect who in wartime changes her profession to nursing to help improve conditions in British hospitals.

Heroic off- as well as onscreen, Leslie Howard's career ended as it started—thanks to a world war. He was doing secret wartime work for his government as well as broadcasting for the Allied cause. His final job was narrating *War in the Mediterranean* (1943).

On June 1, 1943, Howard was aboard a commercial BOAC (British Overseas Airways Corp.) flight from Lisbon, Portugal, to London. Three hours after takeoff, over the Bay of Biscay north of Spain (whose fascist dictator Franco favored Hitler and Mussolini), the plane was shot down by a squadron of eight Luftwaffe fighters. The four crew members and thirteen passengers were all killed.

It was later theorized that the plane was a decoy, that the Nazis had planned to assassinate British leader Winston Churchill, believing he was on that flight. Or, simply, that Leslie Howard was the target—an internationally known Jewish anti-Nazi celebrity and activist.

In those days Jewish stars were rarely known to be Jewish. Comedian Joan Rivers was dead serious when remarking, "You can have Rhett Butler, I'll take Ashley Wilkes! Leslie Howard. . . . In those days if you were Jewish you had to change your name and keep it a big dark secret. We were pressured and scared into thinking we couldn't have a career, otherwise.

"But if more people had known how many admired figures were Jewish, more voices would have been raised against those people and politicians who allowed the Holocaust to happen."

Hattie McDaniel was the first black actor of either gender to win an Academy Award. Hard to imagine, but pre-pictures she was a vocalist with a dance band. Born in 1895, the hefty Hattie didn't try movies until 1932. She went on to play a small army of maids, in support of among others Marlene Dietrich, Mae West, Katharine Hepburn, Shirley Temple, Jean Harlow, and Carole Lombard—had she but written her memoirs. . . . Most famously, and Oscar-winningly, she was the redoubtable Mammy to Vivien Leigh in *Gone with the Wind*.

Singer Minnie Riperton said, "I admire Ms. McDaniel because although she was obese and couldn't be a movie star back then, her Mammy was a force of nature. She held that little war-torn family together . . . with a will of iron. To me it showed it's not so much what you play, but how you play it."

McDaniel's elder siblings Sam and Etta were also actors, and Sam in particular often got small roles, sometimes via Hattie's influence. Though she usually played ladies' maids, she was a virtual costar to Claudette Colbert in the 1934 version of *Imitation of Life*, far less famous than the 1959 version with Lana Turner. The story revolved around two mothers, one white, one black, and their daughters. A major casting difference is that in 1934 Hattie's lighter-skinned daughter trying to pass for white was played by a light-skinned black actress, Fredi Washington. The '50s film cast a Caucasian in the crucial role.

Sandra Dee, who played Turner's daughter in the remake, offered, "I got to see the earlier movie and I hope [producer] Ross Hunter forgives me for saying this, but it just did seem more real to me. Of course it was in black-and-white, but ours was just so much more theatrical."

Hattie demonstrated her musicality in Warners' *Thank Your Lucky Stars* (1943), a wartime musical entertainment partly pitched to servicemen overseas that enlisted virtually all the studio's star roster—even Bette Davis sang and danced in it. McDaniel was delightful performing "Ice Cold Katie." Her weight and poor health caused her to leave movies behind in 1948. Her big-screen swan song was *The Big Wheel* (released in 1949), starring Mickey Rooney. Hattie played Minnie, another mini part inadequate to her talents and personality.

In 1945 she'd begun starring in the radio sitcom *Beulah* about, as expected, a maid. In 1950 the series transferred to television and brought McDaniel back (occasionally in a musical vein). *Beulah* continued on radio until 1954. The TV series ended in 1953 and Hattie McDaniel died of breast cancer in 1952 (the radio and TV versions continued with replacements).

Between Hattie McDaniel and Sidney Poitier in the '60s there was one other, often overlooked black performer who was Academy Awarded. James Baskett (1904–1948) gained an honorary Oscar for portraying Uncle Remus in Disney's *Song of the South* (1946). The picture revolves around a troubled boy who goes to spend a summer on his grandmother's plantation and the storyteller who comforts him with tales of Brer (for Brother) Rabbit, Brer Bear, and Brer Fox. Baskett as Remus also sings the film's Oscar-winning song, "Zip-A-Dee-Doo-Dah."

Upon its release *Song of the South* was picketed in several cities but became Disney's most popular release of the year.

She was born Thelma McQueen in 1911, and her two famous roles are Prissy in *Gone with the Wind* and Joan Crawford's maid in *Mildred Pierce* (1945). Incredibly, **Butterfly McQueen** isn't listed in the latter's credits, though her character wasn't silent. The tendency in "golden age" films was to under-credit, but even so.

Unlike Hattie McDaniel, whose Mammy was a gratifying role for her, Butterfly was disappointed at being in *Gone with the Wind*. "I didn't know she'd [Prissy] be so stupid." McQueen's most famous movie line is the in-hysterics, "Miss Scarlett, I don't know nothin' 'bout birthin' babies!"

At thirteen Thelma was dancing professionally. At twenty-four she danced the butterfly ballet in *A Midsummer Night's Dream* and gave herself a new name. She made her Broadway debut in *Brown Sugar* (1937). Prissy was her first movie part but her second to be seen, because the all-female *The Women* (also 1939), in which she fleetingly appears as a cosmetics counter girl, got released first.

She also appeared in the all-black musical *Cabin in the Sky* (1943) starring Lena Horne and the 1946 David O. Selznick western *Duel in the Sun*, nicknamed "Lust in the Dust," with Jennifer Jones and Gregory Peck.

McQueen's screen career yielded small satisfaction. She resented roles requiring her to wear a kerchief over her head. "Can you imagine," she said in 1975, "that some women cover their heads not for a paying job but just because some religion that men came up with centuries ago orders them to do that?"

Butterfly was a life member of the Freedom From Religion Foundation, which she included in her will. A self-described human rights activist, she was particularly interested in women's and civil rights. At sixty-four she obtained a college degree in political science. McQueen never married, unlike her *Gone with the Wind* costar, who had four reportedly unsatisfactory marriages and no children (two of the husbands apparently took Hattie for her money).

Butterfly played Oriole on the TV series *Beulah* from 1950 to 1952. When she left she was replaced by Ruby Dandridge, Dorothy's mother. She was in a 1975 TV version of *The Adventures of Huckleberry Finn* and won an Emmy as the fairy godmother Aunt Thelma in the TV movie *Seven Wishes for a Rich Kid* (1979).

Toward the end of her life McQueen did cameo screen appearances. Her last part was in *The Mosquito Coast* (1986), starring Harrison Ford and River Phoenix. She declared, "People list me as a movie actress, but I haven't done much of that.... When they try and interview me for information or gossip about the pictures I was hardly in, I don't know what to say. I usually say, 'No, thank you.'"

Alas, Butterfly McQueen never penned her autobiography. Away from the cameras she now and again performed on radio, stage, and television but also worked at Macy's, gave tap and ballet lessons, was a waitress, a maid, a personal companion, and a taxi dispatcher.

Tragically, Ms. McQueen died in 1995 at eighty-four in her tiny Augusta, Georgia, home, burned over 70 percent of her body after trying to light a kerosene heater that set her clothes on fire.

HAIR OF GOLD: TAB HUNTER, BRIGITTE BARDOT, KIM NOVAK, AND TROY DONAHUE

Hollywood deals in stereotypes, and blonde hair on an actress signifies sex. It doesn't on a man, not to the targeted "average" male heterosexual moviegoer. A blond actor may even be sexually suspect, and for a long time blond hair hampered actors' careers: for instance 1930s semi-star Gene Raymond, closeted but better known as Jeanette MacDonald's husband. Alan Ladd had to overcome being short and blond before finally achieving stardom.

Elvis Presley didn't consider his dark blond hair suitable for movies. Or stardom, for that matter. He dyed it black—the darker, the butcher. Blond "pretty boys" of the 1950s like Tab Hunter and Troy Donahue weren't taken very seriously as actors. No doubt the most successful blond actor is Robert Redford, who gained gravitas by becoming a director.

Conversely, at one time or another almost every female star has been blonde. Many blonde stars haven't been seen as their brunette selves since their teens or early twenties. Mae West was so protective of the blonde image she believed compensated for her maturity and non-slimness that she refused to autograph photos of her pre-Tinseltown self if they were brunette. She would offer to buy the picture, and if the fan refused she often became incensed, sometimes declaring the photograph was of somebody else, not her.

Uniquely reversing the Hollywood habit was Joan Bennett (1910–1990), younger sister of blonde star Constance Bennett, at one time cinema's top-paid actress. In time the lovely Joan tired of what she called "insipid, namby-pamby good-girl roles . . . I was always pining for some fellow." When raven-haired Austrian import Hedy Lamarr became a sensation in *Algiers* (1938), in which Charles Boyer did not say, "Come wiz me to the Casbah," Bennett switched from blonde to black hair for the rest of her career. The benefit was better box office and roles, playing femmes fatales in several 1940s noir classics.

(In 1951 when Joan's cheating husband, producer Walter Wanger, found out she was cheating with her agent Jennings Lang, he shot him in the groin. Lang lived and Wanger briefly went to prison, but neither man's career suffered—Wanger later produced the Elizabeth Taylor *Cleopatra*. But the scandal stopped Joan Bennett's career cold. When she was vetoed for a major role in *We're No Angels* [1955], Humphrey Bogart—one of the first stars to oppose the political witch hunts of that era—announced that he wouldn't make the picture without Bennett.)

Arthur Gelien, a stunning blond ex–ice skater, was relabeled **Tab Hunter** by the same agent who named Rock Hudson, Troy Donahue, and several other, mostly gay, future stars. His looks led him toward Hollywood and, for a while, big-time teen popularity at Warner Bros. His first movie was ironically titled *The Lawless* (1950). During the antidemocratic and homophobic postwar McCarthy era, a guy could be arrested for having a male pajama party in his home. It happened to Hunter.

Sexy yet likeable, Tab (1931–2018) was a major studio asset but not viewed as a major talent. Like Marilyn at Fox, he was more eye candy than a contender for dramatic roles offered to darker-haired and more brooding performers. His apex was the 1958 musical *Damn Yankees* (UK title: *What Lola Wants*). But where he'd seemed comfortable enough with girlish love interests like Natalie Wood, Tab was less so with more womanly sexpots like Gwen Verdon in *Damn Yankees* and Sophia Loren in *That Kind of Woman* (1959).

In the '60s his box office plunged, as Tab and his fans matured and he remained single. Post-Warners he sometimes had to settle for minor parts or head for Europe to work. In the '70s he also did TV movies and in the '80s felt comfortable enough to do campy films like John Waters's *Polyester* (1981) and Paul Bartel's *Lust in the Dust* (1985), both with Divine. Enduringly good-looking, Hunter no longer felt the need to vainly try to recapture long-past success.

"I didn't always enjoy those ['50s] pictures. . . . Now I pick and choose what I think is cool or fun to do. I'm not afraid to take chances. . . . No one can predict what's going to be a hit anyway, so why worry?"

Tab Hunter declined to use and hide behind a female, actress or otherwise, for publicity and hire-ability. He lived happily with Allan Glaser, his life partner of thirty-five years. Tab finally came out in 2005 via his memoirs, *Tab Hunter Confidential*. (In the 1950s *Confidential* magazine terrorized secretly gay and lesbian stars by threatening to expose them.) In 2015 Tab's book became a popular documentary by the same title, produced by Glaser.

The actor, who loved horses and enjoyed a Southwestern-ranch lifestyle, last acted in 1992, in *Dark Horse*, the story of a troubled girl (Natasha Gregson Wagner, Natalie Wood's daughter) who bonds with a horse. Did Tab Hunter miss acting? "No, because unlike a lot of the people I knew in the business, acting was what I did for a living, a nice living. But it wasn't who I became."

—◆—

Many fans and nonfans inside and outside France said **Brigitte Bardot** (born in 1934) did the smart thing, retiring from movies before forty. She was publicized as the first "sex kitten," and her dozens of movies between 1952 and 1973 were chiefly notable for her sexiness and increasingly frequent nudity.

Almost single-handedly Bardot enabled the breakthrough of the X-rated Continental film into the international market. She once announced that Marilyn Monroe was not a sex symbol, as she never appeared nude, even topless, onscreen. Brigitte (pronounced Bree-zheet) classified Marilyn as "a romantic symbol" and herself as a and *the* sex symbol.

Though she was appealing in pictures like *Helen of Troy* (1954, not in the title role), the Frenchwoman didn't stand out or capture global attention until 1956. Again, no matter the performer, it takes a combination of the right actor with the right script and role. The star-making vehicle was *Et Dieu crea la femme* (in the United States: *And God Created Woman*, in the UK: *And Woman . . . Was Created*; UK censors were especially chary of "blasphemy").

The director was Bardot's then-husband Roger Vadim, who in the '60s directed new wife Jane Fonda in *Barbarella*. In Vadim's then-shocking film Bardot was a happy-go-lucky temptress to whom marriage, her own or anyone else's, didn't mean anything. The setting was the French Riviera, where the sex symbol and latter-day animal-rights activist would single-handedly make her adopted hometown of St. Tropez internationally famous.

In the United States none of her subsequent films was as famous. The nationalistic Bardot declined to work in Hollywood and didn't receive many offers to do so, on account of her accent in English and the fear that even clothed she might create controversy. However, she did a cameo in the Hollywood movie *Dear Brigitte*, in which a small boy (Billy Mumy, eventually on TV's *Lost in Space*) has an improbably obsessive crush on her, so his parents (James Stewart and Glynis Johns) take him to France to meet his idol.

In Europe Bardot was box office gold for a long time, though few if any of her vehicles became classics. Many or most were basically exploitation flicks; her name was often judged enough to draw in paying customers. Talent, first-rate scripts, and directors were often cited as in short supply.

Bardot's continuing fame was abetted by her marriages, divorces, and feuds, including with her only son. Repetition, time, younger competition, and more permissive films dented the sex symbol's appeal and it did seem wise to throw in the proverbial towel or what was left of it with two 1973 releases, *Don Juan 1973, ou Et si Don Juan etait une femme* (UK title: *Don Juan, or If Don Juan Were a Woman*) and finally *Colinot Trousse-Chemise* (UK title: *The Edifying and Joyous Story of Colinot*).

<hr />

Marilyn Novak toured the United States opening refrigerator doors as "Miss Deep Freeze." In L.A. she accompanied a friend auditioning for an agent and while sitting in the waiting room was discovered by a Columbia talent scout. The studio eventually chose to build her up to replace its former top draw Rita Hayworth.

But first the Chicagoan had to change her first name so as not to act in the shadow of another blonde Marilyn who'd become a superstar in 1953, the year **Kim Novak** entered pictures. In turn, "Kim" had had to insist on keeping her paternal surname, since Slavic names were frowned on in Hollywood.

The beauty's rise was rapid, for in 1955 she costarred in the hit *Picnic*. By 1960 she'd starred in such films as *The Man with the Golden Arm*, an early film on drug addiction, *Pal Joey* with Rita Hayworth (the two got along fine despite publicists' hopes), *Bell, Book and Candle* (whose ending premise about a witch marrying a mortal inspired TV's *Bewitched*), and Alfred Hitchcock's *Vertigo*.

In the 1960s, post-Columbia and post–golden age, Novak's career faltered and as one critic said, she started playing blowsy parts too early—for instance Polly the Pistol in Billy Wilder's much-publicized flop *Kiss Me, Stupid* (1964). She followed it with a remake of Bette Davis's breakthrough film *Of Human Bondage*, which had already been remade—the comparisons flattered the original. *The Amorous Adventures of Moll Flanders*, intended as a female answer to the critical and popular period hit *Tom Jones*, with cleavage galore, also flopped.

Kim Novak made nine films during the decade, then returned in 1973 in a—gasp—TV movie, a sure sign (back then) of a movie star's come-down. Then *Tales That Witness Madness* in England, another telefilm, then *Massacre at Blood Bath Drive-In*.

Her last widely seen motion picture was the 1980 Agatha Christie *The Mirror Crack'd*, with Elizabeth Taylor, Rock Hudson, Tony Curtis, and Angela Lansbury as Miss Marple. Kim, forty-seven, looked fantastic, not just in scenes with the one-year-older but much heavier (at the time) Liz.

Novak moved north to Carmel, then again to Oregon for privacy and to have space for her beloved animals. Her interest in acting seemed to wane, perhaps partly because the pickings were such poor quality. Studios and their writers didn't focus on attractive, personable, and talented mid-aged females. In her heyday Kim had turned down *Days of Wine and Roses*, *Breakfast at Tiffany's*, and *The Hustler*.

In 1990 she played a woman who falls in love with a widower (Ben Kingsley) with objecting offspring in *The Children*. Unfortunately her swan song occurred back in 1991, a terrible waste. *Liebestraum* concerned a professor of architecture who goes to visit his terminally ill mother. In an interview published online in 2018 Kim Novak revealed, "The script was wonderful. I was playing a dying woman with dementia. What a part! I was so excited.

"Had I known that the part was written by [director Mike Figgis] about his own mother, whom he hated, I might have had second thoughts. I also didn't know he'd cast his girlfriend in the ingénue lead. He took out all the cruel feelings he had on his mother on me. I have never been treated so viciously by anyone. I rose above it and my performance was really good.

"He cut my part to shreds to highlight his girlfriend and did his best to destroy me as a human while directing me. It was such a horrible experience that I said I'd never go back to make another movie, and I never have."

⌒‿⌒

"It's hurt my career that sometimes I get confused with another blond actor, but he's gay," said a disingenuous **Troy Donahue**, alluding to later openly gay Tab Hunter. Born Merle Johnson (1936–2001), Troy was a renamed client of renowned agent Henry Willson, whose biggest client was Rock Hudson.

Donahue once averred his hair wasn't blond but "butter-colored." His hair and good looks got him hired for movies in 1957, but in his tenth film he still had a minimal role, as a violent racist in the 1959 hit *Imitation of Life*. His next picture, *A Summer Place*, with Sandra Dee, was his breakthrough, and he became an instant heartthrob. Troy was less likeable and more stiff on screen than his fellow Warner Bros. star Tab, and unlike Hunter eventually involved himself heavily with drink and drugs, also gaining the weight that consumed his good looks.

In 1964 Donahue was married off to costar Suzanne Pleshette, herself bisexual or lesbian. Pleshette, later better known for television than films, declined to discuss the marriage: "It was only a matter of months, hardly worth talking about." Troy later had a longer marriage, but if he was gay or bisexual he never came out (he did have an initially sexual relationship with Henry Willson).

Post-Warners Donahue tried shedding the teen-dream image, with little luck. Robert Hussong, a talent agent for Tony Perkins among others, recalled, "A friend who handled T.D. discovered that when his client wasn't cast in leads his disappointment spilled into the bottle and occasionally he'd fail to show up on schedule. Once or twice is too often. He only hurt himself."

As with Tab Hunter, Troy Donahue's hire-ability suffered from him being perceived as a nostalgia symbol and an ex-hunk (even if still good-looking), and also from the bias that blond performers—both genders—have less range. In 1974 Troy appeared briefly in *The Godfather Part II* as Merle Johnson (!), a former fling of Connie Corleone (Talia Shire, Francis Coppola's sister).

Most of Donahue's parts were in B-movies or less, and after he let his looks go (which actresses at the time didn't dare or they wouldn't get hired) his value was mostly as a '50s Name. Thus he was included in a 1999 telefilm titled *Shake, Rattle and Roll—An American Love Story*. More happily, he was second-billed in his comedic swan song *The Boys Behind the Desk* (2000), helmed by actress Sally Kirkland. Rip Taylor, Sylvia Miles, and talk show host Joe Franklin also appeared.

Taylor reminisced, "I'd met Troy when he was still a golden boy, but not a very happy boy. The last time, he did look kind of bleary but he seemed more chipper . . . happy to be among us, all working pros. We all had a good time."

Troy Donahue died of a heart attack at sixty-five.

SHIVERS: BORIS KARLOFF, BELA LUGOSI, AND VINCENT PRICE

Once upon a time horror movies scared people (especially children). They combined real-life fears and anxieties with preternatural creatures . . . and one-in-a-million foreign performers like Boris Karloff and Bela Lugosi.

Then audiences matured—education and World War II helped—and those monsters didn't seem that scary anymore. Even before the new set of anxieties engendered by the atomic age, people were starting to view nonwar villains and boogeymen with amusement. Horror was turning campy. Its new king was Vincent Price, whose sadistic sneer often seemed about to give way to a snicker. Horror hadn't yet degenerated into sexist slicing and slashing. Horror was still fun.

~

One might never have heard of **Boris Karloff** had *Dracula* star Bela Lugosi not turned down the role of the Frankenstein monster. Of course one might never have heard of Bela Lugosi had Lon Chaney not died of cancer before he could step into the vampire's no doubt bespoke shoes.

Although the Hungarian was five years older than the Englishman born William Henry Pratt (1887–1969), Boris—known to his large family as Billy—started in movies a year earlier, in 1916. Like a good horror-movie star, Karloff kept much of his past and his private life secret, but he did emigrate from Britain to Canada and then the United States, doing assorted jobs before trying moving pictures.

He passed some fifteen years in minor roles, usually villains, in loads of movies. Sara Karloff listed *Frankenstein* (1931) as her father's eighty-first film. His wonderful speaking voice with the trademark lisp was of no consequence in silent pictures and his Russian names may have worked against him, for he wasn't yet associated with the horror genre. Boris much objected to the term "horror movies," which reminded him of horrible movies. He preferred "terror movies" but the media didn't oblige.

As a star, Karloff explained his stage name as owing to some Russian ancestors, but he had a secret: He was part Indian. Bigotry in the United States and United Kingdom was such that any origin other than European was looked down on. Daughter Sara has said she knows of no Russian ancestors on either side of the family. By old age the actor's skin tone had darkened, and in a family photo taken when he returned to England he and his brothers, several of whom had served in the diplomatic service, were clearly of partial Indian descent.

After the understandably willing Boris Karloff undertook the role of Dr. Frankenstein's cadaverous creation in 1931, he was launched on the greatest horror-movie career of all, eclipsing Bela Lugosi before long. *Frankenstein* was an even bigger hit than *Dracula* earlier the same year.

Karloff began creating a stunningly varied gallery of characters in '30s classics like *The Old Dark House*, *The Mummy*, and *The Mask of Fu Manchu*. He also appeared in occasional non-horrors like *Scarface*, *The House of Rothschild*, and *Charlie Chan at the Opera*. In 1935 he reprised the monster in *The Bride of Frankenstein*, considered by many the best-ever horror movie (however, the actor disliked that the monster now spoke). The '40s continued his gallery of doom.

Boris, who'd experienced unfair and unsafe working conditions over his long career, was one of the thirteen founding members of the Screen Actors Guild in 1933—at the time, pro-union activity was frowned on by the very well-paid men who ran the studios and could damage an actor's career.

By 1948 and the hit horror-comedy *Abbott and Costello Meet Frankenstein*, Karloff had left the monster behind. Rather, the next year he costarred in the campy *Abbott and Costello Meet the Killer, Boris Karloff*. The 1930s and early '40s were the golden age of horror movies. But after World War II with its real-life horrors, the genre was considered more comic or campy than scary and was increasingly spoofed. The good-natured Boris sometimes joined in the fun.

His versatility enabled him to play kindly souls as well as villains and ghouls, but as he aged he became less threatening and played non-diabolic "mad scientists" more often. He also acted in legitimate theatre in hits like *Arsenic and Old Lace*, where his name was part of the script, and as Captain Hook in *Peter Pan*. Karloff's elegant voice was heard on myriad recordings, whether horror-themed (e.g., Edgar Allan Poe poems), fairy tales, or other literary classics.

In the 1960s the actor extended his talent into such television roles as a transvestite in the "Mother Muffin" episode of *The Girl From U.N.C.L.E.* and the voice of the Grinch (its expressions modeled on Karloff horror films) in the Dr. Seuss classic *How the Grinch Stole Christmas*, which became an annual holiday TV highlight.

In the '60s Boris, who never tired of working, moved into ensemble semi-horror films like *The Raven* and *The Comedy of Terrors*, working with actors such as Peter Lorre and Vincent Price. He also essayed the so-'60s genre of beach-blanket flicks in *Bikini Beach* and *The Ghost in the Invisible Bikini*, and acted in "straight" films like *The Venetian Affair* and *Targets*, in which he played a horror icon named Byron Orlok.

Confinement to a wheelchair due to severe arthritis didn't prevent Boris Karloff from working. When asked, he traveled to Mexico to do Spanish-language films. He was still popular at the box office, albeit in very low-budget terror films, sometimes horrible ones.

Determining which was his final movie isn't easy, as some foreign titles weren't released in the United States and some that were made in 1968 or 1969—the year of his death in London from bronchitis and pneumonia—were released a year or two or more later: also several had two or more different titles.

Two of his last pictures, *The Fear Chamber* and *House of Evil*, were unreleased as of 1981 but by now are likely on DVD—perhaps under different titles. Candidates for Boris Karloff's swan song include *The Incredible Invasion*, *Alien Terror*, or *The Snake People*, aka *Isle of the Snake People*. One critic sniffed, "They're all the same movie." True, they're far from the many classic Karloffs, but they prove the enduring appeal of the king of horror and his somewhat terrifying work ethic.

—————

When Boris Karloff referred to the elder Bela (pronounced Bay-la, not Bella) Lugosi, he often said "poor Bela." It wasn't condescending. **Bela Lugosi** (1882–1956) got a raw deal—and part of it was his own doing.

He was born Bela Blasko but took his stage surname from his hometown of Lugos, Hungary. In his teens he yearned to act. His father violently objected, so Bela ran away for good. Handsome and suave, in time he became a Hungarian stage star. His roles included Armand in *The Lady of the Camellias* and Jesus Christ. He made silent films in Germany before leaving for the United States.

In New York he lucked out when he got cast in the play *Dracula*, which became a hit. As with myriad stars of hit plays and musicals, stage success in no way assured being cast in the film version. But eventually Lugosi lucked out again and in 1931 became an international star. Nothing like *Dracula* had been seen before. "I have made quite the sensation," said Bela, who could also have said I have created a monster, for the role would ultimately become a trap.

When Universal, the studio behind Dracula and Frankenstein's monster, not to mention the Mummy, the Werewolf, and umpteen sequels featuring each and combinations thereof, offered Lugosi the monster role in *Frankenstein* he was put out. "Anyone at all can play this *thing*," he said of the creature composed of parts of corpses. "I am an *actor!*" Apart from the monster having no speaking lines, Bela felt that the requisite heavy makeup, padding, and elevator boots would render any actor playing the monster all but unrecognizable.

Where Karloff's *Frankenstein* follow-ups were usually leads, Lugosi's *Dracula* follow-ups were sometimes small roles (*International House* starring W. C. Fields, *Island of Lost Souls* starring Charles Laughton) or leads in pictures that weren't big hits and/or haven't stood the test of time like *Murders in the Rue Morgue* and *White Zombie*. In 1932 Bela starred as *Chandu the Magician*, a Saturday-morning serial. Serials equated to a TV series in later decades and were avoided by most stars.

The crux of the difference between Karloff's and Lugosi's fortunes was that Bela truly was a foreigner, with a thick accent and a perhaps necessarily hammier way of acting in English. Boris was an Englishman with an upperclass accent and refined, eerie voice. At the time, Hollywood idolized British culture. Tinseltown stars were trained to shed their regional American accents and acquire a pseudo-English sound. Brooklynite Barbara Stanwyck was taught to say "good ahfternoon" and nearly all non-British surnames were anglicized so stars wouldn't be correctly identified with their German, Italian, Slavic, or other ethnic backgrounds.

Also, where Karloff saved money and requested a salary he felt he deserved, the more show-off-y Lugosi entertained (mostly members of the Hungarian community) lavishly, saved little, and was willing to work cheap. The studios noted his financial desperation and valued him accordingly.

Fan magazines often compared the kings of horror. Though very different, each was the youngest in his family and the rebel in terms of Dad's wishes, each married several times, each had only one child. When Karloff and Lugosi were paired in several memorable movies—starting with *The Black Cat* in 1934—the Englishman was always billed first and paid better. By the time of their final collaboration, *The Body Snatchers* (1945), Bela's role was far smaller, as was his remuneration. Debts forced his move from a house to an apartment.

After Karloff had passed on reprising the monster in 1943, Lugosi took the role. After Karloff completed his run in *Arsenic and Old Lace*, Lugosi took the role. Following *Abbott and Costello Meet Frankenstein* in 1948 in which Bela reprised Dracula yet again, he went to England to appear in *Mother Riley Meets the Vampire* (US title: *Vampire Over London*). Increasingly, Lugosi had been restricted to vampire roles. Karloff said he'd avoided them because "I don't like blood."

Boris explained, "I don't think poor Bela even knew what typecasting was. I don't think it concerned him. Until the money stopped coming in. Then he believed that the system had done it to him."

By the 1950s Bela's career was a joke. He couldn't find work and was glad of attention from teenage fans who sometimes visited his apartment. Worsening health put him into more than one hospital, where he became addicted to pain-killing morphine. Fond of interviews, unlike Karloff, Lugosi told his sad story to the press, which alienated the studios. He looked gaunt but vowed to beat his addiction, and did.

When he finally got work, it was mostly in thirteenth-rate productions via Ed Wood, a cheerfully inept and woefully underfunded amateur moviemaker. He at least esteemed Bela Lugosi and treated him like a star. Where Boris made film after film in more than one country and it's hard to definitively name his final effort, it's all too clear that Bela's swan song, his third film for Ed Wood, was *Plan Nine from Outer Space*, widely labeled "the worst movie ever made" and not released until 1958. Lugosi died of a heart attack —and was buried in his Dracula cape—soon after filming commenced.

Wood replaced the star with a chiropractor acquaintance who had to hold the Dracula-like cape over his face for the entire movie. *Plan 9*'s flying saucers were hubcaps and paper plates, its tombstones were made of cardboard, and its "aliens" were costumed in pajamas. Perhaps as well that the once-proud Hungarian didn't get to view the finished product. (The 1994 movie *Ed Wood* starring Johnny Depp contains numerous inaccuracies, and though it won a supporting Oscar for Martin Landau as Bela Lugosi, it exaggerates the one-sided "feud" between the two titans of terror.)

Alas, Bela didn't live as far into the television age as Boris and so didn't enjoy the huge resurgence of popularity of his past work, resurrected on the small screen. Together and separately, Karloff and Lugosi embodied thrilling characters in "terror movies" which have never been topped and rarely equaled.

— ⁓ —

"To me acting meant the stage. When I got to play Prince Albert [Queen Victoria's husband] I was elated," remembered **Vincent Price** (1911–1993). "Hollywood was nowhere on my agenda. . . . Hollywood's biggest weapon is money. It's the magnet that pulls us greedy actors to that side of the country."

Yet Price came from affluence, for his family owned Price Baking Soda, founded by his grandfather. Due to his posh voice and cultured mien, Hollywood and the public often assumed Vincent was English. Far from macho, he was often cast as wastrels and suspicious or two-faced characters. These traits would push him toward villain roles and then into horror, reviving what had been a supporting actor's career in A-pictures. Price became a leading star in horror movies, usually considered B-pictures in economic and prestige terms.

Vincent's screen career spanned from 1938 to a 1990 motion picture and a 1992 TV movie. He sometimes said he resented the downgraded status of horror films, explaining that they could be as good or lousy, as lavish or low-budget as non-horror pictures. "The story's the thing, as is the part. I'm relieved I don't get cast as ordinary husbands or businessmen in gray flannel suits. Playing the villain is far more fun!"

Besides acting, the man was an art connoisseur, collector, and lecturer, with a degree in art history. He founded the Vincent Price Art Museum in Los Angeles and at one time co-owned an art gallery with actor George Macready, who specialized in non-horror villains, most famously Rita Hayworth's fascist husband in *Gilda*. Vincent also loved to cook and cowrote cookbooks with wife Mary, "my best friend and a very fair-minded critic."

As he got older, his silken voice and purring manner consigned Price almost entirely to campy and horror roles. One exception was an elderly Russian friend of the sisters played by Bette Davis and Lillian Gish in *The Whales of August* (1987). Looking back, he offered, "I've been in classics like *Laura* and clinkers like *The Bat* and *The Tingler* that lots of people have nevertheless enjoyed. . . . How many performers can say they got far more lead roles in the second half of their career than the first? It's nearly always the other way round."

With the 3-D cult classic *The House of Wax* in 1953, Price had achieved horror stardom. He went on to star in Roger Corman cine-tales based on Edgar Allan Poe and campy William Castle non-classics, as well as oddities like *Theatre of Blood* and *The Abominable Dr. Phibes*, often filming in England. "I feel utterly at home in England—just name the century." Price's big-screen swan song was in Tim Burton's quirky *Edward Scissorhands*, starring Johnny Depp. Vincent played the mysterious and powerful Inventor whom the young protagonist seeks out.

As happens all too often to senior stars, Vincent Price's ultimate appearance two years later was anticlimactic. Not just because it was a telefilm (so rarely approaching big-screen quality or originality)—*The Heart of Justice*, a forgettable murder mystery starring Eric Stoltz—but because it proffered too small a role to a larger-than-life performer. Costar Bradford Dillman told the Australian press in 1994, "I come from sort of an in-between time that bridges when being a star meant being unlike anyone else—distinctive in looks, voice, everything, like Mr. Price. I'm frankly not that interesting . . . a few from my time are. Since then, plenty of clones. I discussed this with Mr. Price, he was very diplomatic. A real gentleman. . . . I'm afraid those days of wonderful human difference and innate, excellent manners are gone."

TRAGEDY: HEDY LAMARR AND JEAN SEBERG

There are tragedies and tragedies. The following two actresses' include having to hide one's heritage, extreme looks that limit a career and cause its early end, humiliating criminal publicity, bad plastic surgery, universally bad reviews, being targeted by the FBI and blacklisted in one's own country, losing a baby following libelous and fictitious publicity, repeated suicide attempts, and a grimly successful suicide.

— ∼ —

Hedy Lamarr, considered by many the most beautiful movie star ever, was renamed after silent star Barbara La Marr, known as "the girl who was too beautiful." She died at the ripe age of twenty-nine from a combination of nephritis, pulmonary tuberculosis, and crash diets while trying to make a comeback.

By contrast Hedy lived to eighty-six. She called her envied face a "mask" that hid her personality and made men talk at her, not with her, when they talked at all. She claimed her face brought her six unsatisfactory husbands.

The Austrian-born Hedwig Kiesler (1914–2000) hid being Jewish all of her life: understandably so with her first husband, an arms manufacturer who supplied the Nazis; less so in Hollywood and the country it entertained, particularly in the final decades of her life.

Prior to Winona Ryder, Hedy Lamarr was the most famous star arrested for shoplifting. The first time, in 1966 at the May Co. department store in Los Angeles, generated international headlines. She was still of public interest, a beautiful star who hadn't filmed since 1957. Among the stolen items were greeting cards and bikini underwear. The second time, in 1991 at a drugstore, she was elderly, almost forgotten, living quietly in Florida. The stolen items were laxatives. In both cases her reaction was to sue the store in question for defamation.

Austrian-born Hedy Lamarr considered her beautiful face a mask that kept away personal happiness and attracted six unsatisfactory husbands. It did, however, bring her stardom. The secretly Jewish actress coinvented a radio guidance system to aid against Nazi jamming of US and UK torpedoes during World War II.

In the early '30s Hedy Kiesler made a handful of German-language films before the Czech picture *Extase* (1932, *Ecstasy*). It featured the eighteen-year-old nude, floating in a pond apparently having an orgasm. Though it included no sex it was deemed pornographic and brought Kiesler international notoriety. It also caused her older, controlling husband to try to buy up all copies and destroy them.

Hedy was off the screen until 1938, by which time she'd escaped to Hollywood, signed with MGM, and been renamed. She debuted in English in *Algiers*, an "overnight star" and for a few years a huge sensation. Few of her films have held up over time and fewer became classics. Her biggest hit was *Samson and Delilah* (1948). Almost immediately after, she went into B-movies and stayed there.

Lamarr coproduced some of her late films and sometimes worked in Europe. A 1954 Italian film was *Eterna femmina* (Eternal Female), retitled *The Face That Launched a Thousand Ships* for the US and UK markets. She terminated her movie career in 1957 with two contrasting efforts. In the all-star color spectacle *The Story of Mankind* she had a few minutes as a beautiful but too-mature Joan of Arc, a teenager when she was burned at the stake. In Lamarr's swan song, the black-and-white *The Female Animal*, she was an actress afraid of aging but competing with daughter Jane Powell for the attentions of younger George Nader.

"Hedy felt she had little to offer . . . less and less as time passed," said Nader. "She didn't much carry the action in her movies. She . . . decorated them. Her characters weren't about much more than their looks."

Mentally she had more to offer. During World War II she reportedly helped Howard Hughes improve airplane designs. With composer George Antheil she coinvented an early version of a frequency-hopping spread-spectrum radio guidance system to help Allied torpedoes avoid jamming by the Axis Powers. During and after her film career Lamarr took out several patents and told friends she enjoyed being an inventor more than an actress.

"Hollywood has always sold and often sold out to a very wide but often narrow-minded market," remarked Vincent Price, her costar in *The Story of Mankind*, "so Hedy fundamentally had to hide that she was Jewish and highly intelligent." Her and Antheil's technological contributions were barely publicized. Their inductions into the National Inventors Hall of Fame in 2014 were posthumous.

Despite leaving movies in the late 1950s, Hedy Lamarr remained very conscious of and careful about her looks. She remained stunning well into middle age but whether she finally had too much plastic surgery or chose incompetent surgeons, she wound up looking sadly frightening. She died in Orlando, later to be rediscovered and reevaluated in books and a documentary as an inventor and an example of what can be lost when only surfaces arc valued.

———

Producer-director Otto Preminger reputedly considered thousands of young female hopefuls before choosing one for his 1957 film of Shaw's play *Saint Joan*. The fresh natural blonde from Iowa was beautiful and somewhat boyish. Joan of Arc was certainly boyish. But the much-heralded film debut of **Jean Seberg** (1938–1979) was almost universally panned.

Nonetheless Preminger cast her the following year in his film of the French bestseller *Bonjour, Tristesse* (Hello, Sadness) starring Deborah Kerr and David Niven. Jean played Niven's precocious daughter, then switched to comedy in *The Mouse That Roared* with Peter Sellers and made her most famous picture, the French New Wave classic *A bout de souffle* (*Breathless*, 1959).

Better appreciated in France than her own country, Seberg alternated working there and in Hollywood. Her American films of the '60s included *Lilith* with Warren Beatty and Peter Fonda, the flop musical *Paint Your Wagon* with Lee Marvin and Clint Eastwood, and the big hit *Airport* as Burt Lancaster's love interest.

In 1963 she married French writer Romain Gary and in the late '60s became politically active, helping fund the NAACP and advocating for Native American rights (she bought $500 worth of basketball uniforms for an "Indian" settlement near her Iowa hometown). When Seberg began supporting the militant Black Panthers, she drew J. Edgar Hoover's attention and enmity.

The FBI director informed President Nixon and his top staff (later infamous due to Watergate) of his plan to "neutralize" Jean Seberg, who was several months pregnant. On April 27, 1970, a false and harmful letter was "leaked" to syndicated columnist Joyce Haber about the actress being pregnant by a prominent Black Panther. (Julie Andrews, who badmouthed almost nobody, once stated that the nasty Haber merited heart surgery—and that the doctors should go in through her feet.)

The story ran in the *Los Angeles Times*, *Newsweek*, and other outlets. At the same time, Hollywood studios were pressured not to hire Seberg, and she was effectively blacklisted.

Devastated by the vendetta, Jean overdosed on pills and went into premature labor. Her baby girl died two days after being born. Seberg held a press conference and presented her dead baby to reporters to prove the father was white. There were subsequent suicide attempts, each on the anniversary of her child's death. Jean and Romain divorced in 1970.

Jean Seberg then worked mostly in Europe, in French, Italian, and German productions. Her last English-language effort costarred Kirk Douglas in the story of a teacher separated from his son who plots revenge against his ex-wife. Titled *Mousey* (1974), the Canadian "thriller action drama" aired on TV in the United States and was released to British cinemas as *Cat and Mouse*.

Jean's final movie was *The Wild Duck* (1976), a German film of Norwegian Henrik Ibsen's nineteenth-century play. She played the lead role of Gina but reportedly lost the will to perform further, spending her last few years chronically depressed. On August 27, 1979, Jean Seberg disappeared. There were public pleas in France for her safe return, but twelve days later she was found dead at forty from an overdose of barbiturates, nude in the back seat of her white Renault.

Her funeral at Paris's Montparnasse Cemetery was attended by *Breathless* costar Jean-Paul Belmondo and by Jean-Paul Sartre and Simone De Beauvoir. In 1980 Jean's ex-husband Romain Gary shot himself in the mouth.

THE RAT PACK: PETER, SAMMY, FRANK, AND DEAN

Humphrey Bogart and his drinking buddies were known as The Rat Pack. The posthumous, more famous Rat Pack comprised primarily singing actors—Frank Sinatra, Dean Martin, and Sammy Davis Jr., along with (initially) Peter Lawford for his White House connections and Joey Bishop for . . . curbing their enthusiasm? Also a few "floating" members. But mostly the following four.

———

"Peter was ambitious. He liked to indulge himself, but he wanted to get ahead. More, I won't say at this time."

Closeted actor Cesar Romero referred to the fact that **Peter Lawford** and fellow MGM player Tom Drake, best known as Judy Garland's beau in the classic *Meet Me in St. Louis* (1944), had a 1940s affair. When Drake, in love with Lawford, didn't want it to end, Peter threatened violence (the Englishman's mother acknowledged her gay or bisexual son as "a queer man-loving chap").

Peter (1923–1984) was put into pictures in 1930 and 1931, then returned while still a juvenile in 1938. He never achieved top-rank stardom but ensured his heterosexual credentials and social prominence by marrying Pat Kennedy, sister of John F. Kennedy. They had four children (son Christopher, a sometime actor, died at sixty-three from a heart attack). After Peter and the late president's sister divorced, he returned to same-sex affairs, but not to Tom Drake, five years his junior but an ex-actor (Louis B. Mayer was probably the most homophobic studio head) and a car salesman.

Bette Davis, a Kennedy supporter and Lawford friend, helped get him a prominent role in *Dead Ringer* (1964), but Peter wasn't the male lead—improbably, Karl Malden was. The faded but still handsome English American had several mostly supporting roles still in his future, but his best work was behind him, at MGM where he supported bigger stars like June Allyson, Esther Williams, and Jane Powell.

Most of Lawford's later roles and projects were eminently forgettable, but there were plenty of them, for the charming actor and socialite cultivated new connections and retained the memory of Camelot. The Kennedy connection was a big factor in Peter's Rat Pack membership. Wry comedian and talk show host Joey Bishop eventually bragged about being its "last Rat" and survivor. Born Joseph Gottlieb, he commented twenty years after Peter's death, "He spent more time on his social life than his career and developed sort of a dubious reputation."

Lawford incautiously told the press he smoked marijuana with his children. He remarried more than once (one wife wrote a biography quoting Peter about the sexual act that his then-date Nancy Davis—later Reagan—performed for him). Although a pal to Elizabeth Taylor, Lawford secretly sold a story about her rehab experience (which he'd shared) to a tabloid.

Despite being possibly the last person to speak with Marilyn Monroe, on the phone the night of her death, several insiders believed Lawford could have been a better and more helpful friend to her. (A few accused Peter of pimping for JFK and/or Robert Kennedy.)

Probably Lawford's best latter-day performance was in *That's Entertainment!* (1974) as Peter Lawford, one of the popular documentary's hosts. His final effort was a little-seen UK comedy, *Where Is Parsifal?* (1984), starring Tony Curtis. Peter's minor role was a has-been movie star named Montague Chippendale. Due to long-term substance abuse that impacted his liver and kidneys, Lawford's 1984 heart attack proved fatal. He was sixty-one and had remarried months before his death.

His ashes were placed in the small but prestigious Westwood cemetery where Marilyn Monroe and Elizabeth Taylor's parents are buried. A 1988 financial dispute with Lawford's widow led to his remains being removed and scattered at sea. Reportedly, the *National Enquirer* paid the outstanding cemetery bill in return for photographic rights to the watery disposal.

"I wasn't molded for [movie stardom]. I mean apart from my being short and skinny and one-eyed and dark, you dig? But I could sing . . . and back then, sounding white helped a lot, man."

Sammy Davis Jr. (1925–1990) followed his parents onto the stage, performing in vaudeville, dancing, singing, telling jokes—often on himself—and occasionally acting. "They stuck me in a few movie shorts when I was a kid and, I have to admit, very cute. Then I went away, I mean from pictures . . . and came back. But my acting credits weren't worth saying out loud till my thirties. And for anyone who's wondering, I lost my left eye in a car accident, back in 1954."

In 1958 Davis costarred opposite Eartha Kitt in the sex-vs.-religion drama *Anna Lucasta*. She later opined, "Sammy was interesting . . . intense. Too intense for pictures. His looks limited him mostly to hep cats and hoodlum characters. . . . All that intensity and nervousness was better put to use singing."

In 1959 Davis played Sportin' Life in *Porgy and Bess* but was most widely seen the next year in the popular Rat Pack caper *Ocean's Eleven*. How Sammy became part of the "in" group headed by Dean Martin, Frank Sinatra, and Peter Lawford has several explanations. Over the years two of Davis's replies were "I was their mascot" and "They needed a little contrast, color-wise."

Color contrast ended the platonic friendship between movie star Kim Novak and Sammy and his family, with whom she'd shared Sunday dinners. The tabloid press insinuated an interracial affair, and Kim's studio boss threatened Davis with the loss of his other eye if he didn't stop socializing with the valuable blonde property. Davis complied but semi-retaliated by temporarily marrying Mai Britt, a blonde Swedish actress.

(Novak often reiterated that she and Sammy had never been lovers, and Linda Lovelace of *Deep Throat* fame, referring to Sammy's bisexuality, revealed that he'd asked if he could practice fellatio on her male manager while she watched and gave him tips.)

Best known for singing, Davis appeared on TV umpteen times and in several movies, often in small roles, at times merely musical, as in *Sweet Charity* (1969), starring Shirley MacLaine, where Sammy as Big Daddy performed one "hip" musical number. "The silver screen wasn't that silver for me, baby. . . . I got deleted, I had unsold pilots, sometimes I sang but you didn't see me. One reason was my broken nose—I didn't have a Grecian profile, but I think it helped my singing."

Davis's Las Vegas scenes in the James Bond film *Diamonds Are Forever* were deleted and one of his later song hits was "The Candy Man" from *Willy Wonka and the Chocolate Factory*, in which he didn't appear—an English actor sang the song in the movie.

When Sammy did costar, the film could be dismal, like the intended comedy *Salt and Pepper* (1968) with Peter Lawford. Sammy recalled, "Peter and I owned a Swinging '60s London nightclub ... there's this Chinese mystery chick in there but then somehow it gets to be about overthrowing the government of England!"

Davis did better on TV, including memorable appearances on *Rowan & Martin's Laugh-In*, where his "Here comes de judge!" became a national catchphrase (borrowed from a black comic named Pigmeat Markham).

Sammy Davis Jr. achieved and retained stardom as a singer, in Las Vegas and elsewhere. In 1987 he toured with Dean Martin and Frank Sinatra, later with Liza Minnelli. His final acting assignment was a minor role in a juvenile holiday picture, *The Kid Who Loved Christmas* (1990). In 1989 he acknowledged, "It's flattering being asked to be in something. It's also not so often when you're older, but they sure pay more these days than when I was young!"

Nonetheless when Sammy Davis Jr. died at sixty-four he was in debt to the IRS. He'd predicted, "I'm sure we'll come to a mutual agreement ... some settlement that won't break me or the Infernal Revenue Service." Rather, there were several lawsuits involving his estate. But the music lives on.

———•———

"He did the smartest thing," said Frank Sinatra Jr. "Tastes in music change, but there's always movies. Dad got in, and hung in there."

Like not that many popular singers, **Frank Sinatra** (1915–1998) significantly augmented his musical stardom via the movies. So did Bing Crosby, Doris Day, Dean Martin, and Barbra Streisand. To a far more limited extent, so did Peggy Lee, David Bowie, and Olivia Newton-John.

Tom Jones, sexier and more attractive than Sinatra, didn't. Helen Reddy, a 1970s hit-spinner best known for the anthem "I Am Woman," starred in *Pete's Dragon*, a partly-animated Disney flop: "Making a movie takes ages. It's not very interesting. It may or may not hit the mark and is less lucrative than spending the same amount of time singing live." Film stardom, however, is for the long run.

Unlike the sexy and attractive Elvis, Sinatra—plain, skinny, often dour—didn't seem a natural for movies. His 1941 screen bow, the prophetically titled *Las Vegas Nights*, was unpropitious. Like Elvis, Frank was often assigned trivial pictures, with titles like *Reveille for Beverly* and *The Kissing Bandit*. His best early films were easily the three musicals he did with Gene Kelly. Sinatra wasn't a box-office draw and wasn't considered a dramatic actor. By the early 1950s Hollywood had written him off. Atypically, Frank humbled himself to plead with Columbia boss Harry Cohn for the role of the doomed Private Maggio in *From Here to Eternity* (1953), starring Montgomery Clift, Burt Lancaster, and Deborah Kerr. The supporting role won Sinatra a supporting Oscar (Donna Reed won one for the same movie).

There followed a lengthy string of motion picture leads, most music-free. Some were in hits, some weren't. The actor also directed one feature, *None But the Brave* (1965), set during World War II. A non-hit, it was praised for its even-handed treatment of the Japanese.

Sinatra said he especially liked playing cops. Despite his predilection for Mob figures, he avoided portraying hoods. He'd long since paid the price for his Mafia connections when he partially remodeled his Palm Springs home for President Kennedy to stay at, even adding a helicopter landing pad. White House staff then informed Frank that JFK would instead guest at singer-actor Bing Crosby's home, due to Sinatra's dicey image. The offended Democrat converted to Republican and single-handedly destroyed the helicopter pad. He also cut ties with Peter Lawford, who he felt could have done more to intercede with his brother-in-law.

Frank's final film, the ninth and last he produced, was to have been directed by Roman Polanski before legal problems over sexual abuse of a thirteen-year-old girl intervened. In *The First Deadly Sin* (1980) Sinatra played a detective hot on the trail of a serial killer. In a minor, hospital-bound role, Faye Dunaway was his disease-stricken wife. Frank's screen career spanned four decades.

In 1984 he did a cameo as himself in the multi-star *Cannonball Run II*, in 1988 he lent his singing voice to *Who Framed Roger Rabbit*, and in 1995 he signed off in a made-for-TV comedy-drama titled *Young at Heart* (the title of one of Sinatra's song hits) as a fictional version of himself.

Besides *From Here to Eternity*, Sinatra's more memorable films include *The Man with the Golden Arm* and *The Manchurian Candidate*. But he is best remembered as a singer and recalled as "the chairman of the board." Said Joey Bishop, "Frank was famous for trying to skip movie rehearsals. He was too impatient . . . and he liked getting his own way. The rest of us weren't very uptight, we liked having fun too, so usually Frank got his own way.

"I think Dean had the most fun of us. He didn't drink as much as people thought but he knew how to let the star thing, the ego, slide into the background. Dean kept it real. Frank kept it under control, or tried to."

"[Sinatra] and my father were really more associates than buddies," disclosed Dean Paul Martin, also pointing out that in record sales **Dean Martin** often surpassed Frank Sinatra.

The less ambitious, more laid-back Martin, born Dino Crocetti (1917–1995), received and probably sought only a fraction of the publicity his singing rival did. For instance, Sinatra left his wife, mother of their three children, for movie star Ava Gardner. Later he wed the much younger Mia Farrow, whispered in some quarters to possibly be his own daughter via an affair with actress Maureen O'Sullivan (Tarzan's Jane). Sinatra's final wife was formerly married to a lesser Marx Brother. Frank Sinatra Jr. was recurringly rumored to have planned his own kidnapping for publicity, and daughter Nancy Sinatra became for a time an actress and singing star—one of her/their hits was a duet with Dad titled "Somethin' Stupid."

In the mid-1960s Dean Paul Martin, still known as Dino, was part of a briefly popular teen-boy singing trio called Dino, Desi & Billy (the other son-of was Desi Arnaz Jr.), but Dean Paul (a tennis player and actor) was "proud my father didn't use his kids or wives for publicity."

Dean Martin became famous as half of Martin and Lewis. Basically he was the suave, self-confident singer while Jerry Lewis was the comic foil and sometime idiot. (Dean's nose job had reputedly been financed by comedian Lou Costello; comedian Milton Berle quipped that pre-rhinoplasty Crocetti habitually looked like he was eating a small banana.)

After the inevitable split with Lewis, Martin went on to a successful film career and hosted a long-running TV variety series. He also enacted a cross between James Bond and Hugh Hefner in four Matt Helm movies between 1966 and 1969 but declined a fifth installment.

Martin's final role was in Burt Reynolds's *Cannonball Run II* (1984)—but not as himself, unlike Sinatra. Reynolds had long admired Dean, "the essence of cool. Nothing fazes the guy, nothing's that important. . . . If Dean Martin isn't his own stereotype, I say he's a great actor."

In 1987 Dean Paul, a member of the California Air National Guard, was killed in a military airplane crash at thirty-five. Dean Sr., father of four, was said by some friends to be shattered, losing much of his will to perform. "Dean was proud of his son and closer to his children than most stars," said producer Samuel Goldwyn Jr. "That death hit the whole family very hard, they were very united."

Dean and Frank Sinatra, touring with Sammy Davis Jr. in 1987, grew apart when the bereaved father's increased alcohol intake occasionally affected his concert performance. At one point Sinatra was heard to growl, "Get that drunken bum off the stage!"

"Dean loved entertaining people, it made him feel good," said comedian Rip Taylor. "Unlike most of us, Dean didn't do Vegas for the dough. He did it because he had fun. People who worked with him had fun. . . . I think he stopped when the heart went out of him. It wasn't fun for him anymore."

After decades of a full schedule singing, recording, and concertizing, working in films and on his TV series, and hosting the Dean Martin Celebrity Roasts, the entertainer put his career on the shelf and lived out the rest of his years with family and a few friends. "He was not in perpetual mourning, as has been said," corrected Joey Bishop. "But Dean didn't laugh much anymore. He wasn't exactly melancholy . . . let's just admit he wasn't looking forward anymore."

BRUCE LEE AND BRANDON LEE

"American movies don't acknowledge us. They fear us and ignore China's people and longstanding achievements," asserted **Bruce Lee**.

In Tinseltown the martial-arts master couldn't attain more than a few supporting roles, let alone a lead. His Hollywood highpoint was the non-villainous Kato, valet and sidekick to star Van Williams in the 1966-'67 TV series *The Green Hornet*. (Not to be confused with Cato, the servant and sparring partner of Inspector Clouseau in the Pink Panther movies, played by London-based Burt Kwouk.)

Lee continued, "Did you ever see heroic, intelligent Charlie Chan cast with an Oriental actor? Or evil and intelligent Fu Manchu, for that matter? At least they admit our intelligence.... But to this day, important Oriental roles go to Caucasian actors.... We get to play the servant or #1 son."

Several Hollywood casting directors informed the 5'8" actor that his good looks were complemented by a significant screen presence and the bonus of his ability to do his own impressive stunts. *The Green Hornet* placed Lee above the radar, but less as an actor than a stuntman. Insiders later pointed out Bruce's burning ambition to become internationally famous.

"My father didn't want stardom for its own sake," stated Brandon Lee. "But he wanted to prove it could be done. He didn't want to be limited... not by height, ethnicity or cultural ignorance. He felt martial arts embodied discipline and dignity.... What he really liked was the idea of being a teacher."

Bruce was born Lee Jun-fan in 1940 in San Francisco's Chinatown (his mother was half-Caucasian) but raised in Hong Kong. Frustrated and angry at not scoring the lead in the *Kung Fu* TV series (it went to a Caucasian actor), Lee left Hollywood to start over. Martial arts were integral to many of the movies made in Hong Kong, East Asia's film capital. Bruce hoped to introduce Western moviegoers to martial arts, especially kung fu. His handful of starring vehicles, including the 1973 hits *Enter the Dragon* and *Return of the Dragon* (he directed the latter), did just that.

Penetrating international boundaries, Bruce Lee became a household name. Rumors swirled like recalcitrant crows around a scarecrow about the mysterious, not very sociable star. Some involved his seemingly superhuman strength, his diet and health routines, possible drug addiction including steroids, and Lee's possible connections with Hong Kong's underworld. A cult developed around the star and his philosophy. Some fans felt Bruce was starting to take himself too seriously, as something beyond an entertainment figure.

Others believed he'd become obsessive and was working too hard. In his last film he played a kung fu master battling drug lords. Grimly titled *Game of Death*, it was incomplete at Bruce Lee's sudden death in 1973 at thirty-two of a cerebral edema partly caused by legal drug interactions (the cannabis found in his system was not a contributing factor).

Lee's specific kung fu moves made it difficult to shoot unfilmed scenes using his stand-in. Director Robert Clouse eventually completed *Game of Death* with a new cast. Assorted delays and disputes kept the movie from reaching cinemas until 1978. "Hong Kong filmmaking is anything but transparent," observed critic Gene Siskel. "The mysteries surrounding *Game of Death* remain unsolved . . . but add to the mystique of the short-lived phenomenon called Bruce Lee." (The film was also the swan song of Hollywood actor Gig Young [see the Murder-Suicide chapter]).

"Because my father died young and in perfect physical shape," said Brandon Lee, "there is a ridiculous bunch of theories about what 'really' happened." One theory held that Bruce Lee's life had been threatened by a criminal syndicate and he'd staged his own death and was still alive—somewhere in the world.

"Some stories are totally nuts but others are more like wishes," added Brandon. "A lot of his fans didn't want to let him go . . . so one way or another they try and hope that he's not really gone."

———

Bruce Lee's marriage to teacher, writer, and martial artist Linda Lee Cadwell had produced a son and daughter. Without becoming the martial-arts phenomenon that his father was, **Brandon Lee** nonetheless had an expectant following the moment he entered acting. He noted more than once that he wasn't trying to replicate Lee Sr.'s career. "Our backgrounds and outlooks aren't the exact same. But for movies it does center on action."

Brandon's career began with the TV movie *Kung Fu: The Movie* (1986), followed by *Kung Fu: The Next Generation*. He moved on to feature films like *Laser Mission*, *Big Showdown in Little Tokyo*, and *Rapid Fire*. His role as Eric Draven (de Raven=the Raven), a murdered rock musician resurrected to avenge his murder and his fiancée's, would have been his biggest to date.

The vehicle was a horror-thriller, *The Crow*, based on a popular underground comic book. Minor accidents had beset the 1993 production in North Carolina. The prop gun had already been used but then wasn't properly reloaded. Ironically the fatal scene was the one in which Draven is shot and killed. A dummy bullet, accidentally jammed in the prop gun's barrel, fired into Brandon's stomach and lodged in his spine. He fell to the floor in pain. At first the crew thought the twenty-eight-year-old was overacting. Lee was rushed to the hospital and several hours of surgery followed, to no avail.

The actor firing the gun was later cleared and the incident officially declared an accident. Footage of the unintended fatality was destroyed before it could be developed. *The Crow* was completed using a body double, with Lee's face digitally inserted. The movie was released in 1994.

Brandon Lee had been slated to portray his father in a 1993 biopic, but the role necessarily went to someone else—Jason Scott Lee (no relation).

SCARLETT: VIVIEN LEIGH

Ironic for Hollywood that an Englishwoman, **Vivien Leigh** (1913–1967), was chosen to enact two of the most iconic Southern belles in US literature—Scarlett O'Hara from Margaret Mitchell's novel *Gone with the Wind* and Blanche DuBois from Tennessee Williams's play *A Streetcar Named Desire*. Leigh won Academy Awards for each portrayal.

The former was the most coveted role in movie history. Vivien won out over some two hundred actresses, including aspiring and future stars like Paulette Goddard (who didn't produce a requested marriage license to Charlie Chaplin) and Susan Hayward plus established stars like Bette Davis (who said she declined because it was a package deal with Errol Flynn) and Katharine Hepburn. Producer David O. Selznick told the latter he just couldn't see Rhett Butler chasing her for ten years.

Vivien Leigh was born Vivian [*sic*] Hartley and chose for her surname her first husband's second name. In England pre-*GWTW* she was known for her personal and professional association with Laurence Olivier, whose name went widely public due to their association. Each was already married, she to an attorney, he to better-known actress Jill Esmond, who later left him for a woman.

Leigh's initially indifferent film career began with *Things Are Looking Up* (1935), then looked up with *Fire Over England* (1937), an Elizabethan-era costume drama costarring Olivier. Flora Robson, who played Elizabeth I, later noted, "Vivien was very likely the most beautiful actress I ever saw. Her problem, such as it was, involved being comely enough to be guaranteed film work but unlikely to be hired to depict a really substantial character."

Charles Laughton, Leigh's costar in the British film *St. Martin's Lane* (1938, US title: *Sidewalks of London*), opined, "Vivien was ambitious. . . . She was also besotted with Larry. But for him the career absolutely came first."

Leigh lobbied unsuccessfully to star in *Wuthering Heights* and *Rebecca*, both featuring Olivier, but she wasn't considered well-known enough in the

Protests that Hollywood chose an Englishwoman to portray Southern belle Scarlett O'Hara in *Gone with the Wind* (1939) were quickly silenced by Vivien Leigh's performance. It earned her an Oscar, to be followed by another for *A Streetcar Named Desire* (1951)—as Southern belle Blanche DuBois. Reportedly, Leigh's Hollywood success helped sour her marriage to actor Laurence Olivier.

States. She was able to benefit from Olivier's American agent Myron Selznick when she got him to arrange an interview with his brother David. The meeting apparently occurred at the Selznick Studio's backlot on the first day of shooting *Gone with the Wind*, with Myron shouting to be heard, "David! Meet Scarlett O'Hara."

George Cukor, the then-*GWTW* director, did a screen test of Vivien Leigh, and thus Selznick's two-year search for Scarlett was over. There were more than a few protests about giving the role to a foreigner. But the film's success, the glowing reviews, and Vivien's performance and Oscar, not to mention the passage of time, made anyone else in the role nigh unthinkable.

(Vivien Leigh worked 125 days on *Gone with the Wind* and was paid $25,000. Clark Gable, who didn't bother with a Southern accent, worked seventy-one days and was paid $120,000.)

Leigh made surprisingly few motion pictures post-Scarlett. Three movies on, she starred in the most expensive British production to date, *Caesar and Cleopatra* (1945). Unfortunately her depiction of Egypt's last pharaoh was kittenish and juvenile, unlike Elizabeth Taylor's resolute and savvy monarch in *Cleopatra* (1963). Two films post-Cleo she was Blanche opposite Marlon Brando's Stanley Kowalski. She'd already played the role onstage in Olivier's London stage production.

The married couple (1940–1960) worked together off but mostly on stage. Vivien passed up several choice screen roles for their stage work, no doubt aware she was a bigger draw than her husband, who often directed their joint ventures, e.g., the play that became the film *The Prince and the Showgirl* (1957) starring Marilyn Monroe in the role Leigh had done onstage. Olivier directed the movie as well.

Sadly, Vivien had contracted tuberculosis in 1945 and was often in poor health. Her mental condition also wasn't ideal, though an accurate diagnosis was elusive, ranging from bipolar disorder to schizophrenia. Leigh, who'd had a daughter by her first husband, suffered miscarriages in the 1940s and '50s and in 1953 was said to have had a nervous breakdown before completing the film *Elephant Walk* (1954). She was replaced by a nineteen-years-younger Elizabeth Taylor and hospitalized.

Psychiatric drugs and electroshock therapy didn't seem to help and may have caused damage. Vivien continued working on stage and screen as her tuberculosis worsened and her behavior became at times erratic. Laurence Olivier felt he couldn't continue with her, and the once-beautiful pair divorced.

After the 1951 *Streetcar* the actress made only three more films. Her penultimate, *The Roman Spring of Mrs. Stone* (1961), was from a Tennessee Williams story about a fading actress living in Rome who meets a handsome but rapacious Italian gigolo (a charmless Warren Beatty with a wandering accent). In real life, Leigh had a younger male companion. In *Ship of Fools* (1965), from Katherine Anne Porter's novel, Vivien headed an all-star cast, again playing a proud and still-beautiful but vulnerable and emotionally wounded woman sailing the Atlantic.

Vivien Leigh died alone in her Eaton Square flat in London from tuberculosis at fifty-three.

EXOTIC: CARMEN MIRANDA, ANNA MAY WONG, AND MERLE OBERON

What's exotic in one country or culture isn't necessarily so in another. Until recently Hollywood deemed "exotic" the people from the world's two by far most populous nations, China and India.

While many people semi-understandably think all Latin America speaks Spanish, in Washington, DC, not many decades back a mentally minor vice president believed Latin Americans speak Latin.

The following actresses were, respectively, Brazilian, Chinese American, and part Indian (as in India, not Native American). The actress who was visibly the most "exotic" or different was afforded the most limited screen career.

━◆━

Interesting how many celebrities who are introduced to an audience as "the inimitable" so-and-so are indeed imitable. Among the most unique and imitable movie stars was **Carmen Miranda**. From the start of her Hollywood career, which lasted from 1940 to 1953, she has been imitated by everyone from Lucille Ball, Mickey Rooney, and Jerry Lewis (in Miranda's swan song) to Carol Burnett and weatherman Willard Scott. The Brazilian Bombshell was a virtual parody of herself. "People like me in movies because right away they recognize me!"

Maria Do Carmo Miranda Da Cunha (1904–1955) made her Brazilian screen debut in 1933 in a carnival-themed picture—but then, she was a carnival. She hit Broadway in the late '30s and bowed in Hollywood in 1940 in *Down Argentine Way*. Her movie characters were virtually all the same one: an immensely energetic, likeable and amusing singer—with a bit of dancing thrown in—accompanied by her own band. When allowed to perform more than musical numbers she would fracture English and display comic jealousy over some man.

Her appearances were often the highlight of the film she was in. One French critic observed, "She is like a cartoon intermission happily interrupting

179

the middle of a motion picture." Another reviewer noted, "Our neighbor from way, way down south is colorful even in black-and-white."

Helping boost Carmen's career was the US government's Good Neighbor Policy, intended to urge Latin American nations into the Allied side during World War II. Critic Gene Siskel said, "Miranda was so unusual she couldn't help but stand out. . . . She was utterly foreign yet completely non-threatening and unmysterious. . . . During that time of food rations all those luscious fruits on her head didn't hurt."

Carmen's costumes, invariably full-length and featuring high platform heels, were skimpy for their day, typically exhibiting some portion of her midsection—but not of course the belly button, which was taboo. Her studio, Fox, was scandalized when it was discovered she didn't wear panties. Dancing partner Cesar Romero recalled, "In one scene I was lifting Carmen and twirling her. A photographer caught the moment, and for a while Miss Miranda's career was in jeopardy. . . . Had the photo gone public it could have sent her right back to Brazil.

"[Studio chief] Darryl Zanuck was able to suppress the photo and destroy any copies." At least one copy survived and has been reproduced in a few books.

The war years were Carmen's heyday. Postwar her popularity dipped dramatically and she seemed much less relevant. The actress was so stereotyped she couldn't be cast in dramatic roles or even as a regular human being. Nor did she choose to return to Brazil, where some compatriots disparaged her for having emigrated to and succeeding in the United States. However, whenever possible she emphasized that she was a Portuguese-speaking Brazilian, where most English speakers might have assumed she was Hispanic and Spanish-speaking.

In 1947 she teamed with another autofact, Groucho Marx. *Copacabana* (a nightclub named after the Rio de Janeiro beach) was a positive change for Carmen Miranda in that virtually all her movie roles had been supporting ones. This time she was the female lead and one of the two stars. But the B-picture was black-and-white and didn't fare well at the box office. There followed supporting roles in two A-pictures in color, then three years off-screen (she did do small-screen musical appearances) before her finale in the Martin and Lewis vehicle *Scared Stiff* (1953), in which she was imitated by one of the picture's two male stars.

Asked about her many imitators, Carmen offered, "I love it! I love them! Flattering is the sincerest form of imitation, yes?"

Alas at fifty-one Carmen Miranda died from a heart attack. (Her half-sister Aurora had a small but memorable part in a film-noir classic, *Phantom Lady* [1944]. Eleven years younger, Aurora outlived Carmen by fifty years.)

~

Anna May Wong had an unusual career. Not because she had small roles in A-pictures and starring roles in B-pictures. Nor because she enjoyed greater success in Europe than her own country (the United States). Nor because the young Anna differed markedly from her mid-aged self. It was unusual because the leading lady only got to kiss her leading man once (not in the United States). She was allowed to play romantic scenes with Caucasian actors but not kiss them—except John Loder, a husband of Hedy Lamarr, in *Java Head* (1935), made in England.

"I am not the color yellow," she protested, "It should not matter, but I am lighter than most southern Italians. Please don't assign me a color."

The father of Wong Liu Tsong (1905–1961) was a laundryman. He forbade her (her first names meant Willow Frost) to go to the movies and despaired that she disliked needlework, preferred baseball, and played marbles with boys. Once Anna broke into the movies, Mr. Wong refused to see her on the screen.

Anna May Wong became the only Hollywood star of Chinese origin. There were well-known Chinese, Japanese, and Korean actors, plus American actors of East Asian origin. But no other stars until Bruce Lee in the 1970s. As for East Asian characters, if the role was large it was assigned to a Caucasian. Besides, most such characters were villains or menials. Charlie Chan—played by a Swede, an American Caucasian, an Englishman, etc.—was the exception.

Growing up in Los Angeles, Anna was fascinated by motion pictures and determined to appear in one, which she did as a teen in actress-producer Alla Nazimova's *The Red Lantern* (1919). She continued happily, at first not minding small roles. Briefly but memorably she was seen in Douglas Fairbanks's very popular and impressive *The Thief of Bagdad* (1924). But Wong's roles were usually stereotypical, so she left Hollywood for England and the Continent, where she enjoyed considerable success on stage and screen. There, she sometimes had lead roles, and her characters weren't necessarily defined by race.

"Europe has a longer history than the United States . . . not as long as China's, but they can better appreciate different cultures and peoples. They can place them in context rather than fear them."

However, she returned to her family and based herself in the United States. In 1932 she received her best-known role, in the classic *Shanghai Express* with Marlene Dietrich. There followed adventure and mystery films like *Limehouse Blues, Daughter of Shanghai, Dangerous to Know, Java Head, King of Chinatown,* and *The Lady from Chungking.* Most were "exotic" and further stereotyped her.

In the late 1930s Wong became very concerned with Japanese military aggression against China, and active once the United States declared war against Japan. She explained, "If Americans generally think we are all the same, we are no more 'the same' than French or English and Germans. They are all European but the Germans are attacking the English and the French. . . . It is governments and fascist regimes that are wrong, not entire nationalities or races."

Anna was away from movies between 1942 and 1949. She returned in a too-small role in an excellent B-picture, *Impact.* Although in her mid-forties, she had aged visibly and looked, understandably, hardened. She then stayed away until 1960, as a maid in a Lana Turner vehicle, *Portrait in Black*—sadly, that was her swan song. Wong owned an apartment building in Santa Monica that took up much of her time, but not enough to explain her long screen absences. Keye Luke, best known as Charlie Chan's #1 Son, said, "I speak not to invade her privacy. People ask about Anna May Wong. They remember her.

"But they assume I knew her well because of our common ancestry. . . . I knew her slightly. I think she was shy. She had several female friends but did not socialize outside her circle."

Actor and restaurateur Philip Ahn was of Korean origin but often played Japanese villains, ironic because his father, a Korean patriot, was executed by the Japanese. Ahn, who was gay, worked with Anna, and in some of her biographies he has been deliberately and erroneously linked with her romantically—almost certainly less to closet him than her (neither married).

Ahn stated, "I know that the bad treatment dealt to so many non-Japanese [i.e., Chinese and Koreans] in California after Pearl Harbor was one motivation turning Miss Wong against the Hollywood industry. It did so little to explain matters or to lessen stereotypes. . . . She should have and I believe could have worked more. Why she chose not to, I don't comprehend. It was a great loss."

As an "exotic" actress, Anna May Wong, who like Carmen Miranda died prematurely from a heart attack, had very limited screen options. As an individual with integrity, even fewer.

Merle Oberon (1911–1979) was often described as an exotic beauty. Yet she claimed to be from Tasmania, Australia's southeastern island state. So how did she come by her un-Aussie looks? In those days the media didn't press. What a star said was accepted as truth.

Estelle Merle O'Brien Thompson's name reflected her father's heritage, if not his being posted in India, ruled at the time by Britain. Her mother was, depending on the source, half-Indian or Indian and reportedly gave birth to Merle at age twelve. The story goes that the ambitious Queenie, her nickname, passed off her mother as her maid when she went to England to become an actress. After her mother died there, she buried her in an unmarked grave.

The actress covered her tracks. It's hard to discern her life's fictions from the facts. That she was reputedly named after Oberon, king of the fairies in Shakespeare's *A Midsummer Night's Dream*, is ironic in view of the star's personal fairy tales and the fact that on and off the screen she would rub shoulders with royalty. Merle bowed on screen in 1930 and gained a spotlight in the prestigious international hit *The Private Life of Henry VIII* (1933), which won Charles Laughton the Oscar. She played a stunning, not-very-English-looking Anne Boleyn.

The following year she was in *The Private Life of Don Juan* and *The Scarlet Pimpernel* with Leslie Howard. In 1937 while making the unfinished *I, Claudius* (decades later an A-list TV miniseries) she suffered facial damage in a car accident that fortunately wasn't permanent. Merle's career leaped ahead when in 1939 she wed Alexander Korda, perhaps Britain's leading film producer (they divorced in 1945, when she wed cameraman Lucien Ballard— from whom she divorced in 1949).

That year, in Hollywood, she starred in her most famous role, the lovelorn Cathy in *Wuthering Heights*. With the 1940s her career declined due to less interesting films and parts, and in the '50s she made but a handful of films, most notably enacting Josephine, Napoleon's first and favorite wife whom he divorced because she didn't produce an heir. The biopic was *Desiree* (about the Corsican's younger love) and Napoleon was Marlon Brando, a startling look-alike.

In the '60s Oberon did a cameo as herself at the Oscar ceremonies in *The Oscar* plus two movies, period. In *Hotel* she was a duchess trying to stay one step ahead of the law. Biographer Charles Higham noted, "Merle Oberon's type was passé by the 1950s. She looked foreign, sounded British and had an air of regal aloofness. . . . With age, there was less room for her in the movies [but] she was wealthy enough not to lower herself into third-rate projects or to work at all."

Merle's private life had superseded her acting career. Some said she collected trophy husbands. Her third, Bruno Pagliai, whom she wed in 1957 (till 1973), was possibly the richest tycoon in Mexico. The pair adopted children, and their homes were distinctly regal. Invitations to lunch, dinner, weekends, or weeks at a time were eagerly accepted by Hollywood stars, including former costars, and European royalty. Queenie's mother would have been amazed.

Steve Cochran, Oberon's costar in *Of Love and Desire* (1963), revealed, "She's a born romantic. She loves being in love, with each leading man, as I've heard it. She told me she'd be happy to make nothing but love stories. . . . The problem is insecurity. Merle doesn't know how good-looking she is."

The actress had always tried to offset her high forehead with piled-up hair and elegant hairdos. As she aged her complexion became less pale. She remained beautiful, an intriguing combination of vulnerable and aloof. But her type (apart from her age) was less relevant to the 1970s. Merle Oberon's swan song was the partly self-financed *Interval* (1973), her first film in seven years. The exotic locations in Mexico's Yucatán Peninsula backgrounded the story of a jaded but vulnerable woman of the world who falls in love with a much younger painter. Insiders said the actress was playing herself and/or going through an emotional crisis.

"She'd fallen out of love with Bruno long before," a mutual friend of Merle's and Audrey Hepburn observed. "She stayed with him for the children and of course the lifestyle and their 'set.' But Merle wasn't old . . . she wanted one more great romantic adventure." She got it.

Merle fell in love with her twenty-five-years-younger costar Robert Wolders, decided to retire, and ended her sixteen-year marriage to Pagliai to remarry in 1975. Living in Malibu, she socialized much less often but was said to be happy.

After her death from a stroke, Wolders became Audrey Hepburn's younger companion until her death, then the companion of ex-actress Leslie Caron, and spent two decades with Henry Fonda's widow Shirlee.

The posthumous novel *Queenie* by Simon & Schuster chief Michael Korda (Alexander's nephew) was a bestselling 1985 roman à clef about the amazing journey that took its protagonist from India to London, Hollywood, Acapulco, Malibu, and the heights. One hopes Queenie's secret didn't weigh too heavily upon her.

MARILYN MONROE

In her day, **Marilyn Monroe** (1926–1962) was not a favorite of the media. She was criticized almost as often as she was ridiculed, as when she studied Method acting and said someday she hoped to appear in stage classics like *The Brothers Karamazov.* The press, comedians, and insensitive fellow actors, male and female, jumped on and perpetuated the *Karamazov* reference.

The story of Marilyn's rise to Mt. Olympus is probably the best-known star biography. No father, and an increasingly mentally ill mother who placed Norma Jeane in one foster home after another. However, most were with relatives. Norma Jeane married young in order not to be sent to an orphanage when her latest foster family moved out of state. While she was working in a parachute factory during World War II, a photographer took color photographs (then rare) of her, and she began appearing on magazine covers. Marilyn had a lifelong love affair with the still camera.

The movie camera was another story. She was insecure when speaking and emoting. Female coaches were required to assure her she had done all right in a given scene (to the ire of many a movie director). Monroe's lifelong quest was to expand her talent. She didn't realize and wasn't told that she was a gifted comedienne. She also fared well in early dramas like *Don't Bother to Knock, Clash by Night*, and *Niagara.* As a star she rarely got a role where she wasn't a showgirl.

Eventually her reputation for tardiness became public knowledge. What the media didn't always know and never reported was that she suffered from severe menstrual cramps that often delayed her appearance on a set. She was also prone to infections and bad colds.

Directors like Billy Wilder made a public issue of Marilyn's tardiness, which became exaggerated with the retelling and in the media. Yet her directors, including Wilder, admitted they'd work with her again—as did Wilder after *The Seven Year Itch* with *Some Like It Hot.*

John Huston, known for dramatizing himself and his directorial efforts, went very public about the delays involved in Marilyn's last completed film, *The Misfits* (1961), which was Clark Gable's swan song. As a result, much of the press blamed the leading lady for Gable's fatal heart attack shortly after filming ended. Little mention was made of the macho actor, nearing sixty, insisting on doing demanding stunts on location under the grueling Nevada sun.

As a blonde sex symbol Marilyn Monroe wasn't extended the same dramatic opportunities by 20th Century-Fox as brunette sex symbol Elizabeth Taylor, who was being paid $1 million (a record salary) by Fox to star as *Cleopatra*. Taylor's delays on the costliest film yet made exceeded Marilyn's on *Something's Got to Give* and weren't just health-related. She was pursuing a stormy relationship with married costar Richard Burton that at one point led her to try suicide.

Marilyn was probably the least well-paid major movie star and in her mid-thirties was concerned with her future. After seeing herself un-svelte in a *Misfits* scene in a bikini, she went on a serious but not extreme diet. The result was that shortly before her death she looked as beautiful as she ever had, proved by filmed costume tests for *Something's Got to Give*. It was the first time she played a mother, something female leads preferred to postpone as long as possible.

Intended for a 1962 release, *Give* costarred Dean Martin as the husband who believes Monroe, lost at sea, is dead, and is about to marry Cyd Charisse when Marilyn shows up. A copy of director George Cukor's lavish home was built on the Fox lot. Marilyn did miss many days of filming but also worked hard and effectively when she did show up. The eventual claim that thanks to the irresponsible leading lady there was almost no usable footage was a lie disproved by the subsequent compilation and decades-later screening of about forty minutes of excellent footage.

When Fox fired Marilyn Monroe it made worldwide headlines, for it was a first. What got far less press was her subsequent rehiring after renegotiating her undervalued contract for a much better salary, still not in Liz's league, and for another Fox picture. As for the sad-suicidal-Marilyn stories, she was making plans for the future. She'd recently bought her first house and traveled to Mexico to buy furniture and also brought back a temporary Mexican boyfriend.

Monroe was doing lengthy photo sessions with several top photographers, partly to prove she was in prime physical shape, not drug-wasted like some periodicals claimed. She also planned shortly to visit friends back east and was reportedly busy reading scripts. A number of film projects planned for Marilyn were inherited by other stars, for instance *What a Way to Go!* (1964) with Shirley MacLaine. *Something's Got to Give* was posthumously refashioned into a 1963 Doris Day movie titled *Move Over, Darling.*

In her lifetime it was little-known that Monroe was an avid reader who preferred socializing with authors rather than actors. She also had political opinions she knew better than to make public at the time, for instance her distrust of Richard Nixon and contempt for the Shah of Iran and his destroy-Israel agenda.

In the past Marilyn had attempted suicide more than once, her miscarriages being one motive, but she wasn't suicidal when she died of a drug overdose in the early hours of Sunday, August 5, 1962. Los Angeles "coroner to the stars"Thomas Noguchi was, not for the first time nor the last, too eager or too pressured to "solve" the death and declared it "suicide."

Though she divorced three times (less than half Liz's total), Marilyn kept in touch with Joe DiMaggio's troubled son and Arthur Miller's elderly father and, like Elizabeth Taylor, didn't unconvert from Judaism post-divorce. Had she lived, her love for animals would according to friends probably have moved her toward animal-rights activism à la Doris Day or Brigitte Bardot. Day saw her relatively brief yet extremely successful show-biz career as just a precursor to her pro-pets work. Bardot retired before the then-big-deal Four-O. Might Marilyn have done the same?

We can never know what Marilyn Monroe might have chosen to become. We do know what she became: a goddess.

MURDERED: RAMON NOVARRO, SHARON TATE, AND SAL MINEO

Over time, there have been numerous notable Hollywood murders, including several murdered by their nearest if not their dearest. The following three were killed by perfect strangers. Or rather, the opposite of perfect.

He was the second most popular Latin Lover of the silent era, after Rudolph Valentino, and starred in the most expensive silent movie, *Ben-Hur* (1925). But by the second half of the twentieth century **Ramon Novarro** (1899–1968) was largely forgotten. His name turned up a few times on *I Love Lucy* via old Mrs. Trumble (Elizabeth Patterson), who babysat for Lucy Ricardo. Although she mispronounced his name "Raymon Navarro," he was her favorite movie star and long-ago crush.

Tom Tryon, who gave up acting to write fiction, had a bestseller in 1976 with *Crowned Heads*, comprising four stories, each focusing on a thinly disguised movie star. One was Ramon Novarro (the story based on Greta Garbo became the Billy Wilder movie *Fedora*).

Cousin to Mexican actress Dolores Del Rio, who later followed him into Hollywood pictures, Novarro was billed as Ramon Samaniegos, his real name, in his first four films, starting in 1916. In 1921 he had a small role in the hit *The Four Horsemen of the Apocalypse*, reportedly secured for him by its star—his friend and possible lover—Valentino. The Italian's departure from MGM over a denied raise increased Ramon's opportunities there. Boyish, sincere, very handsome and likeable, and with no accent in silent movies, he made his name in adventure films like *The Prisoner of Zenda*, *Scaramouche*, and *The Arab*.

After *Ben-Hur* the hits continued with *The Student Prince*, *The Pagan*, and *In Gay Madrid*. One Hollywood myth has it that Novarro was among the stars felled by talkies. Untrue. In 1930 he did *Call of the Flesh* in English, Spanish, and French versions and in 1932 was Garbo's leading man in MGM's *Mata Hari*. Another bit of nonsense has him uttering the line, "What's the matter, Mata?"

Various factors contributed to Novarro's celluloid decline: changing audience tastes (foreign actresses were also becoming less popular), growing too mature for boyish roles, grittier pictures (e.g., gangster flicks), Ramon tiring of back-to-back-to-back movies and giving more time to his singing career, plus the fact of his remaining single and the suspicions it raised. He could only confess that he was seriously considering becoming a priest for so long.

Additionally, by the time of the much-strengthened movie censorship that took full effect in July 1934, various studios, MGM in particular, had dismissed those gay actors who declined to marry a woman for show. Louis B. Mayer blackballed the Mexican in Hollywood, so he worked in Europe for a time. In 1935 he played the London Palladium with his sister Carmen. They toured the Continent and were a hit (three of Ramon's five sisters became nuns).

Novarro had tried his hand at directing with the 1930 *La Sevillana* (the Spanish-language version of *Call of the Flesh*) and *Contra la Corriente* (1936, Against the Tide). He concertized on tour, in 1937 did *The Sheikh Steps Out*, and in 1940 made *La comedie de bonheur* (French for The Happy Comedy). In 1942 he made a Mexican film, not filming in Hollywood until 1949, by which time he was playing only small roles and had reportedly begun drinking too much.

His penultimate film was *Crisis* (1950), with Cary Grant as a vacationing US doctor forced to operate on a Latin American dictator (Jose Ferrer). In 1960 friend and gay director George Cukor gave Ramon a small part in *Heller in Pink Tights* starring Sophia Loren. In the late '50s Novarro began appearing in guest roles on TV dramas, explaining, "I am no longer too handsome." His last such was a priest on a 1968 episode of the Hispanic-themed TV western *High Chaparral*.

Like a number of Hollywood actors, Ramon eventually used a discreet male-escort service that sometimes involved prostitution. He may have met the fatal Fergusons through one of the brothers' brother-in-law, who allegedly worked for the service. The two had heard a rumor that Ramon Novarro kept $5,000 in cash at his home. He invited them over, but the would-be tryst went horribly wrong when he denied the cash rumor and Paul Ferguson bound his hands and feet and proceeded to beat the elderly man to death.

Ramon choked on his own blood while Tom Ferguson made a long-distance call to his girlfriend in Chicago to brag about the murder. What didn't happen was that Ramon died with an Art Deco dildo, supposedly given him by Valentino, shoved down his throat. The myth originated in Kenneth Anger's book *Hollywood Babylon*. When the brothers left behind Novarro's corpse and home they took with them a total of $20.

The trial was a travesty, with Ramon Novarro's sexuality on trial as much as the co-conspirators. Found guilty, they were sentenced to life imprisonment. Tom was released after six years and Paul nine. Each was later rearrested for other crimes. In 2005 Tom Ferguson killed himself. Paul Ferguson received a sixty-year sentence for raping a woman in Missouri.

Sharon Tate (1943–1969) is mostly remembered for her role as a tragic blonde sex symbol (reputedly based on Carole Landis or Marilyn Monroe) in *Valley of the Dolls* (1967) and for her horrific death at the hands of the "Manson family" while pregnant by husband Roman Polanski.

After Sharon, a military brat, relocated to Verona, Italy, with her family she became a semi-celebrity there when her photo was published in a local US military newspaper. Next step? Her film debut via a small part in the Italian-made biblical picture *Barabbas* (1961), starring Anthony Quinn. "She was a very pretty girl," Quinn later said. "But her personality didn't jump out at you. It wouldn't in the next twenty pretty girls, either. Not at that age. . . . She was quiet and respectful."

In Hollywood it didn't take time for Tate to be noticed by film executives and such, but it took time for public notice through non-token roles in widely released films. "She had a quality of speaking so softly," noted Deborah Kerr, "that one tended to lean in to hear her. She enunciated better than most American girls, so there was no trouble understanding her. But one did have to pay attention."

In 1966 Tate had a significant part in *Eye of the Devil*, a classy black-and-white chiller starring Kerr and David Niven. "Had Sharon Tate come along earlier she might have become a genuine sex symbol," Niven stated in 1972. "By the time she came along the whole sex-symbol thing was disappearing. . . . As for earlier days, Miss Tate was completely modern in look and manner."

Sharon's breakthrough year was 1967. She was in *Don't Make Waves*, starring Tony Curtis, who observed, "The more you experience her on the screen the more you realize there's more than just a beauteous blonde there." In *The Fearless Vampire Killers* she played the unpanicked damsel in distress opposite unlikely hero Roman Polanski. And she was one of the starring trio of Jackie Susann heroines—the one who dies—in *Valley of the Dolls*, with Patty Duke and Barbara Parkins.

Duke found Tate "natural and unaffected. . . . Most of the lookers in this town are stuck on themselves. Sharon didn't have an arrogant bone in her body."

Whether Sharon Tate would have become an ongoing leading lady or been mostly restricted to smaller decorative roles, who can say? "You couldn't see her playing a foreigner or in period pictures," felt Orson Welles, "but her talent could have expanded over the next few decades."

Welles, Vittorio Gassman, Vittorio De Sica, and Terry-Thomas costarred with Sharon in her final movie, *Twelve Plus One* (1969), also known as *The Thirteen Chairs* and *Una su tredici*. Whether making a European comedy that wouldn't obtain wide US distribution was a sign of a languishing career or a nod to a European husband's connections is hard to tell. However, the three *Valley of the Dolls* principals didn't reap the expected box-office follow-ups in the wake of its huge success.

Back in Hollywood Sharon took time off while she was expecting and Roman was busy in Europe. Meanwhile, Charles Manson, an aspiring musician (as Hitler was an aspiring painter), had contacted music producer Terry Melcher, Doris Day's son, who brushed him off. Manson thus targeted Melcher for death. But Terry and girlfriend Candice Bergen had moved out of 10050 Cielo Drive in Los Angeles's Benedict Canyon. It was being rented by Tate and Polanski.

The night Manson's zombies made their way up the estate's driveway Sharon was entertaining guests Abigail Folger, heiress to the "mountain grown" coffee fortune, hairdresser Jay Sebring, Wojciech Frykowski, and Steven Parent—the victims.

The murders caused more than consternation in Hollywood. Varying degrees of paranoia set in, and homes were rigorously secured against intruders. The insensately evil Manson remained unremorseful and later tried to fatally stab a judge with a pencil. He got to live out his life at public expense in prison. Every several years the news has reported the justifiably denied parole of one or other of his "family" of killers.

"I wasn't a child actor, I was a teen idol." Two-time Oscar nominee **Sal Mineo** (1939–1976) corrected an Italian journalist who noted how difficult it was for male child stars to transition to adult stardom (less difficult for girls, e.g., Elizabeth Taylor and Natalie Wood).

Salvatore Mineo, who declined to change his surname to Miller or Maynard, was a teenybopper favorite known as the Switchblade Kid due to his big-screen portrayals of mostly sympathetic juvenile delinquents. Ironically, he would die—bleeding to death on the floor of his carport—via a hunting knife repeatedly inflicted by a career criminal who was later, again, set free.

It was real-life juvenile delinquency, unpublicized at the time, that pushed Mineo into show business. He was arrested for stealing gym equipment from his Bronx school and hiding it in the caskets that his father made for a living. Rather than reform school, Sal's parents' pleas led to his placement in a performing arts school. That led to dramatic connections and adolescent roles in Tennessee Williams's play *The Rose Tattoo* and in *The King and I*.

Rose Tattoo star Maureen Stapleton recalled, "Sal was somewhat small for his age, but a big personality and big, big eyes . . . and a charming smile. When I eventually heard he went out to Hollywood I wasn't at all surprised."

Sal's roles were small but in pictures starring names like Paul Newman, Tony Curtis, and Charlton Heston. In one case, he lucked out when the movie's intended male lead, Jeff Chandler, dropped out, replaced by Tony Curtis—the actor who'd been cast to play Chandler as a youth didn't resemble Curtis. Mineo did. Sal's big break was being cast as part of the trio also comprising James Dean and Natalie Wood in the future hit and classic *Rebel without a Cause* (1955).

"My character Plato," Sal explained in 1974, "has been called the first gay teenager in American movies. It's obvious now he has a crush on Jimmy. I did too . . . I often get asked if Jimmy and I had an affair, and we could have. But they forget how young I was. In those days people were more careful. Not always—Nick Ray, *Rebel*'s director, had an affair with Natalie, who like me was jail bait.

"Anyway, Plato dies in the end, so the sympathy for him probably helped get me the [Oscar] nomination. My other nominated character also gets killed off, come to think of it."

Thanks to his connection with Dean, Sal had a small role as a Mexican in *Giant* the following year. It starred Rock Hudson, Elizabeth Taylor, and Dean, who was posthumously Oscar-nominated but didn't win.

Mineo was soon starring in pictures aimed at the teen market but also in *The Gene Krupa Story* (1959) as the famous drummer. Its lackluster box office was a harbinger; many in the business believed Sal (no longer a teen but looking like one) could only carry a film in juvenile roles. Producer-director Otto Preminger gave Mineo a youthful supporting role in *Exodus* (1960), about the founding of modern Israel. "Dov got me another nomination that I didn't win, but I was proud of having two . . . it showed I wasn't a flash in the pan. Or so I thought back then."

However, Sal's Dov, a concentration-camp survivor, cost him a role in *Lawrence of Arabia* "because the producers caved right in to [King] Hussein's anti-Jewish ban after they decided to shoot the movie in Jordan." The Arab leader boycotted Jewish actors and all actors who appeared in *Exodus*.

Mineo continued in supporting roles, with few exceptions. One was *Who Killed Teddy Bear?* (1965), which he termed "a psychopath flick that flopped. It was a gamble. The money men hoped it would cause a big stir like some other far-out '60s movies that pulled in a big youth audience."

Sal's final big-screen role was a smart chimpanzee named Dr. Milo in the 1971 sequel *Escape from the Planet of the Apes*. He was eighth-billed, unrecognizable, and got killed off early. "I did it for the money." By then he was no longer in demand. Rumor had it his sometime boyfriend Roddy McDowall (who appeared in each *Apes* epic) got him the part. Thereafter, Sal did occasional small-screen appearances—"hardly one a year"—in TV movies or series, concluding with the 1975 documentary *James Dean, the First American Teenager*.

That Hollywood knew Sal Mineo was gay may have influenced his career downturn. But he pointed out, "I'm short-ish and have an olive complexion. If I'd been born later I could have been one of the ethnics, like Hoffman, De Niro and Pacino. . . . I discovered a novel, *Midnight Cowboy*, tried to get it produced with me as Ratso Rizzo—Italian-American, see?— but someone else made it later, and Dustin Hoffman, Jewish, not Italian, got the role," and an Oscar nomination.

Mineo noted more than once the difficulty of making the transition from supporting actor to lead. "It's hard to not be pigeonholed as what you start out as. You're only allowed one image."

Sal turned to the stage. He starred in and directed the gay prison drama *Fortune and Men's Eyes*. Doing so was tantamount to coming out, and there were no further movie offers. Sal prospered in the theatre and was due to open in Los Angeles in a starring bisexual role in *P.S. Your Cat Is Dead*. He was living in a West Hollywood apartment, having had to sell his house (many years before, he'd bought his parents a pricey house in Mamaroneck).

Returning home one night after rehearsals he encountered a thug in his carport who stabbed him to death at the age of thirty-seven on February 12, 1976. Neighbors in the apartment complex heard Sal's agonized pleas for help.

The bigoted media tried to connect the murder with the actor's non-heterosexuality and with possible drug use. Or, another stereotype, with supposed dealings with Mafia types. Or a gay lovers' quarrel. The killer was a stranger, a career criminal named Lionel Ray Williams who'd been in jail before. He was twenty-one in 1978 when he was arrested. In prison Williams bragged about killing "a big white celebrity." He hadn't known Sal Mineo's identity while stabbing him.

Eventually Williams was set free, later returning to jail for another crime, nowhere as horrific as the slaying of Sal Mineo, who happened to be in the right place at a very wrong time.

ATTICUS: GREGORY PECK

"Single-mindedness is the most important factor in a successful actor's career," said the star born Eldred **Gregory Peck** (1916–2003). "It means refusing to give up. It means putting your work before everything else, except your family."

The same would appear to be the philosophy of Peck's most famous character, attorney Atticus Finch in *To Kill a Mockingbird* (1962). The kindly father, fierce in the courtroom, earned him a fifth Oscar nomination and the award itself. His perhaps other most famous role was the obsessive Captain Ahab in *Moby Dick* (1956). Contrary to Peck's peaceful and benign image, he didn't avoid emotionally virulent characters, as in *Duel in the Sun* (1946, nicknamed "Lust in the Dust"; a film by that name was made decades later with Tab Hunter and Divine) or *Moby Dick* or *The Boys from Brazil* (1978) as the Nazi doctor Josef Mengele. "I very seldom get offered bad boys," he remarked at the time of the latter film.

One of Gregory Peck's best-known pictures was *Gentlemen's Agreement* (1947), among the first to examine anti-Semitism and a Best Picture Oscar winner. "I'm all for good entertainment . . . but I'm not one of those who decry a good message if it's wrapped inside an entertaining picture. There's nothing wrong with a message that opens people's eyes."

One of his best-loved efforts was *Roman Holiday* (1953). He recalled, "It was one of the first Hollywood productions to go on location, and a number of my peers were very surprised I was willing to do so. I was surprised they were surprised. If the script is good, I'll go anywhere it requires. . . . Little did I know how good the leading lady [new star Audrey Hepburn] would be."

In Peck's final movie, *Other People's Money* (1991), he was a business-man battling to save his firm from a hostile takeover by rotten little Danny DeVito. The picture wasn't a hit.

Like many longtime superstars, Gregory Peck at seventy-five didn't look forward to spending the rest of his career in minor roles, so he retired from acting. Besides focusing on family and friends, he traveled internationally with a one-man show of his movie clips, answering questions from admiring audiences. The community-minded Peck was a former president of the Academy of Motion Picture Arts and Sciences. Though he'd been asked to run against Ronald Reagan for governor of California and declined, he urged his son Carey to run for Congress, which he did twice, narrowly losing to a Republican opponent.

In 1998 Peck came out of retirement because of an offer he couldn't resist, albeit a supporting part. He agreed to play Father Mapple in a TV miniseries remake of *Moby Dick*. That role in his 1956 movie had been filled by Orson Welles. Britisher Patrick Stewart played the small-screen Captain Ahab.

"It was a fitting punctuation to my acting career," explained Peck. "It was sort of closing a circle. . . . In one's eighties one can't realistically expect offers of leads in film or television. This was just the right move."

The move earned the star a Golden Globe award for Best Supporting Actor in a Series, Miniseries, or Television Film. Following the usual career trajectory of a star, Peck had followed up lead roles on the big screen—in latter-day hits like *The Omen* and character parts like *MacArthur*—with leads in special TV events, until they too petered out.

The miniseries remake of *Moby Dick* wasn't the first time Peck took a small role in a project he'd once headlined. In 1962 he'd costarred with Robert Mitchum in *Cape Fear*, playing another decent lawyer, forced into battle with psycho ex-convict Robert Mitchum. During the climactic fight scene where Peck defends his family, he accidentally packed a powerful punch whose result the brawny Mitchum felt for days. In 1991 Martin Scorsese directed a *Cape Fear* remake starring his then-preferred leading man, Robert De Niro (Nick Nolte played the attorney). Peck took the fleeting role of the vengeful De Niro's lawyer. "I'm not overly fond of the remake syndrome, but in this case the talents before and behind the camera were very reassuring."

Peck had been able to mostly avoid trashy scripts and projects over the decades. Mitchum, by contrast, rationalized, "Making movies is a routine or a rut, like nine-to-five for most people. You have to have something to do, and if it's actually worthwhile, so much the better."

"Greg was very much a family man," offered friend and costar Lauren Bacall. "The suicide death of his son Jonathan in Santa Barbara was a very private and very heartfelt grief. Greg spent even more time with his loved ones after that. . . . I can tell you that his last years, when he was no longer acting, were very far from empty years."

(As to the unusual first name of Harper Lee's *To Kill a Mockingbird* protagonist, her friend and fellow Monroeville, Alabama, native Truman Capote informed film historian Carlos Clarens, "Back in old Roman days Atticus was a name for an upstanding man of ethics. Harper also told me she admired the Atticus Circle, a very early group that hoped to advance equal rights for [gay] people like us.")

ACCIDENT: SUSAN PETERS, JAMES DEAN, JAYNE MANSFIELD, AND CHRISTOPHER REEVE

Not many but too many acting careers have been cut short by accidents, most often mechanical, i.e., car or airplane crashes. Other causes, as here, include firearms and horses. One of the most gruesome cases was movie tough guy Charles McGraw (1914–1980), best known for *The Narrow Margin* (1951) and *Spartacus* (1960). He fell through a glass shower door and bled to death.

One of the saddest Hollywood endings was that of **Susan Peters** (1921–1952). Under her birth name of Suzanne Carnahan she appeared in thirteen films starting in 1939. In 1942 she debuted under her new name, making nine movies that year and in 1943 when she was named Star of Tomorrow and wed actor Richard Quine (later a director and a suicide). MGM was grooming Susan for stardom.

On New Year's Day, 1945, Susan was involved in a duck-hunting accident when the trigger of a .22-caliber rifle she was handling unexpectedly discharged. The bullet severed her spine, paralyzing her from the waist down. Her career was terminated overnight. Jack Lemmon, a friend of director Quine, told film historian Carlos Clarens, "Richard said the years after were hell on earth. For Susan of course . . . physically, but the professional loss. . . . She yearned somehow to resume acting.

"It also took its toll on their marriage," which ended in 1948, the year Susan Peters was able to make her screen comeback in a Columbia picture, *The Sign of the Ram*, acting from a wheelchair. She played a controlling woman who alienates loved ones and ends tragically.

"In those days," added Lemmon, "a younger character in a wheelchair practically had to die by fadeout. If you were old and in a chair, that was different."

The dark and depressing film didn't appeal to moviegoers and effectively ended Susan's big-screen career. Instead, she acted in appropriate stage roles in *The Glass Menagerie* and *The Barretts of Wimpole Street*. Peters was also a wheelchair-bound attorney in a 1951 TV series titled *Miss Susan*.

"Susan never gave up on Hollywood," said Mickey Rooney, her costar in *Andy Hardy's Double Life*. "Hollywood gave up on *her*. It didn't have to. Mr. [Louis B.] Mayer kept Lionel Barrymore going in several [wheelchair] roles. ... The truth is, people didn't want to see a female in a wheelchair."

Despite trying to keep busy, following the end of her life in movies and her marriage, Susan Peters sank deeper into a depression made worse by a chronic kidney infection and capped by self-starvation. She died at thirty-one.

—◆—

Public sorrow over the death of twenty-four-year-old **James Dean** (1931–1955) was unequaled since the 1926 death of Rudolph Valentino at thirty-one. He'd starred in only three films—*East of Eden* (1954), *Rebel without a Cause* (1955), and *Giant* (1956)—yet Jimmy Dean impacted hugely upon the emerging teenage audience that was beginning to be recognized and courted in the 1950s.

Two-time costar Sal Mineo, promoting the 1975 documentary *James Dean, the First American Teenager*, said, "Monty Clift and Brando came along and changed acting into something emotional that men could do too. Jimmy followed suit but Monty and Brando were grown-ups ... Jimmy was more of a teenager, a contemporary Peter Pan hanging on to youth and trying to tell his own truth."

Growing up, Dean was criticized by his father for taking to poetry. "I once saw Jimmy holding a little book of poetry," recalled *East of Eden* costar Julie Harris. "He was holding, or clutching, it tight. Like a security blanket."

Pre-stardom, Dean worked on the New York stage, then did a handful of forgettably small parts in forgettable films. Stage costar Geraldine Page believed the actor would have preferred to be a poet but "He was terribly ambitious and in a hurry, almost as if he *knew* ..." that his time was limited.

In *Eden* James played the son of a madam. Jim Backus of *Gilligan's Island* played his father in *Rebel*, noting, "In the first two, Jimmy was anguished. His characters were tormented. Then in *Giant*, it seems to me, he focused on envy and revenge. Whatever Jimmy expressed, you always kept your eyes on him."

Though not exceptionally handsome, Dean became a sex symbol to millions. Sal Mineo pointed out, "In *East of Eden* he had a brother—Richard Davalos, right? There was a scene, the two in the bedroom, absolutely platonic, but they censored it out. Jimmy and another handsome dude . . . too homoerotic.

"Jimmy could project sexuality. Several times when he smiled at me, it was downright sexual, and we both knew it. Dumb kid that I was, I didn't push it."

The ambitious Dean partook of the Hollywood casting couch and boasted that he'd been fellated by five of the biggest names in the business. After his death an underground rumor spread that Jack Warner had had him killed because James planned to come out of the closet. Several who knew him said he would never have come out; his career came first.

In a 2019 *Closer* magazine interview Carroll Baker, who played Dean's love interest in *Giant* and attended the Actors Studio with him, was quoted, "It became my well-considered opinion that Jimmy was in fact asexual. Girls I knew who had been close to Jimmy only spoke about how he held their hands and how innocent he had been, never touching them." Surprising that an eighty-eight-year-old who worked in Hollywood couldn't guess why Dean was asexual where girls were concerned.

Baker added that although married, "Hedda Hopper wanted me to say I was having a love affair with Jimmy! It was so distasteful and unfair." Ironically, actor William Hopper (*Perry Mason*), only child of the far-right homophobe, was gay.

Platonic friend Eartha Kitt stated, "Jimmy's private life was exceedingly private. But in those days, in public, he did what he had to do. He went around with [Italian actress] Pier Angeli more than the others. . . . After he died, several publicity-seeking actresses said they'd been secretly engaged to Jimmy. I never pretended. We were just wonderful friends.

"After Jimmy died there were also those who disliked him but didn't dare say so, the reaction to him was so intense."

One who disliked him and didn't say so for years was Rock Hudson, the first-billed star of *Giant*. Insiders had predicted a discreet affair between the male costars, but they shared an instant dislike precipitated by James's surly attitude. He considered that Rock—he ridiculed the made-up name—was coasting on his looks and mainstream image. Second-billed Elizabeth Taylor got along with both but admitted, "Jimmy was rude, he didn't treat Rock as he should have."

One star who voiced antipathy toward the late James Dean was Humphrey Bogart, who called him out as overrated and a product of the new teen culture. Jack Warner eventually expressed disgust for Dean's self-destructiveness. When the actor was posthumously nominated for a *Giant* Best Actor Academy Award, Warner didn't mount a campaign for him, being interested only in living actors who could continue generating profits for the studio.

Sal Mineo admitted, "Jimmy wasn't an easy personality. He had some conflicts. . . . I know he was sweet to me 'cause I was real young and not a threat. I don't know how his career would have gone if he'd lived. . . . After he hit it big in *East of Eden* he did start making some enemies.

"Jimmy was ambitious but also reckless, like with cars and speeding. He was almost defiant about breaking speed limits. . . . When I heard he'd crashed near Salinas [California] I almost felt it was inevitable."

Jo Van Fleet, who won a supporting Oscar as the mother in *Eden*, guessed, "Did he build himself up only to tear himself down? There are contrary personalities like that, and there were different rumors. . . . But I couldn't say."

Dean's death left behind several projects that instead were filled by and made stars of Paul Newman and Steve McQueen. James Dean had been Elvis Presley's favorite actor. He commented that the star's death made him a more careful driver. "Such a waste. . . . He was able to act out what a lot of teens were feeling."

Julie Harris observed, "Every decade or so since Jimmy's death there's some young actor who's advertised or hailed as 'the new James Dean.' You notice not one of them has stood the test of time anywhere like the original."

In the 1950s **Jayne Mansfield** was known as the poor man's sex symbol (next to the classier Marilyn Monroe) and for the oversized bust she never tired of thrusting into the public eye. Her motto was nothing risqué, nothing gained. Today she's most often identified as TV star Mariska Hargitay's mother and with her death in a car accident near New Orleans in which she was *not* decapitated.

Rumors of headlessness were fueled by a wig found at the death site. The accident also killed two men and Jayne's inseparable Chihuahua. Born Vera Jane Palmer (1933–1967), she'd lightened her hair and affected a little-girl

Jayne Mansfield struggled to be a second Marilyn Monroe, often sliding into self-parody as a busty "dumb blonde." Her films' quality diminished quickly and she wound up doing exploitive documentaries and driving cross-country for personal appearances. Jayne died at thirty-four in a car crash (she was not decapitated; her wig came off).

voice in her attempt to crash the postwar parade of Hollywood blondes. When success eluded her—she screen-bowed in 1950 in *Prehistoric Women* but didn't make another movie until 1954—she redoubled her publicity efforts, later declaring, "Publicity can be terrible. But only if you don't have any," and further dumbed down her image.

Asked whether it was wise to be known solely for her body, Mansfield replied, "A girl doesn't get very far in pictures if she's known for her brain."

Urban legend held that the pneumatic blonde had a genius IQ. Contrarily, costar Tony Randall from her most famous movie, *Will Success Spoil Rock Hunter?* (1957), quipped, "One day [on the set] Jayne said she had a terrific idea. The director stared at her, then said, 'Treat it gently, dear. It's in a strange place.'"

Also in 1957, Jayne found a feud and a new man. Mae West's popular nightclub act featured a line of musclemen, the most celebrated being the current Mr. Universe, Hungarian Miklosi "Mickey" Hargitay. Mansfield caught the act at the Latin Quarter (owned by Lou Walters, Barbara's father) and the two began dating, much to Mae's fury. The ambitious Hargitay publicized the relationship, insinuating both women (West was sixty-four, Jayne twenty-four) were fighting over him. Mae characterized her rival in tawdry terms—"When it comes to men, I heard she never turns down anything but the bedcovers."—virtually forcing Mansfield to respond in kind. West also pretended she'd never had any romantic interest in Hargitay and would replace him with the new Mr. Universe as soon as a new one was crowned (Mickey had seen to it his contract didn't lapse until then). The bodybuilder made several ungallant cracks about the old West, with his future wife and mother of their children siding with him.

After Jayne's death Mae West proclaimed, "She was so full of evil that one day her head just popped off and exploded." (A TV movie about Mansfield and Hargitay starred Loni Anderson and Arnold Schwarzenegger.)

Where Marilyn made relatively few films, Jayne made too many. Her usually mediocre 1950s vehicles looked good by the 1960s, when she appeared in *The Loves of Hercules*, *The Fat Spy*, *Las Vegas Hillbillies*, and other equally forgettable flicks. In between Z-movies Jayne toured the country, working live and exploiting herself ever more aggressively. British film historian David Quinlan put it succinctly: "The seemingly inevitable downward spiral through men, drink, drugs and semi-nude appearances in nightclubs has been graphically depicted in a thousand newspaper stories."

Mansfield's final bow in a movie was in *A Guide for the Married Man* (1967), starring Walter Matthau and another beautiful blonde who would die young, Inger Stevens. Jayne's role was typically brief and bubble-headed.

A documentary titled *The Wild, Wild World of Jayne Mansfield* was uncompleted at her death. By turns tacky, bizarre, and rather touching, it featured ex-husband Mickey Hargitay. Some Mansfield pictures weren't released in the United States, including foreign-made ones. Some were only released posthumously. Jayne made another documentary, *Mondo Hollywood* (1967), inspired by the hit Italian documentary *Mondo Cane* (meaning Dog World, as in dog eat dog).

"When I first heard I had 'movie-star looks' I told myself don't go for the quick bucks and become some male model who's flung aside by 30. . . . Or some movie actor who's past it at 40 or 50," said **Christopher Reeve** (1952–2004). "I just wanted to work on the stage, in front of an audience."

The dedicated and handsome actor spent years in regional and New York theatre, finding success in plays like Lanford Wilson's *Fifth of July* and opposite Katharine Hepburn in *West Side Waltz*. Naturally, Hollywood came a-calling and in 1977 Reeve screen-debuted in the Charlton Heston submarine clunker *Gray Lady Down*. But his looks, naturalness, and low-key charm pushed him to international stardom when he won the coveted role of the Man of Steel in the comic-book hero's comeback, *Superman* (1978).

Best friend Robin Williams recalled, "Chris didn't want to be a Hollywood pin-up . . . did not want to make it on his looks. But Superman! He was awed by the prospect. How can you turn Superman down? That's sacrilege."

In the 1950s TV's Superman was George Reeves, "a nice guy but too old for the part and not remotely as buffed as Chris Reeve," offered Jack Larson, the actor turned writer who played *Daily Planet* photographer Jimmy Olson. "Our series was made on the cheap. It was aimed at kids, not adults.

"Since then, there was no serious attempt to bring Superman back in a major production until now," in 1978.

Through 1987 Reeve starred in four Superman movies. Margot Kidder, who played the new Lois Lane, felt, "When times get worse, or when our leaders—like, politicians, I mean—are worse, I think that's when you see more movie superheroes. People want heroes or leaders who truly are good guys."

The boyish Reeve was able to avoid being trapped by his most famous role via a variety of films and roles, starting with the ultraromantic *Somewhere in Time* (1980) with Jane Seymour. He then played gay opposite Michael Caine in *Deathtrap*, starred as a sexually active *Monsignor*, as a nineteenth-century anti-feminist in Merchant/Ivory's *The Bostonians*, shared the TV-themed *Switching Channels* with Kathleen Turner and Burt Reynolds and *Remains of the Day* with Anthony Hopkins and Emma Thompson. Reeve seemed set to age handsomely into further leading but interesting roles when he suffered the disastrous 1995 horse-riding accident that left him paralyzed and in a wheelchair.

Years of therapy and hoped-for cures followed. Christopher's acting career was sidelined but not terminated. His final full role, as opposed to too-brief appearances on the TV series *The Practice* in 2003 and *Smallville* (about a very young Clark Kent/Superman) in 2004, was in a TV remake of the 1954 *Rear Window*. The Hitchcock murder mystery had starred James Stewart, immobilized due to a broken leg, peering through binoculars at apartment-house neighbors, one of whom turns out to be a killer. The Cornell Woolrich story had long since appealed to Reeve, who said he would have taken the role even if he hadn't been wheelchair-bound.

"The irony," concluded Margot Kidder, "is that what happened to the actor and the man who played Superman so beautifully seemed too incredible, so unreal. . . . It's fitting that Chris, with what he went through and how he mentally rose above it, in the end proved himself to be a real, not a fictional, hero."

SILENTS: MARY PICKFORD, LILLIAN GISH, AND RUDOLPH VALENTINO

Most silent stars who died before the sound era or didn't continue working in it are today little remembered. Mary Pickford is remembered because she was so big, Lillian Gish because her name reverberated through the many decades that witnessed the longest screen career of all, and Rudolph Valentino because of his huge impact as the original Latin Lover and because he died young . . . that helps.

———

The biggest if not the most interesting star of the silent era after Charlie Chaplin was **Mary Pickford** (1893–1979). She was Canadian, as were the first four actresses to win the Best Actress Academy Award (Marie Dressler, Janet Gaynor, Pickford, and Norma Shearer).

Born Gladys Smith, Pickford was "America's Sweetheart." Nearly all her shorts and features were silents. She emoted from 1909 to 1933. She was most famous for playing little girls well into adulthood in features like *Tess of the Storm Country, Poor Little Peppina, The Schoolteacher and the Waif, Honor Thy Father, The Little American, Rebecca of Sunnybrook Farm, A Little Princess, Pollyanna, Little Annie Rooney,* and two versions of *Tess of the Storm Country.*

In the late 1920s she focused on playing females her own age. Probably no other former superstar's movies are so rarely seen as those of Mary Pickford. Her Oscar-winning turn in *Coquette* (1929) and her swan song *Secrets* (1933) occasionally turn up on old-movie channels (she also appeared in a 1935 short, "Star Night at the Cocoanut Grove").

"Little Mary," another popular nickname, was a cofounder of United Artists in 1919, with Chaplin, Douglas Fairbanks, and director D. W. Griffith. In 1920 she became bigger than ever—he did too—by marrying dashing screen hero Douglas Fairbanks, her second husband. She was firmly retired from acting by 1936 when they divorced, but it caused a scandal—divorce was very much a negative and a rarity, and their marriage had seemed solid as the Rock of Gibraltar. The couple's Beverly Hills home, Pickfair, was America's closest thing to Buckingham Palace.

A prior Pickford scandal involved her brother Jack, whom she helped make a star. His wholesome image was shattered when he died from a drug overdose in 1933. That a movie star could be an addict was a public outrage. A less popular star than Pickford could easily have been tainted by the scandal's aftermath.

One of Mary's more memorable adult roles was in *Coquette*, in which she defied her father's choice of suitor for a more down-to-earth man. When her preferred suitor is killed, her father is put on trial and Pickford's in a pickle, torn by conflicting loyalties. The result was an Academy Award.

In her 1933 finale, *Secrets*, the setting was the 1860s, with Mary defying her father's marital choice of a British lord for a humble clerk. The ensuing drama includes cattle-rustling out west (the US West), the loss of the couple's son, and Mary's outsmarting the cow-stealers. Pickford turned forty in 1933 and terminated her acting career. She became widely publicized as a businesswoman, specifically a production executive. "The very fact of her being a founder of United Artists and attending board meetings with men impressed the general public," commented writer Doug McClelland. "But she wasn't terribly active.

"She produced fewer pictures than intended and nothing really major. Associates said she liked the grown-up image and power that the word 'executive' conveyed. . . . Pickford also tended to her investments and since she had no children was more involved with the rest of her family."

In 1937 Mary wed actor Charles "Buddy" Rogers, eleven years her junior. It was a companionate marriage, and once she lapsed into alcoholism and senility he became her minder. They remained wedded until her 1979 death after a stroke. By then she'd become a recluse.

Every decade or so, Mary Pickford's return to the screen was anticipated. She was purportedly offered (as was the highly offended Mae West) the role of faded silent-screen star Norma Desmond in Billy Wilder's *Sunset Boulevard*. In the mid-1950s she considered starring in *Storm Center*, the cautionary story of a librarian who refuses to remove a controversial book from the collection because of a few witch-hunter types. The theme was controversial during the McCarthy era and Pickford, who later campaigned for Nixon against John Kennedy, backed out. The 1956 film starred Bette Davis.

"Mary Pickford's appeal seems incomprehensible, even freakish, to us now," said journalist Lance Loud. "She needs to be seen in the context of a society that was still emerging from the Victorian age. . . . The fact that in her adult roles she was occasionally at odds with authority was daring then.

"She retired much too early . . . and after she did, she did much too little. She had the resources and influence, she could have made a positive difference. But she merely sat on her laurels, growing brittle, anti-modern and more and more distant. . . . It would appear, anyway, that she wasted over half her life."

—✦—

Lillian Gish (1893–1993) had possibly *the* longest screen career, spanning 1912 to 1987. Born Lillian De Guiche, she became famous with sister Dorothy Gish in pictures directed by the pioneering D. W. Griffith. Her 1969 autobiography was titled *The Movies, Mr. Griffith and Me.* Dorothy, most of whose shorts and features were silents, left films for marriage and the theatre, doing only a handful of talkies.

Elder Lillian possessed more dramatic intensity, more ambition, and more independence. She directed one movie, *Remodeling Her Husband*, in 1920, but never wed. Her first few years she did shorts, which were the standard. Via popular features she became one of probably the three most popular silent-era actresses, with Mary Pickford and Gloria Swanson.

Her silent hits included the classics *Judith of Bethulia, The Birth of a Nation, Intolerance, The Hearts of the World, Broken Blossoms, Way Down East, Orphans of the Storm, La Boheme, The Scarlet Letter,* and *The Wind.*

Gish's talkie debut was *One Romantic Night* (1930). But by then the longtime star was considered old hat. She did one more film in 1933, then departed for the theatre, where she could be relevant and was popular. "Self-improvement, it is vital. . . . The theatre is set up to encourage, even demand improvement."

In 1942 Lillian Gish returned to the screen without making a big impact. Still gracefully pretty, she looked middle-aged at least and usually received "old lady" parts. She never again worked frequently in films. Her future director Charles Laughton later said, "The shall we say classic Miss Gish was for all intents and purposes another person. She was a girl. She stayed a girl a very long time. But not in the debatably absurd way that Miss Pickford did, playing girl children."

In 1955 Lillian performed her most famous sound role in Laughton's *The Night of the Hunter*. Her partly symbolic role was the confident, comforting protectress, shotgun and all, of the children "hunted" by Robert Mitchum. Praised but not popular then, the picture has grown significantly in stature over the decades.

Her few subsequent pictures include one of Audrey Hepburn's least seen films, the western *The Unforgiven* (1959), *The Comedians* with Richard Burton and Elizabeth Taylor (1967), Robert Altman's *A Wedding* (1978), and her penultimate film, Alan Alda's *Sweet Liberty* (1986). Her swan song was *The Whales of August* (1987), directed by Lindsay Anderson, starring Bette Davis and Gish as cohabiting sisters on the New England coast—Bette as the soured blind sister and Lillian as the optimistic, friendly one who entertains Ann Sothern and Vincent Price.

The screen sisters' relationship was mirrored and exaggerated in that of the real-life legends. "Bette had battled her way back to working but the stroke's effect was still quite evident," offered Anderson. "She was brave, eager to film and not at all passive. . . . Bette was some fifteen years younger than Lillian and inclined to be impatient. And I think it's no secret the lady is rather competitive."

Davis sometimes grew impatient with the slower Gish, approaching her mid-nineties. Bette's manner was direct, at times brusque. She was also impatient with the weather and other factors that slowed down shooting on location. (While filming *Death on the Nile* [1978] under the blazing Egyptian sun, she informed the press more than once that in her heyday Jack Warner would have built Egypt for her on the studio lot.) After one lengthy setup for a closeup of Lillian Gish, a technician was heard to remark that the star had photographed beautifully.

Bette sniped, "Well, she should! She was there when they invented closeups."

The more diplomatic Lillian was quoted, "That face! Have you ever seen such a tragic face? Poor woman. How she must be suffering! I don't think it's right to judge a person like that. We must bear and forbear."

Always anxious to work, Davis had previously gone to England to make an Agatha Christie TV movie with Sir John Mills and Helen Hayes as Miss Marple. Mills said of working with Bette, "I was never so scared in my life. And I was in the war!" Helen Hayes commented, "While Bette Davis has indeed always been one of my idols, she did make mincemeat out of poor

Lillian when they made *The Whales of August*, a lovely picture. Lillian swears she'll never act again.

"So first she drove me from the screen, now she's driven Lillian. She's making a clean sweep of everyone our age!"

Before Ann Sothern received a supporting-Oscar nomination, many hoped in vain that Gish would be honored with a Best Actress nomination, if not the award itself. (She'd received an honorary Oscar in 1970.)

Unfortunately Lillian Gish's final film (and Bette Davis's last completed film) died at the box office. A psychological portrait of two contrasting siblings, it had little action but its cast was sterling, and emotionally it held the mature, or intelligent, filmgoer's interest. One immature critic's review dwelled on the combined ages of the four principals. In any case, Lillian Gish didn't end her storied screen career in support and she played a character who was warm, adventurous, and life-affirming.

The actress lived to ninety-nine.

—◦—

Most women loved him, most men resented him. Being a foreigner in the United States during the anti-immigration 1920s didn't help. He was born Rodolfo Alfonzo Raffaele Pietro Filiberto Guglielmi di Valentino d'Antonguola (1895–1926).

Sheik condoms were named after **Rudolph Valentino**'s most famous film. "Rudy," the movies' first male sex symbol, returned in his swan song to his most famous role—or close to it—in *Son of the Sheik* (1926). He was the first actor to become a star because of his looks and sex appeal, and paid dearly for it.

Much about Valentino's early life is murky. Apparently he left Italy for Paris at seventeen, then arrived in the United States at eighteen in 1913. After he became a star it came out and was widely published that in 1917 the vice squad raided the Alwyn Court apartment at 180 W. 58th Street of Mrs. Georgia Thyme, arresting her and a male visitor named Rodolfo Guglielmi. The "charges involved white slavery and blackmail, and although Mr. Guglielmi insisted he had been framed, he spent three days in jail."

Valentino was reportedly arrested twice for suspicion of petty theft and blackmail and sent to the Tombs prison. Whether that was separate from the 1917 arrest and jail sentence is unclear. Supposedly he then kept "clean" thanks to wealthy sugar daddies and then as a "taxi dancer," paid to dance with women at afternoon tea dances (as did future actors Clifton Webb and George Raft). Besides earning ten cents a dance, Rudolph may or may not have pimped.

He was rumored to have engaged in prostitution with either or both sexes during leaner days, but the rumors may have been prompted by spite and xenophobia. Whether he was "gay for pay" but primarily heterosexual is unknown. "Even yet, it's typically assumed the man was infatuated with women," said film historian Carlos Clarens, "on no more evidence than that he was infatuated with women on the silver screen. But it is called acting. . . ."

Valentino, sometimes nicknamed Vaselino for his slicked-back hair, took his movie roles as a lover—another nickname: the Latin Lover—to heart. He injected passion into his love scenes and was "too emotional" for most male reviewers but big box office for armies of female moviegoers.

The patriarchal press criticized the star for doing ads for Valvoline Face Cream, for wearing and popularizing wristwatches (considered "effeminate" at the time), for wearing cologne (likewise), and also for wearing a "slave bracelet" given him by his second wife, who was also—unofficially—his manager. She announced that "A real union is a spiritual one, not one of the flesh," which helped engender jokes that Rudy believed "to consummate" meant to make chicken soup.

The fledgling actor did a film in 1914, then nothing until 1916. He went west, arriving in Hollywood an unknown in 1917. His roles grew and several of his efforts were rereleased once he attained stardom. His 1920 picture *The Married Virgin* was later renamed *Frivolous Wives*, as the original title was too close to home. Valentino's first marriage was reputedly arranged by actress-producer Alla Nazimova, a Russian lesbian (and Nancy Davis Reagan's godmother) who at one point was the movies' highest-paid actress.

First wife Jean Acker was a leading lady and a lover of Nazimova, whose lavish Hollywood home later became the fabled Garden of Allah hotel. On their wedding night Jean refused Rudy entry to the bedroom, and when he persisted she left him for actress Grace Darmond. The one-day marriage was one of moviedom's shortest. (She, better known than he at the time, may have wed to gain heterosexual credentials, important then as now for box-office potential.)

In 1921 Valentino scored big in *The Four Horsemen of the Apocalypse*. He also played Armand (as Robert Taylor later would opposite Garbo) opposite Nazimova in *Camille* and redoubled his stardom as *The Sheik*, an international sensation that dared to imply rape but copped out by having Valentino's Arab character turn out to be a Brit in a burnoose. Henceforth Rudy would incarnate exotic lovers introducing innocent American or English girls to "forbidden love" by sweeping them off to his tent or temple or palace.

When Rudy starred in *Blood and Sand* in 1922 (memorably remade with Tyrone Power and Rita Hayworth), he was disparaged in the press for not actually fighting the bull. A reviewer wrote, "The expensive Signor Valentino is shown making passes at a bull which is only half in the picture. As [comedian] Will Rogers observes, we shall probably never learn the identity of the hero who held the bull's tail."

Rudy's divorce from Acker came after, not before, Rudy's second marriage, thus he was found guilty of bigamy. It was later theorized that his remarrying was meant to repair damaging publicity about his private life and therefore image.

Second wife Natasha Rambova was really Winifred Hudnut of Salt Lake City, a costume and set designer who'd worked with and perhaps bedded Alla Nazimova. When Rambova walked out on a male associate who habitually bedded most of his female assistants, he shot her in the leg, souring her on domineering men. After she and Rudy wed—he called her "the Boss"—she basically took over his career, including demands that Paramount boost his salary.

The studio resented her involvement in his career and some of her designs were ridiculed. Rudy was upbraided by male critics for *The Young Rajah* (1922), in part of which he posed topless, wearing an outfit mostly consisting of ropes of pearls. Studio chief Adolph Zukor ordered a clause in Valentino's contract barring Natasha from the lot. She thereupon insisted he quit Paramount, and he did. Rudy was off the screen until reaching a lavish agreement with United Artists in 1924.

Part of the agreement was that Rambova was banned from his sets. Furious, she left Rudy. Before their divorce she threatened to write a tell-all book about him (after his death she wrote a play about him featuring many thinly veiled characters, but it went unproduced). During divorce proceedings it came out that the second marriage too had gone unconsummated. The press had a field day.

Meanwhile in 1924 Valentino returned to the screen in *Monsieur Beaucaire*. Critics disliked the title they couldn't pronounce plus the sight of Rudy topless and sporting a beauty mark on his cheek. He made only a few more pictures before 1926 and his *Son of the Sheik* swan song.

The star was humiliated by the stinging reviews and ongoing criticism, which was harsh. A month before Valentino's death an editorial titled "Pink Powder Puffs" in the *Chicago Tribune*, which billed itself as "the world's greatest newspaper," accused the star of feminizing American male culture. It demanded, "Why didn't someone quietly drown Rudolph Guglielmo, alias Valentino, years ago?" The rabid writer felt "man began to slip when he discarded the straight razor for the safety pattern. . . . What has become of the old 'caveman' line?" He blamed "Rudy, the beautiful gardener's boy," for corrupting young American males via his screen characters, his private life, and his public image.

The mortified Italian challenged the writer to a duel. But the actor was suffering from appendicitis and a perforated ulcer that resulted in peritonitis and septicemia. Prior to an ineffectual operation, as Valentino lay dying and struggling with the pain, he asked, "And now do I act like a 'pink powder puff'?"

Publicity intended more to profit the studios' posthumous reissues of the Latin Lover's movies than the late thirty-one-year-old's ego was created by "the Lady in Black" who visited Rudolph Valentino's tomb annually and was eventually, reluctantly revealed to be a hired actress or series of actresses. And that's showbiz.

ELVIS PRESLEY

Just as he ran every facet of singer **Elvis Presley**'s career, his manager Colonel Tom Parker ran Elvis's movie career. Into the ground.

Presley (1935–1977) might be alive today if he'd only opposed Parker, who insisted on an exorbitant, deal-breaking percentage of the music rights to the 1976 movie remake of *A Star Is Born* starring and co-produced by Barbra Streisand. Every *Star Is Born* remake has been a hit, and Elvis had not appeared on the big screen since 1969 and needed a hit. When Barbra proposed costarring, Elvis agreed. From a commercial standpoint it made sense in terms of the project and the singer-actress. Artistically the role was substantial, dramatic, and a challenge, unlike earlier Parker-approved parts.

Personally it was an intriguing and unexpected choice, since Presley would have portrayed a self-destructive singing star (not that much of a challenge). Kris Kristofferson later got the role, and the film was a big hit.

Elvis had tired of trivial and repetitive roles in unoriginal, decreasingly popular pictures. "They keep trying to make *G.I. Blues* and *Blue Hawaii* over and over again, and all they do is move the scenery around a little."

Had Elvis costarred in *A Star Is Born* his screen career would have revived with a jolt and he'd be a viable leading man again, not a washed-up actor whose movies were often joked about. No doubt—unless he reverted to always obeying "Tom Parker" (born Andreas Cornelis [*sic*] van Kuijk)—he'd have then made more films, certainly more interesting ones than his 1960s vehicles.

Parker had seen to it that Presley rarely had a major or scene-stealing costar. His one major leading lady was Ann-Margret in *Viva Las Vegas* (1964), his biggest hit movie. (Two major costars were Dolores Del Rio and Barbara Stanwyck, but they played his mother and his boss, respectively.) On Elvis's behalf Parker had declined a number of worthwhile screen projects, including one with Robert Mitchum, Presley's favorite living actor after James Dean died.

But more important than worthy roles and costars, had Elvis resumed his movie career he would have ended his total reliance on performing live. Once Tom Parker got proof that Elvis was a huge draw in Las Vegas and elsewhere, he sent Elvis out on tour after tour. The grueling pace and emotional demands and late hours (Elvis had long suffered from insomnia) fueled Presley's need for drugs. That was of less interest to his manager than the fact that the tours were under Parker's control, unlike films, where he'd had to contend with producers, directors, and studio executives.

The rock 'n' roll idol's celluloid career had started well. He was third-billed in his debut, *Love Me Tender* (1956), which was renamed after the song Elvis sang in it. His fans made it a hit and thenceforth he was always first-billed. Early films like *Jailhouse Rock, King Creole, Flaming Star*, and *G.I. Blues* were critically praised, and *Blue Hawaii* was a big hit as well as yielding Elvis's biggest-selling album.

Tom Parker settled for churning out formulaic Presley pictures, each featuring some romance, a little comedy, a fight or two, and plenty of songs to provide another big-selling movie album. The songs got blander and blander because Parker insisted that composers writing for Elvis sign over their rights, as in "work for hire," and sometimes even give Presley unearned cowriting credit. No established composer would agree to that.

Of *Double Trouble*, one of three 1967 Elvis flicks, Presley stated, "You mean it's come to this? Those damn fools got me singing 'Old MacDonald' on the back of a truck with a bunch of animals. Man, it's a joke and the joke's on me." On the other hand, nobody put a gun to his head to force him.

During Elvis's celluloid run of thirty-one mostly interchangeable pictures, he had very few song hits. It wasn't just the Beatles that dethroned him on the charts; it was also Colonel Parker, whose greed and lack of taste or long-range vision for his sole client harmed his musical as well as cinematic careers. Parker eventually took 50 percent of Elvis's income, apart from side deals Elvis never knew about.

Elvis also never knew that Parker was an illegal alien (1909–1997) from Holland who may or may not have killed a woman in his small hometown. He fled the country the day after the murder and somehow entered the United States, possibly through Canada. Under a new name he worked in carnivals for several years. One of his carnie acts was "Colonel Parker's Dancing Chickens"—a hot plate sprinkled with sawdust atop which chicks hopped to keep from getting burned, to the tune of "Turkey in the Straw." Parker also painted sparrows yellow and sold them as canaries.

For a while Parker managed country singer Eddie Arnold, who unlike Elvis stood up to the tyrant and eventually fired him. But the Presleys were dirt-poor and when the fast-talking "Colonel" made a millionaire, for starters, out of Elvis he practically became the family's patron saint. Costar Deborah Walley said, "Tom Parker did a lot for Elvis. He did even more for himself. . . . Elvis would have become a star no matter who managed him. There was no sane reason for him to stay so beholden to that man. He let him almost strangle his career."

Parker could have saved his client millions of tax dollars yet avoided all tax dodges, legitimate and especially otherwise. He feared any contact or trouble with the US government. More egregiously, Colonel Parker turned down—did Elvis never wonder why?—all requests for his client to perform overseas. Europe, Japan, Australia, and elsewhere would have paid millions per visit, but Andreas wasn't a US citizen and had no passport. He wouldn't have been allowed into another country nor been allowed back into the United States.

(Elvis's only performances outside the United States were a few, early on, in Canada. Surprisingly, Parker didn't accompany him. With time he grew increasingly possessive, calling Elvis "my boy." When Presley was stationed in Germany with the US Army and was requested to sing for the troops the "Colonel"—who claimed to have served in the US military but no records ever proved it, and the media never pressed him—vetoed Elvis doing so. "If they want to hear my boy sing they'll have to pay, just like anyone else.")

Besides a lack of quality, Elvis's filmic output suffered from too much quantity. 1969 saw release of three Presley pix. First out of the pipeline was *The Trouble with Girls—and How to Get into It*. The title says it all. Then came *Charro!*, whose poster proclaimed, "A different kind of role. A different kind of man." Not really. It was a western and for the first time clean-shaven Elvis wore stubble. Finally, in time for Thanksgiving, there was *Change of Habit*, with Elvis Presley as a doctor (that's believable) romancing a nun (that's tasteful).

Popular gossip had it that Elvis slept with "all" his leading ladies up until Mary Tyler Moore as the nun. She said she kept it platonic. She wasn't the first. Early on, Presley asked two-time costar Dolores Hart for a date. She declined. Not very long after top-billing the hit *Where the Boys Are* (1960), Hart left Hollywood to become a nun (currently an abbess).

After Dr. Presley's swan song, he did two successful film documentaries—for Elvis was more interesting than the generic characters he played. He'd made a big singing comeback via television and went on to record successfully, in and out of Memphis. Elvis made his first public appearance in over eight years at the huge new International Hotel in Las Vegas in 1969. But he didn't open the hotel's showroom, the biggest in town. That assignment was left to new super-star Barbra Streisand. Parker didn't want that extra psychological burden laid on his client. When Elvis sold out every show, seven nights a week, two shows a night, of his monthlong contract, Colonel Tom Parker was delighted. It was the start of eight years of live performances, throughout the USA. It was also the beginning of the end.

SUICIDES, PREDESTINED: GEORGE SANDERS AND SPALDING GRAY

Authorities often hurriedly close a celebrity death case with "suicide." Tidy, and easy to assign or shift blame.

There are as many reasons for suicide as there are people who (old-fashioned and judgmental term) "commit" it. Some finally choose it because they've lost a loved one. Brian Keith, seventy-five, was undergoing chemo-therapy for lung cancer when his daughter deliberately shot herself in 1997. Later that year he too placed a gun to his head and pulled the trigger. Charles Boyer, seventy-eight, and his longtime wife had lost their only son to suicide. After she died, he took his life in 1978.

Then there are those who probably or certainly didn't do it, except officially. Actor Nick Adams, thirty-six, was found dressed, propped against his bedroom wall, dead from paraldehyde and Promazine. "Coroner to the stars" Thomas Noguchi ruled the 1968 death "accidental—suicidal and undetermined." Friends and relatives cried foul, for there were no drugs or needles at the site.

Most upsetting was the case of sixty-two-year-old actor Albert Dekker, who served in California's state legislature from 1944 to 1946. Because he opposed the political witch hunts he was blacklisted and for some years denied work in Hollywood. In 1968 Dekker was found nude kneeling in his bathtub, a scarf covering his eyes, a hypodermic needle in each arm, a noose hanging around his neck from the shower's curtain rod, obscenities scrawled in lipstick on his chest, stomach, and buttocks, plus he was handcuffed and his mouth gagged with something like a horse's bit. The official cause of death: "accidental asphyxia."

For the following two men, their past comments and actions left little doubt that suicide was the cause of death.

George Sanders (1906–1972) was the personification of cynicism. He didn't smile, he sneered. He was suave, civilized, sophisticated, often sinister, and sometimes got hissed in cinemas when he made his onscreen appearance. Except for his two B-film series as The Saint and The Falcon, Sanders was nearly always a villain. Or at least a creep, as in his Oscar-winning role of Addison DeWitt in *All About Eve* (1950).

The Russian-born Englishman married four times. He wed two of the three Gabor sisters: Zsa Zsa from 1949 to 1954 and her older sister Magda in 1970 for a matter of weeks. He had no offspring, once stating, "I cannot bear children. In either sense of the word." His autobiography, *Memoirs of a Professional Cad*, published in 1960, is one of the most candid and entertaining in that semi-fictional genre.

"My mother was quite famous," he explained, "for a horticulturalist. My father wasn't famous—he made rope." George began in British films but his contract was transferred to 20th Century-Fox soon after the company formed in 1935. His cultured speaking voice meant he never played average people. Its distinctive quality often sounded like he had a snooty cold.

Sanders's ninety-plus films included classics and hits like *Rebecca*, *The House of Seven Gables*, *The Moon and Sixpence*, *The Picture of Dorian Gray*, *The Ghost and Mrs. Muir*, *Forever Amber*, *Samson and Delilah*, *I Can Get It for You Wholesale*, *Ivanhoe*, *Call Me Madam*, *Death of a Scoundrel*, *Solomon and Sheba*, *Village of the Damned*, *The Quiller Memorandum*, *The Jungle Book* (as the voice of Shere Khan the tiger), and *The Kremlin Letter*.

By the 1960s George was older and movies were being cast younger. Smooth villainy was often replaced with guns and violence. The actor made several films in Europe and returned to TV, which he said he disliked and never watched, though he proved an icily demonic Mr. Freeze on *Batman*. In 1957 he'd hosted *The George Sanders Mystery Theatre*, but it lasted only thirteen episodes.

The actor's romantic menace had by the late '60s turned to menace, period, and George failed or didn't bother to crack the horror market then dominated by Vincent Price. His roles had become more peripheral, the films less distinguished. Lee Radziwill, younger sister of Jacqueline Kennedy Onassis, starred in a 1967 TV remake of the 1944 noir classic *Laura*. She said of her costar, "He wasn't as jaded as he liked to seem. He was a gentleman but he was bored.

George Sanders's characters were invariably witty, haughty, and cynical. He won an Oscar as "venomous" gossip columnist Addison DeWitt in *All About Eve* (1950). Two of his wives were Gabor sisters. At sixty-five, in a Mediterranean resort in Spain, George chose suicide. His note began, "Dear World, I am leaving you because I am bored."

"He was a fine actor, his voice was a gift, yet he seemed anxious to do the work—do it well—and be away. After all he'd done as an actor I don't doubt he felt his best work was past and that he'd done it all."

Speaking with British actor David Niven in 1937 Sanders had asserted he would someday end it when he'd had enough of life and future disappointments. "He told me," said friend and fellow actor Brian Aherne, "he was tiring of gloomy characters in gloomy pictures." Sanders's last pictures had titles like *Endless Night*, *The Night of the Assassin*, *Doomwatch*, and *Psychomania*.

Asked by British *Photoplay* how many films he'd made, Sanders replied, "I've no idea. It's a silly question. Some of them surely went unreleased or only saw the light of day in a few countries. Anyway I couldn't care less."

His UK-made swan song *Psychomania* (1973, also known as *The Death Wheelers*) was, according to *Weekly Pix*, "aimed at the drive-in brigade. . . . Mr. Sanders, always well clad, plays a Mr. Shadwell, elegantly aloof from Nicky Henson's motorcycle gang who keep dying off only to be retrieved to some semblance of life."

By the time of his last film George's health was deteriorating. He told few that he didn't feel up to par but allowed that he was being treated for depression. He'd sold his mansion in Majorca, Spain, and moved into a hotel ten miles south of Barcelona. On April 24, 1972, he went to bed after asking to be woken early next morning. Come morning, when he didn't respond the hotel manager entered George Sanders's room and found him dead. He'd consumed five bottles of the barbiturate Nembutal, washed down with vodka.

At sixty-five he chose to retire from life itself. His suicide note read, "Dear World, I am leaving because I am bored. I feel I have lived long enough. I am leaving you with your worries in this sweet cesspool—good luck. Love, George."

Spalding Gray (1941–2004) was one of the most successful monologists ever, but also an actor in films like *The Killing Fields* (1984), *Beaches* (1988), *King of the Hill* (1993), and *The Paper* (1994). His monologue film *Swimming to Cambodia* (1987) earned him a cult following. In it he elaborated on his minor role as a US consul in *The Killing Fields* and commented on the war in Southeast Asia.

Born into affluence in Rhode Island, Gray had a lifelong obsession with his mother's 1967 suicide. It may or may not have been the major factor in his suffering from depression. "When a parent takes his own life and takes it away from you, as my father did," said actress Mariette Hartley, "it fixes suicide in your mind as the ultimate and worst thing to avoid."

Gloria Vanderbilt witnessed the suicide of one of her sons. "I wanted to join him . . . it was a strong feeling. But I had another son," Anderson Cooper.

Introverted and admittedly obsessive, Spalding Gray dove inward for much of his professional material and in the 1970s became involved with avant-garde theatre. Friend and associate Ron Vawter noted, "He liked having an audience, preferably a live one," adding, "Soon after we met he freely shared his views on suicide, which he talked about almost as a fond goal." A former date said, "With him, suicide was almost a sort of duty he preferred to put off. But a duty. . . ."

Spalding's monologues, often painfully honest, attracted growing audiences. "I enjoy shocking people when it's not for shock's sake alone," he stated. Some of his filmed monologues became cult classics, like *Monster in a Box* (1992), about his efforts to compose a novel. "A psychiatrist I'd never met told me he made a study of me. He informed me I was both shy and exhibitionistic. I chewed on that . . . I had to agree. I am fond of dichotomies." In 1976 Spalding had appeared as an escaped convict in a porno movie titled *Farmer's Daughters*.

A Hollywood casting director felt, "Gray had a good future as an actor. He had an enviable platform, good looks, acting ability and a special brand of charisma. But he didn't seem to think he was worth casting.

"He preferred to go on doing his own things, which were good but had a very limited audience compared to what we had to offer."

Spalding attempted suicide several times, more so after passing fifty-two, his mother's age at her suicide. In late 2003 he jumped from New York's Sag Harbor Bridge into calm water and was rescued by a policeman. More than a few lines in his monologues indicated obsession with a watery death. Because he often joked about suicide, most friends believed he didn't take it seriously.

A big cause of Gray's mounting desperation was the aftermath of a 2001 car accident in Ireland that reportedly injured him psychologically as well as physically. He was taking antidepressants and undergoing therapy, yet his suicide mania persisted. Spalding apprised a friend "that someday he'd get it right."

His movie swan song was *How High* (2001), a drug-oriented comedy in which he played Professor Jackson. In 2003 he appeared in a short, *The*

Paper Maché Chase, as Dr. Calhoun. "It's funny how often I'm perceived as an authority figure . . . I get to play a doctor, when I can barely look after myself."

On January 10, 2004, Gray and his family attended an afternoon showing of the movie *Big Fish* (2003), by whose end he was crying. At 6:30 p.m. he said he was going out to visit friends. That night the Manhattan weather reached a low of 1 degree Fahrenheit. Around 10:30 p.m. Spalding phoned home and told his six-year-old son he was just checking in.

The next day his wife called the police to say he was missing. On January 12 a Staten Island Ferry employee declared he'd seen Gray disembark on the night of January 9. It was speculated that perhaps he'd been "practicing." There was no news for two months. On March 9 a body was dragged out of the East River. Only Spalding's black corduroy pants were recognizable. The coroner identified Spalding Gray from his dental records.

CAUGHT: LIZABETH SCOTT

Her birth name was Emma Matzo, she was Jewish (surprise) and lesbian or possibly bisexual (surprised?) and she was publicized as "The Threat"—to another Jewish beauty with a husky voice (heterosexual). Back then their nonmainstream faith wasn't made public. But the one's nonmainstream sexuality was trumpeted by *Confidential* magazine in 1954 and cut short her career.

— ❧ —

Lizabeth Scott (1922–2015) was two years older than Lauren Bacall (born Betty Perske) and made her screen debut a year after her, in *You Came Along* (1945). The picture wasn't high-profile and didn't star a major actor—Robert Cummings, not Humphrey Bogart. So Scott couldn't create the same impact as Bacall nor the ongoing publicity that came with falling in love with a famous costar of the opposite sex, marrying him, and having children. Lizabeth's second was an A-picture but starred a long-established actress.

Leaving behind Scranton for Manhattan, Scott, who wanted to be a nun (!), had made little headway. "There was one period of five months when I was always hungry. My folks wanted me to come home and they cut my allowance to $12 a week. Out of that I paid $6.25 for my room. From what was left I ate, though sometimes I would have to buy stockings or something, out of my eating money."

In 1942 after several dozen auditions Lizabeth became understudy to Tallulah Bankhead in Thornton Wilder's hit play *The Skin of Our Teeth*. Tallu liked her but never missed a performance. Years later, rumors proliferated that *All About Eve* was based on the women's professional and private relationship, for *Eve* had Sapphic undertones (though not via its main character).

When she couldn't get theatre work, the slinky Scott did fashion modeling. She was taken to Hollywood by Hal Wallis, a top Warner Bros. producer who went independent, also signing Dean Martin and Jerry Lewis,

Polly Bergen, Corinne Calvet, and Shirley MacLaine. He groomed Lizabeth as an "answer" to Lauren, who often went on suspension. The sultry, often tight-jawed Scott proved a formidable film noir star in several mostly 1940s pictures, costarring with Humphrey Bogart, Burt Lancaster, Kirk Douglas, Robert Mitchum, Victor Mature, Dick Powell, Charlton Heston and others, including Elvis Presley (not as his love interest) in her penultimate movie.

Scott inherited several good roles declined by Bacall and Veronica Lake. Her characters were often on the wrong side of the law but difficult for the hero to resist. One film historian in the 1980s described Lizabeth's screen persona as "tough babes who ended up with no more than they deserved." He also used code to summarize her private life: "Has never married."

Wallis's wife, actress Martha Hyer, remarked, "Lizabeth was stubborn but smart. She was seen about town with Hal, generating publicity. But her private life was private. She would not participate in manufactured romances.... To her detriment, she didn't kowtow to Hedda and Louella," Hollywood's reigning columnists.

"I think she realized early that a career based on looks and type more than versatile talent was limited . . . someday it would end, though not as soon as it did. With her intriguing personality she should have lasted decades longer.... But she was smart about buying real estate and when she no longer had work, she didn't have to work. Her investments cushioned her."

Scott was also smart-smart. During one summer off, she audited USC courses in philosophy and political science. The homophobic Hedda Hopper, who often dropped mean-spirited hints about gay, lesbian, and bisexual performers, declared Lizabeth's intellectual pursuits "perplexing."

Several Scott pictures are now cult films. One is her second, *The Strange Love of Martha Ivers* (1946). The film noir with the deliberately ambiguous title has been labeled "a three-lez flick" for its female stars Barbara Stanwyck, Lizabeth Scott, and Dame Judith Anderson (whom Stanwyck kills). It was also the film debut of Kirk Douglas, who for the first and perhaps last time wore glasses as Stanwyck's husband but not her love interest, played by Van Heflin. Douglas later revealed that Stanwyck was cold to him.

"On my first picture I could have used a verbal pat on the back. But nothing. Well into shooting, the big star informs the supporting player I was good. 'Too late! Too late,' I said to her." Of Scott, Douglas noted, "I knew not to make a pass at Stanwyck. I was advised not to try with Lizabeth Scott. We had hardly any scenes together but I later understood why I was advised not to try."

The 1950s ushered in a cascade of blondes but blonde Scott, pushing thirty—an age when some actresses retired or were demoted to playing mothers—wasn't the desired type. The golden age of noir was passing, and younger, sunnier and/or more voluptuous blondes were the ticket, e.g., Doris, Debbie, Jane Powell, Lana, Marilyn, Kim, Dorothy Malone, Bardot, Gloria Grahame.

By 1953 Lizabeth's career high point was past. Women's roles were more traditional and peripheral, Hal Wallis was focusing on Martin and Lewis, and the glamorous Scott suffered the indignity of being stuck in a second-rate Martin and Lewis oddity titled *Scared Stiff* (1953), whose highlight was Jerry Lewis in Carmen Miranda drag. It was her sole picture that year.

Fan magazines and columnists increasingly wondered why Lizabeth wasn't more visibly social. She told the Universal Press Syndicate in 1953, "I'm not a recluse. Is there anything wrong with a gal just because she doesn't show up at every premiere and party? . . . I do a lot of riding and I have a growing art collection that I'm awfully proud of. . . . I'm having a wonderful time doing just what I want."

The September 25, 1954, issue of *Confidential* featured a story headlined "Lizabeth Scott in the Call Girl's Call Book!!" It was tied in to the arrest of three young women caught in a Los Angeles vice raid—or "vice" raid. "The vice cops expected to find a few big-name customers when they grabbed the date book of a trio of Hollywood Jezebels, but even their cast-iron nerves got a jolt when they got to the S's!"

The tabloid magazine opined, "Liz was a strange girl from the moment she arrived in the cinema city. She never married, never even gets close to the altar. . . . Liz, according to the grapevine buzz, was taking up almost exclusively with Hollywood's weird society of baritone babes." The article pointed out that she called herself Scotty and was seen "from time to time in off-color joints that were favorite hangouts for movieland's twilight set."

Also noted was her prior admission "that she always wore male colognes, slept in men's pajamas and positively hated frilly, feminine dresses. . . . In recent years, Scotty's almost non-existent screen career has allowed her to roam farther afield and on one jaunt to Europe she headed straight for Paris' Left Bank where she took up with Frede, that city's most notorious Lesbian queen and the operator of a nightclub devoted exclusively to entertaining deviates like herself."

The piece concluded, "Insiders began putting together the pieces of the puzzle that was Lizabeth Scott and it didn't take them long to get the answer.

They know the shocking fact that one of the screen's top glamour girls is listed in the little black books kept by Hollywood prostitutes."

Ten months later (the delay is perplexing) Scott sued *Confidential*, as did several celebrities, eventually driving it out of business.

Depending on the source, the lawsuit was either dropped or "settled out of court." Regardless, it garnered more publicity than if the actress had ignored the article. *Confidential* counted on gay celebs not to sue, and most didn't. Jokes about "Mr. Scott" became fashionable, while she became unfashionable in Hollywood. In 1955 she had to go to England to make a low-budget movie, *The Weapon* (1956), that wasn't distributed in the United States till 1957. She played a mother in it. Lizabeth slipped further professionally by appearing in a TV movie, *Overnight Haul*, that however was released to cinemas in Britain in 1956. To complete her Wallis contract Lizabeth appeared in the 1957 Elvis vehicle *Loving You* as the "hard-boiled publicist" who discovers the swivel-hipped singer.

That was the end of a unique star's movie career—for fifteen years. Lizabeth Scott's was one of the earliest cases of homophobic exposure, brought about by profiteering and self-righteous heterosexuals, in contrast to modern outing, brought about by the gay community to expose the harmful hypocrisy of privately gay but publicly antigay politicians, preachers, actors, and other VIPs.

Scott then guested on some TV dramas, cut a record album, and appeared on 1960s game shows like *You Don't Say!* She lived in the same modest Hollywood Boulevard apartment as during her heyday and continued auditing college classes, especially in psychology, and pursued singing lessons. She asserted, "My personal life, my development as a human being, is the most important thing. . . . It's being *for* things. Too many people are against things."

Finally and out of the blue, Lizabeth Scott was asked to costar with Michael Caine, Mickey Rooney, and Lionel Stander in what she was told would be a modern film noir, to be shot in Malta. The semi-comedic *Pulp* (1972) is about a gangster who hires a ghostwriter to pen his memoirs and the investigation that follows a murder at a celebration. Scott played an ersatz princess improbably named Betty and surnamed Cipolla (onion in Italian). The almost token-female role was described by one reviewer as "a man-hungry [!] social climber." The snide character doesn't do much; some of the actress's scenes were reportedly cut.

Unlike vintage noir, *Pulp* doesn't hold one's interest, let alone grab it. Lizabeth Scott's belated return to the screen created more interest than the little-seen result, which was her swan song. She lived another forty-three years and in her seventies still looked great and was often seen out and about in Hollywood, West Hollywood, and Beverly Hills. In her eighties she still resembled Lizabeth Scott. She did not "come out" and did not write her memoirs.

In his memoirs Hal Wallis devoted six lines to his sister Minna Wallis, one of the most powerful though relatively unpublicized agents in Hollywood. Minna was lesbian and apparently a platonic friend of Lizabeth Scott. She told columnist James Bacon, "What Hollywood did to Lizabeth was shameful. But it couldn't have happened without society's complicity."

Scott's fan Lily Tomlin noted, "What happened to her couldn't happen again, thanks to our own visibility and audibility. Not that that helps Lizabeth Scott. . . . God, she was such a star!"

The former Emma Matzo lived to ninety-two (three years longer than Betty Bacall).

BLACKLISTED: GALE SONDERGAARD AND JOHN GARFIELD

The Hollywood political witch hunts were the most publicity-effective of the post–World War II witch hunts that targeted not only Communists—though it wasn't illegal to be a member of that party—but suspected Communists, liberals, gays, Jews, and women and minorities with openly expressed political opinions.

The national climate of paranoia owed partly to the rapid spread of communism in Eastern Europe and then China. Far-right politicians like Senator Joseph McCarthy exploited the fear to gain power and stifle or punish their opponents. Initially the witch hunts were about firing people in government jobs. Gays, Jews, and liberals were the primary targets.

But anything to do with Hollywood got much more publicity, and Congress's House Un-American Activities Committee (HUAC) intimidated the film studios and TV networks into firing and blacklisting anybody named or suspected.

"There were very few Communists in Hollywood," said showbiz columnist Lee Graham. "This is maybe the greediest business on earth. I did know two or three non-practicing intellectual Communists. So what? They couldn't make a communist movie—no such thing. Name one communist movie.

"Like somebody said, the only –ism Hollywood's ever been interested in is plagiarism."

When McCarthy moved to tackle the Army about supposed "communist infiltration" he finally met his match and was toppled. But it took some more time, and the Democratic Kennedy administration, to end the officially sanctioned persecution.

"It was a field day for bigots," declared longtime CBS news anchor Walter Cronkite, "a time of national disgrace."

Others called it Scoundrel Time. Several witch hunters were eventually indicted for bribery, corruption, and other crimes.

———

Gale Sondergaard (1899–1985) was the first winner of a Best Supporting Actress Academy Award. She got it for her first film, *Anthony Adverse* (1936). Sandy Dennis, who won BSA for *Who's Afraid of Virginia Woolf?* (1966), wondered "why on earth it took most of a decade for AMPAS to recognize actors who weren't necessarily stars but who made the movies so special?"

Despite her black hair Sondergaard was of Danish origin. In possibly her most famous role, the Eurasian who blackmails murderer Bette Davis over possession of *The Letter* (1940), she was presented as a villain. "Stereotyping is a form of shorthand. For acting, it's not what you are, it's what you seem.

"I was dark-haired, pale, slim, relatively tall, I enunciated clearly and looked 'foreign.' So I was often a villain, sometimes a foreign one."

In *The Blue Bird* (1940) she was a devious Cat trying to thwart Shirley Temple. Anti-feline stereotyping followed Sondergaard in films like *The Cat and the Canary*, *The Black Cat*, and *Gypsy Wildcat*. She was also the Spider Woman, locking horns more than once with Basil Rathbone as Sherlock Holmes.

"I did play some nice human beings," as in the Oscar-winning Best Picture *The Life of Emile Zola* (1937), about anti-Semitism, and *Anna and the King of Siam* (1946)—the non-musical precursor to *The King and I*—in which Gale played the king's wife (Rex Harrison was the unlikely Siamese king).

But in 1949 her career stopped. Sondergaard's second husband, from 1930 to 1971, was writer-director Herbert Biberman (1900–1971), one of the Hollywood Ten, sent to prison for refusing to name names to HUAC. The actress stood by Biberman. "Don't ever let the Ronald Reagans tell you that there was no blacklist!" said Gale, who from 1949 to 1969 wasn't allowed to work in movies or on television.

The couple could have moved to Europe, as several individuals did, to continue making a living, but chose to remain in the United States. "We weren't about to be chased out of our own country by pretend-patriots," said Biberman.

"There were bigots who compiled lists of anyone they disliked," Gale explained. "They tried to smear them as 'reds' and mailed their lists to politicians and entertainment executives. Some lists became nationally influential, and once your name was on a list it was all but impossible to get it off.

"One 'named' writer went to a studio head and insisted he was an anti-Communist. The rich, uneducated ignoramus, of which Hollywood has never had a shortage, yelled, 'I don't care what kind of Communist you are! Get out!'"

Theatre, with a smaller, more sophisticated audience than the big or small screens, wasn't as affected by the witch hunts, and in the late 1960s Sondergaard performed off Broadway in a one-woman pro-feminist show titled *Woman*. In 1969 Gale made her big-screen comeback in *Slaves*, which tracked the fates of two 1850s slaves of different genders in the American South. It starred Stephen Boyd and Dionne Warwick and was directed and co-written by Herbert Biberman.

Ahead of its time, the well-intentioned *Slaves* flopped. Sondergaard noted, "You could be blacklisted if you'd merely signed a petition for peace, for civil rights, an anti-war petition, against nuclear testing . . . anything could be labeled 'a communist front.' The bullies' goal was to scare people out of speaking up or protesting anything, including discrimination."

Ironically it was her next picture that was titled *Comeback*, followed by a 1973 telefilm, *The Cat Creature*. *Comeback* featured 1930s star Miriam Hopkins as a pseudo Norma Desmond, with Sondergaard as a mysterious housekeeper. "I've played more than one mysterious housekeeper in my day," said Gale, "and more than once I've been mistaken for Judith Anderson," the maleficent housekeeper in *Rebecca*. *Comeback* was shot in 1970 but released in 1974 (also as *Savage Intruder* and *Hollywood Horror House*). It costarred John David Garfield, the late star's son.

A Man Called Horse (1970) starred Richard Harris, with Judith Anderson as an elderly Native American. Its 1976 sequel, *Return of a Man Called Horse*, starred Richard Harris, with Gale Sondergaard as an elderly Native American. "It was a wonderful opportunity because it was so far from me. I enjoy projects that share the realities of other people . . . and let us 'walk a mile in someone else's moccasins.'"

After her return to acting, Ms. Sondergaard guested on several TV drama shows. Her movie swan song was *Echoes* (1982), involving a psychic, nightmares, and murder. "A friend once mentioned that from my screen appearances you wouldn't guess I had anything approaching a sunny disposition. But your disposition depends mostly on you. I had to work hard to keep mine through the difficult times . . . that bad era. Too many innocent people gave in and took their own lives.

"I simply felt that when you do that, in a way the bad people win. In the end, survival is its own reward."

———⁓———

John Garfield (1913–1952) has been called the first Method actor. He incarnated rebels, losers, and loners—vulnerable tough guys. During the late 1930s and early '40s his chip-on-the-shoulder image was rare and gained him wide popularity among teenagers and young moviegoers. His roles as an urban macho man with a soft side would influence generations of actors from Brando on.

He was born Julius Garfinkle, the son of Russian Jewish immigrants. The story goes that when ordered to use a new name and the actor proposed Garfield, Jack Warner said it sounded too foreign—but then the future star informed the mogul that there was once a US president named Garfield.

Growing up partly on tough New York streets, Julius got into fights and was sent to P.S. 45 for problem youths. He directed his aggression toward boxing and acting. His friend playwright Clifford Odets encouraged his talent, landing him in the prestigious Group Theater. Hollywood took notice and John's debut film, *Four Daughters* (1938), was a success and elicited a supporting-actor Oscar nomination.

There was a sequel, *Daughters Courageous*, the next year, but Garfield went on to films with grim and/or socially relevant themes like *Juarez, They Made Me a Criminal, Dust Be My Destiny, East of the River, Castle on the Hudson, Out of the Fog, Tortilla Flat*, and *Dangerously They Live*.

In 1942, along with Bette Davis and music executive Jules Stein, John Garfield founded the Hollywood Canteen. For over three years during World War II, the Canteen provided free food and star-studded dancing and entertainment to thousands of lonely and fearful servicemen passing through Los Angeles, most of them headed for overseas combat.

In 1946 he peaked commercially with two major hits pairing him with female stars: *The Postman Always Rings Twice* with Lana Turner and *Humoresque* with Joan Crawford. The following year he formed his own production company, intending to produce pictures with a social conscience. In *Body and Soul* (1947) John played a slum denizen who becomes a boxing star by selling out to the Mob. It earned him a Best Actor Oscar nomination. In *Force of Evil* (1948) he portrayed a corporate lawyer working in the numbers racket.

Both pictures painted a negative picture of unbridled capitalism; however Garfield wasn't a Communist. His daughter Julie pointed out that many victims of the Great Depression had imagined in communism a possible alternative to economic exploitation and uncertainty, several later turning to socialism instead.

Also in 1948 John costarred in *Gentleman's Agreement*, a Best Picture Oscar winner about anti-Semitism. "My father wasn't just out for himself," said Julie Garfield. "That aspect of Hollywood is the usual one you hear or read about. But my father was a friend to people."

An admirer of the postwar neorealist movement in Italian cinema, John Garfield did the English narration for *Difficult Years* (1950), a dramatic 1948 Italian movie. His swan song was *He Ran All the Way* (1951), about a man committing payroll holdups who meets a young woman (Shelley Winters) and forces her family to hide him from his pursuers.

Although the witch hunters seldom targeted stars—mostly writers, directors, and supporting players—John Garfield, Jewish and liberal and with a career in decline, was sacrificed as an example. Summoned to testify before HUAC, he refused to implicate himself or name names and was blacklisted. When his wife left him soon after, he sank into depression. Garfield had already experienced minor heart problems but his post-HUAC health problems were exacerbated by unemployment, public humiliation, loneliness, and financial worries; he was known to have regularly given money to friends and strangers in need.

For the final eighteen months of his life John Garfield was unemployed and unemployable. On May 21, 1952, he died of a heart attack at thirty-nine. Many fans, friends, and his daughter Julie contended that it was HUAC that killed him.

TOUGH: STANWYCK, MITCHUM, AND McQUEEN

There's tough and there's tough. One type is pretty much internal. Another radiates outward, sometimes intruding on others—in the case of actors, on other characters but possibly also in real life. Psychologist Dr. Betty Berzon elucidated, "Toughness isn't a gender thing and is not necessarily aggression. It has more to do with a shell, a protective carapace that an individual develops, invariably early in life. . . . It's a way of coping. Sometimes not the most positive way, sometimes eventually working against the individual."

And yet tough movie stars are among the most interesting to watch and contemplate.

—~—

Sometimes a movie star's film titles reveal something about the star. Among those of **Barbara Stanwyck** (1907–1990): *Forbidden, Ladies They Talk About, The Bride Walks Out, The Bride Wore Boots, This Is My Affair, The Gay Sisters, The Strange Love of Martha Ivers, The Other Love, No Man of Her Own, To Please a Lady,* and *Walk on the Wild Side.*

Stanwyck's more popular films included *Stella Dallas, Double Indemnity, Golden Boy, The Lady Eve, Meet John Doe,* and *Sorry, Wrong Number.*

The hard knocks for Brooklyn-born Ruby Stevens began early. She was two when her mother was accidentally killed by being pushed off a moving trolley by a drunken man and hitting her head on the pavement. Ruby's father, left to look after the youngest three of his five offspring alone, soon abandoned his family to go work in Panama. Elder sister Mildred, a showgirl—Ruby would follow in her footsteps—was often away on tour, so the little girl and her elder brother were farmed out to one foster home after another.

At eleven Ruby was placed with a Jewish couple, the Cohens. Decades later she stated, "They were the first people ever to brush my hair, care how I looked. They taught me how to use my knife and fork. They tried to teach me nice manners. They tried to stop me from swearing."

Nonetheless at thirteen Ruby quit school to work in a department store. But show business paid better, specifically as a chorus girl, later an actress. (It was during her dancing days that Stevens met, befriended, and possibly bedded fellow hoofer Lucille LeSueur, later known as Joan Crawford.) At nineteen Ruby became a Broadway star. Also in 1926 two theatre bigwigs renamed her by combining the name of a thirty-year-old show with an actress who appeared in it: Jane Stanwyck in *Barbara Frietchie*. In 1927 Barbara Stanwyck made her only silent movie.

No beauty, Stanwyck rose through the celluloid ranks through persistence, personality, and onscreen intensity and sincerity. Marriage, whether love- or business-motivated, has boosted many an actress and actor. Barbara's first, in 1928, was to much older comic star Frank Fay. Hours after the wedding, Stanwyck was on a train heading for a touring engagement. An alcoholic, a known wife-beater and, according to comedian Milton Berle, "the most hated man in our profession," Fay had been married twice before.

Nolan Miller, costume designer for *Dynasty*, said, "I'm not the first to tell that Missy [Stanwyck's nickname] had scars on her chest . . . probably cigarette burns. Apparently inflicted by her first husband."

To save their marriage, Frank and Barbara adopted a son whom she later disowned after he discussed her coldness to him in an interview. When Frank Fay died in 1961 his will didn't include Dion, who'd changed his name to Anthony. Anthony sued and won. Stanwyck chose never to see her grandson.

In 1939 Barbara was urged to marry costar Robert Taylor, who was strongly pressured to marry by his studio, MGM. Then as now, paired celebrities of the opposite sex don't double their publicity, they multiply it. Taylor, born Spangler Arlington Brugh, was considered "too beautiful"—he soon acquired a lifelong mustache—and had been chided in the press for being a "mama's boy." Four years Bob's senior, Barbara was known to wear the pants in the family.

By the 1950s Taylor wished to have children. He and Stanwyck broke up but remained good friends. Barbara's closeted publicist and lifelong friend Helen Ferguson conveniently and often let it be known that after Robert Taylor, Miss Stanwyck could never look at another man. (Barbara renamed one of her movie characters "Helen Ferguson.")

Stanwyck's big-screen swan song was a thriller titled *The Night Stalker* (1965), costarring Robert Taylor and openly gay character actor Hayden Rourke (best known as Larry Hagman's boss on TV's *I Dream of Jeannie*).

Rourke later offered, "Davis and Crawford had already initiated the cycle of semi-horror films starring lady superstars of yesteryear. Barbara Stanwyck hadn't had a hit in a long time but was wary of the genre . . . I don't think she would have signed on if Bob Taylor hadn't been part of the package.

"Unfortunately ours was not one of that genre's successes, commercially or artistically."

But Stanwyck had already transitioned to television after prime film roles dried up and westerns were taken over by the small screen. In between western movies she'd declared, "I'm mad about westerns . . . this is all I want to do. . . . I want to play a real frontier woman, not one of those crinoline-covered things you see in most westerns. I'm with the boys."

In the '60s she costarred in the western TV series *The Big Valley*, thereafter keeping a low profile except for a few telefilms and accepting an honorary Academy Award (her four Oscar nominations hadn't resulted in the prize). When the American Film Institute chose to honor her with its Life Achievement Award Barbara confessed she'd thought they made a mistake and wanted Barbra Streisand.

Stanwyck's final hurrah was the highly-rated TV miniseries based on the bestselling novel *The Thorn Birds*. Several female stars had sought the role of the rich older woman in love with the handsome young priest played by Richard Chamberlain. Among them was Bette Davis, who'd had a small role in an early Stanwyck picture. Barbara won an Emmy Award as the memorably frustrated Mary Carson.

Producer Aaron Spelling persuaded Stanwyck to return to TV as a star of the *Dynasty* spin-off *The Colbys*. Dismayed by its ratings, poor scripts, arrogant costar Charlton Heston, and a character she considered watered-down and underutilized, Stanwyck departed the series after its 1986 first season. Her character was killed off in an airplane crash.

Nolan Miller felt, "Barbara Stanwyck was often better than her material, in television and in motion pictures. . . . Series television isn't an ideal way for an actress to end a career as big and wide-ranging as hers."

"I don't play tough, I am tough. After all I've been through, who wouldn't be?" When the future actor was one year old his father was crushed to death in a railyard accident. **Robert Mitchum** (1917–1997) was so tough a men's deodorant was named after him. "I don't discuss that. They don't send me residuals."

After a string of diverse jobs, Bob Mitchum, as he was initially billed, entered the movies in 1943. "My first year I was slotted into some 20 movies ... I doubt I'd remember any of the titles if I heard them."

To his surprise he was up for an Oscar in a supporting role in *The Story of G.I. Joe* (1945). Mitchum never got an Academy Award, partly because "He has these sleepy eyes and doesn't really seem to act," said Charles Laughton, who directed him in *The Night of the Hunter* (1955). "He inevitably plays a variation of himself ... sometimes himself, which works very well."

Mitchum had a unique face, voice, and walk. "Robert was somebody you had to stare at," recalled Laraine Day, star of *The Locket* (1946). "We all knew on the set he'd soon become a lasting center of attention." Mitchum's supporting role was a painter who, atypically for a Mitchum character, jumps out an office-building window to his death when he's disbelieved about the perfidy of Day's character.

On September 1, 1948, Robert, thirty-one, and a friend, actress Lila Leeds, twenty, were arrested for marijuana possession. "There've been some obscene rumors attached to my name," he told writer Sheridan Morley (son of actor Sir Robert Morley) in 1990. "But the stupidest was I arranged that bust for publicity. . . . Man, in those days publicity like that could kill your career stone-dead." It did kill Lila Leeds's career.

Post-prison, Robert Mitchum resumed acting, excelling in noir thrillers at RKO and later in bigger-budget movies. His film career spanned 1943 to 1997. Blacklisted director Joseph Losey, who helmed *Secret Ceremony* (1968) with Elizabeth Taylor, Mia Farrow, and Mitchum in London, said, "He was proud he didn't have to do a TV series," referring to the many declining movie stars whose series usually drew insufficient ratings. By contrast, a number of minor movie stars like Lucille Ball and Donna Reed or very minor movie comedians like Milton Berle and Jackie Gleason or movie villains like Raymond Burr found big success on the small screen.

Charles Laughton noted, "Robert is not an adept at accents or hiding himself in a role. Yet with only the slightest calibration he is able to play a chilling villain," as in Laughton's *Night of the Hunter* and in *Cape Fear* (1962).

Over the decades, in movies of varying quality the quietly domineering Mitchum was able to play mostly leads and for the most part avoid telefilms. His final role was in a 1997 telefilm, *James Dean: Race with Destiny*. Its title referred to the young star's fatal penchant for car racing; the original title was *James Dean: Live Fast, Die Young*. Casper Van Dien played Dean while Mitchum portrayed George Stevens, the director of *Giant* (1956), Dean's final movie. Mitchum once informed a journalist who inquired if he'd ever wanted to direct, "That would require more interest in any one given film than I've ever been able to muster."

Robert Mitchum's final movie was the Norwegian *Pakten* (1995), shot in English and released in the UK as *The Pact* and the USA as *The Sunset Boys* (perhaps referencing the hit comedy *The Sunshine Boys*), with an "international title" of *Waiting for Sunset*. The top-billed actor costarred with Cliff Robertson and Erland Josephson (of Ingmar Bergman fame). Friends and ex-roommates who met forty-five years ago reunite to grant one man's dying wish to visit Heidelberg, Germany, to see his ex-girlfriend. Once they arrive, townspeople are unwilling to speak about what happened to her.

An unregenerate smoker, Robert Mitchum died at seventy-nine of lung cancer and emphysema.

An actress once asked **Steve McQueen** (1930–1980) why he rode and raced "dangerous motorcycles" despite studio insurers banning such activity during film production. His answer: "To prove I'm still a man."

More than a few male performers—then (Spencer Tracy, Richard Burton) and even now (TV actor David Duchovny)—have equated acting with supposedly compromised masculinity. McQueen was nakedly ambitious yet maintained a deliberate emotional distance from his profession. Robert Wise, who directed him in *The Sand Pebbles* (1966), felt, "He didn't have a terribly wide range but I don't think he felt less than any other given actor. . . . If, as has been said, he felt a lack or shortcoming, I think it had nothing to do with what he did for a living."

Paul Newman's friend and costar Anthony Perkins, discussing the Newman-McQueen rivalry, wondered if Steve's surname wasn't a thorn in his side. Perkins may not have known McQueen's given first name, Terrence. In any case, the actor billed as Steven McQueen in his first four pictures, including *The Blob* (1958), spent part of his youth in reform school and was unfocused until his mid-twenties, when he chose acting. Much of its appeal was the prospect of big bucks.

Home life for the teenaged Terrence had been complicated by a stepfather with whom he didn't get along, sometimes coming to blows. The youth's alcoholic mother sent him to live with his grandparents. When Terrence left home he fell in with bad companions, including petty criminals. The teen was sent back home, but his stepfather convinced his mother to send the under-aged "problem son" to a reform school.

McQueen finally debuted in 1956 in a minimal role in the boxing picture *Somebody Up There Likes Me*, starring Paul Newman, who inherited the proj-ect from the late James Dean. Steve publicly stated that he wasn't unhappy about Dean's demise, as it provided him more opportunities. But another small part drove McQueen to television, where he starred in the western *Wanted: Dead or Alive* (1958–1961). He admitted his favorite parts of the show were his salary, his billing, and using his left hand to fire his sawed-off shotgun. The actor alternated his series with movies, and from his third film on Steve played leads. In future years his agent was instructed to automati-cally turn down TV offers.

McQueen was a leading 1960s box-office attraction. Fans enjoyed his laconic and reliably repetitive image. Unlike Newman, he took few risks with his screen persona and genres. Writer Doug McClelland cited Paul New-man's humor and contrasted his smile with "McQueen's troubled half-smiles . . . McQueen doesn't give much to the camera."

The Sand Pebbles, set in Taiwan in the 1920s, was a major and rare flop. A British biographer later described the star's penchant for "roles of lean, confident, sometimes even psychopathic masculinity, from 1963 through to 1972. After that, he seemed to press the self-destruct button on his career."

McQueen's box office had diminished by 1972 when he costarred in *The Getaway* with Ali MacGraw, whom he wed in 1973. He'd been married to actress Neile Adams from 1955 to 1971. At least one insider felt Neile McQueen, whom Steve had asked to relinquish her career, was the stabilizing influence whose exit from his life left emotional scars. McQueen pressured MacGraw into something approaching seclusion, and, as with wife number one, he preferred her to cease acting—she returned to the screen in 1978 after the inevitable divorce.

As the press had minimal access to the two-star pair, rumors abounded about his turning into a hippie and/or drug addict or alcoholic, or becoming paranoid or ultra-religious or planning to quit acting.

But after costarring with Dustin Hoffman in *Papillon* (1973), the disappointing—to readers—screen version of the international nonfiction bestseller, McQueen teamed with archrival Paul Newman (via "equal bill-ing") in *The Towering Inferno* (1974), produced by Irwin Allen, the "master of disaster" flicks. The stellar duo shared few scenes and no visible ani-mosity. Columnists had expected, even hoped for, possible fisticuffs. There were none. One scribe credited the lack of testosterone-fueled aggression to "laid-back, ever professional Paul Newman."

Post-*Inferno* Steve avoided acting for an unprecedented three years. Reports of occasionally erratic behavior were later ascribed to possible health problems he kept to himself. His bushy beard and "homeless look" prompted fevered speculation. McQueen returned to the screen in 1977 in a commendable but surprising and surprisingly uncommercial choice of vehicle. *An Enemy of the People* was adapted from Norwegian Henrik Ibsen's nineteenth-century play about a progressive citizen whose bravery and integrity cause him to be shunned by his townspeople due to the maneuvering of the town's monied interests.

Another few years off, and McQueen returned in two more typical vehicles, including his swan song. *Tom Horn* (1980) was about "the legendary western scout and outlaw who helped capture Geronimo" and *The Hunter* (1980) was a "crime thriller" in which Steve played a bounty hunter. Unaware of McQueen's health situation, columnist Jim Bacon wondered if these might be the unpredictable actor's final offerings for years to come

"He's hinted that he is sick of acting . . . but then he comes back and acts some more. Surely not for the money. Maybe he has to psych himself up to make the show go on."

Steve McQueen died at fifty from a heart attack following surgery for mesothelioma, a cancer of the chest.

DUKE: JOHN WAYNE

Born Marion Morrison, **John Wayne** (1907–1979) was a football player before he became a cowboy actor. His nickname, Duke, was the name of his dog. He served a long apprenticeship in low-budget westerns and was even a singing cowboy until *Stagecoach* (1939) and his association with director John Ford.

The budgets got bigger and Wayne branched out of the Old West. He became famous as a loner and man of action, too often as a belligerent foe of Native Americans and assorted foreigners. In war pictures he always won. In reality he never served, taking more than one military deferment, starting with his status as a working father—so were numerous movie stars who did serve.

With the years Wayne became controversial, especially during the McCarthy witch-hunt era. Late in life he admitted he'd made mistakes and that people in Hollywood shouldn't have been deprived of their livelihoods because of political differences. When the Panama Canal was ceded to Panama and Wayne voiced approval, he received hate mail from people more right-wing than he.

Lauren Bacall, who with husband Humphrey Bogart was among the first to denounce the political witch hunts, twice costarred with Wayne and got along fine with him. "You have to remember that he came from nothing," she explained. "Such people were often afraid of any political theory they imagined would take away their wealth. . . . It was known his drinking buddies weren't a very educated or fair-minded lot . . . [they] may have been a negative influence."

Wayne also gained critics with ignorant public comments against women's rights, civil rights, and gay rights. He strongly backed the war in Vietnam. "Let him go fight, then," said British costar Laurence Harvey. "He'll find it's not as easy off the screen, and it involves genuine blood and real lives."

When Wayne directed *The Alamo* (1960) and co-directed the Vietnam-themed *The Green Berets* (1968), he made very free with historical facts and was particularly criticized for the former by reviewers and Mexican Americans. But the most ongoing criticism was for his frequent role as what Marlon Brando called the biggest Indian-killer of the silver screen.

When Brando won a second Oscar for *The Godfather* (1972), his award was declined on his behalf by Sacheen Littlefeather, who inveighed against Hollywood depictions of Native Americans as violent barbarians that perpetuated the old line "the only good Injun is a dead Injun." At the award ceremonies' close John Wayne was brought on or charged on, clearly upset.

Surprisingly, the actor—who against Richard Burton and other talents won an Oscar for *True Grit* (1969)—once voiced a wish to appear in a Noel Coward play. Presumably a filmed Coward play, as Wayne didn't have theatrical training. But he knew producers would never cast him in a sophisticated light.

After Wayne costarred with Rock Hudson in *The Undefeated* (1969), set during the Civil War, the younger actor revealed, "I didn't know what to expect. I was nervous, maybe a little intimidated. But I think he was a little intimidated by me . . . he knew several of my movies.

"You know, out of his boots he wasn't quite as tall as I expected."

Robert Mitchum commented that Wayne used lifts in his boots, his shoes, his car, and his boat. "Don't get me wrong. I like the guy, even if he is a bit of a fraud. . . . That tight way he walks? His dresser told me the Duke sometimes wears a corset to hold it in and hold him up when he struts. Don't you love the movies?"

Capucine, Wayne's leading lady in *North to Alaska* (1960), stated, "I compared notes with an actress who worked with him and had a similar experience about a women's tennis match on TV. He was loud, cheering the American and cursing the non-American. [The actress] said to me there isn't much distance from being non-American to 'un-American,' the phrase the witch hunters used as a weapon.

"The point is, instead of a positive patriotism or enjoying a game, it was fanaticism—being against people different from oneself."

John Wayne never gave up westerns, acknowledging, "It's a formula with only so many variations. But it's sure worked for me. . . . I'm comfortable riding horses. I like them—they do what you want them to and don't answer back."

Wayne's swan song *The Shootist* (1976) was strikingly apt. The western screen hero, diagnosed with cancer in real life, played a western hero dying of cancer (while lodging with Lauren Bacall). Many fans deemed it his best performance. The film's emotional high point features James Stewart as Dr. Hostetler sadly and delicately informing John Wayne's character John Bernard Books that he has inoperable cancer. Within three years Wayne would succumb to what he called the big C.

Contributing to the star's demise may have been his unlikely role as Genghis Khan in *The Conqueror* (1956), shot in the Utah desert at Snow Canyon. Producer Howard Hughes may or may not have known that much of the dust from the US government's eleven atomic bomb tests in 1953 in Yucca Flat, Nevada, 137 miles away, had settled in Snow Canyon. Two hundred twenty cast and crew members were exposed to the radioactive dust on location and also back in Hollywood, where Hughes shipped sixty tons of the contaminated dirt for retakes.

Ironic, because John Wayne automatically supported most anything the US government did.

Of the 220 people, ninety-one developed cancer—a figure three times greater than a normal sampling. An uncounted number of Native Americans at the nearby Shivwit reservation sickened and died from the fallout. Director Dick Powell died at fifty-eight of stomach cancer, John Wayne at seventy-two of lung cancer, leading lady Susan Hayward at fifty-eight of brain tumors, Agnes Moorehead at seventy-three of lung cancer, and after Mexican actor Pedro Armendariz, fifty-one, found out he had kidney cancer, he committed suicide.

AGELESS: MAE WEST

"Yes . . . well, yes. I was Mae West's final leading man. . . . An unusual picture, to say the least."

Timothy Dalton, best known as the fourth James Bond, doesn't dwell on his role as the lusty bridegroom of "international superstar Marlo Manners," enacted by **Mae West** in her jaw-dropping swan song *Sextette* (1978), set in a London hotel during their honeymoon. Why? Mae was fifty-three years his senior.

Mae West (1892 or 1893–1980) began and ended her movie career as a sex symbol, albeit in her mid-eighties.

No other actress could have gotten away with it. Among stellar egos, Mae's ranked at the top. She was incandescent with self-belief. One critic described her manhunting persona thus: "She sidles along like a predatory costumed lobster casting her eyes and antennae over the men most likely to."

A legend in her own time as well as her own mind, she made many fallacious claims—including authorship of nearly all her films—and would only compare herself as a movie institution to Charlie Chaplin and as an alleged beauty to Marilyn Monroe. After Monroe married Joe DiMaggio, Mae asked the audiences of her nightclub act, "Why marry a ball player when you can have the whole team?", referring to her adoring lineup of musclemen.

Born in Brooklyn and a child performer, Mae West toured the country in vaudeville before grabbing national notoriety in the 1920s via her prostitution-themed play with the scandalous title *Sex*. It landed her in jail. Her hit play *Diamond Lil* was less offensive to stage censors, but her blatantly sexual image and material long kept Mae out of Hollywood.

West made her screen debut at a more advanced age than most movie stars. In 1932 Paramount defied the censors and cast the then-forty-ish West in *Night After Night* as an ex-girlfriend of George Raft, a hood trying to go straight and enter Society. Barely suppressing contempt for the industry that had shunned her, Mae apprised the press upon her arrival in the film capital,

"I'm not a little girl from a little town making good in a big town. I'm a big girl from a big town making good in a little town."

In her supporting role West made audiences howl when she parks her wrap with a hatcheck girl who remarks, "Goodness, what beautiful diamonds!" and Mae replies, "Goodness had nothing to do with it, dearie." Raft recalled, "Mae West stole everything but the cameras."

The Great Depression was on, losing the studios money, so Paramount opted to film *Diamond Lil.* But since that title was banned by film censors the vehicle was renamed *She Done Him Wrong* (1933) and the character relabeled Lady Lou. Set during the nostalgic—to '30s audiences—Gay Nineties, the picture showcased Mae West walking her soon-to-be-much-imitated walk, talking in her adenoidal twang, strutting, singing, and sashaying in period costumes and picture hats.

Something entirely different, with a star unlike any other, *She Done Him Wrong* was a huge hit. It made a national catchphrase of "Come up and see me some time" (not exactly what Mae said on screen). Audiences demanded more Mae, and Paramount obliged with another huge 1933 hit, *I'm No Angel.* The two pictures may or may not have "saved Paramount," as is sometimes claimed.

However, the patriarchy's censors and "moral" guardians were incensed. Publisher William Randolph Hearst branded West "a monster of lubricity" even though he was married and had a mistress. Some said the ultra-right-winger (during World War II he favored Germany over Britain) was upset that the second-highest paid person in the United States after him was a woman—West.

Religious groups and prudish women's clubs agitated against Mae West. Mary Pickford complained that her "oh-so-carefully brought-up" niece had heard Mae West's racy song "Easy Rider" (about a jockey) in *She Done Him Wrong.* Platinum blonde Jean Harlow's vampy-trampy roles in hit MGM pictures also engendered nationwide complaints. Naturally, it was the complainants who were heard and emphasized, not the masses who made superstars of West and Harlow.

The studios, fearing federal censorship, strengthened local censors' power. The "self-censorship" involved studios submitting their scripts, pre-filming, to the Production Code Administration, whose seal of approval was required for any motion picture to be released to US cinemas. The rigid and bigoted censorship system endured from July 1934 until 1968. "Sin" of any kind, if shown, had to be punished and of course there was a double standard against women and minorities.

Mae West's next film for Paramount, *It Ain't No Sin*, was retitled *Belle of the Nineties* (1934). To diminishing box-office returns, she did another four for the studio, which then let her go. By 1940 she was reduced to working at second-tier Universal and sharing the screen with another star, W. C. Fields, in the delightful comedy *My Little Chickadee*, not a success at the time.

She returned in 1943, again for a second-tier studio, Columbia, in a flimsy vehicle and outright flop titled *The Heat's On* (later renamed *Tropicana*). Thereafter Mae was offscreen until 1970 and her late seventies. She filled in the decades with theatre, starring in *Catherine Was Great* and revivals of *Diamond Lil* as well as minor plays showcasing her as an agelessly irresistible woman of the world. In the '50s she pioneered and toured in a nightclub act featuring beefcake in the muscular persons of bodybuilders. In the '60s camp was "in," Mae's movies were rediscovered, and she recorded various music albums. Discussing camp, West arrogated it to herself: "Camp is the kinda comedy where they imitate me."

During shooting of *Myra Breckinridge* (1970) at 20th Century-Fox, West threw a minor tantrum in front of reporters when one mentioned she'd been put in Barbra Streisand's dressing room from *Hello, Dolly!* She shrilled, "I'd like to see someone break records like me, and then I'll respect them as a star. Till someone can do that, I feel I'm in a class by myself. . . . So don't say they put me in someone else's room!"

Myra was the almost universally reviled film of Gore Vidal's bestselling transsexual-themed novel. *Time* unfairly called it "about as funny as a child molester" and it was unfairly rated X despite almost no foul language and nearly no nudity—after Farrah Fawcett became famous, her topless scene in bed with Raquel Welch as Myra was trimmed from videocassettes.

Though Mae was a supporting character—randy talent agent Leticia Van Allen—she received top billing. Although she looked incredible for her age, she was typically described as looking "like something you discover in a pyramid." Once again, the patriarchy was riled by West relating to younger men the way many men relate to younger women. She and Raquel's Myra (a former male; gay film critic Rex Reed played Myron) treated men, or "boys," as sex objects. Today the comedic film seems harmless and couldn't elicit an R rating.

To Mae, *Myra* had been a personal triumph and she was ready to make a bigger, more dominant comeback in *Sextette* (1978), adapted from a play she'd written decades earlier. "I had so much fan mail about doing another picture, I felt I had to." *Sextette* was camp with a capital K. Its all-star, all-male supporting cast included Timothy Dalton, Dom DeLuise, Tony Curtis, Walter Pidgeon, George Hamilton, Ringo Starr, George Raft, Alice Cooper, Keith Moon, and Regis Philbin.

Playing a six-times married legend, West looked remarkable for her age but walked and talked with less fluidity than in 1970. Her musical performances at times seemed forced, at times amusing. In some scenes her false eyelashes were bigger than her eyes. Her skin looked more waxen than before but remained unlined. Mae's short-term memory came and went, so during shooting her lines were sometimes fed to her through a shortwave radio transmitter concealed in her wig. The media found out and revealed that one day a radio traffic report broke through into her transmitter and on-set Mae was heard to repeat, "Traffic is bogged down on the Santa Monica Freeway. Use of alternate routes is suggested."

Except for fully clothed bedroom suggestions and Westian double-entendres, *Sextette* might have been rated G. Some of Mae's lines were more insinuating than others, which disconcerted some viewers, e.g., "I'm the girl who works at Paramount all day and Fox all night." In one gym-room scene she asks a perky athlete one-fourth her age, "What do you do, dear?"

He answers, "I'm a pole vaulter."

"Ooh, aren't we all?"

Sextette didn't deserve its condescendingly cruel or even vicious reviews (which Mae reportedly was kept from reading). For instance Vincent Canby's in the *New York Times*: "A disorienting freak show . . . a terrifying reminder of how a virtually disembodied ego can survive total physical decay and loss of common sense."

The movie was campy fun, a colorful tribute to Mae West's ego and her rock-solid self-esteem. She began her screen career as a one-time-only supporting character but ended it as what she would no doubt have considered an ageless goddess.

ROBIN WILLIAMS

"I don't always like to work . . . as in the work I sometimes have to do. Or choose. You know? But I don't like not working—makes me a little nervous."

When the high-pressure, manically active **Robin Williams** ended his life at sixty-three, he was working as hard as ever, on a TV series and with three or four (depending on the source) completed films yet to be released and more planned. Asked why he worked so hard, the primarily comic actor (1951–2014) would spew out assorted answers:

"To support my kids and ex wives."

"So my wife will hang around but have quality time without me."

"To create an awesomely impressive filmography. Yes!"

"Idle hands, you know . . . the devil's workshop. Non-union."

"I like to avoid terminal boredom."

"This time, to show my dramatic side—both of 'em."

Actor-comedian Dick Martin, whose comedy-variety TV series *Rowan & Martin's Laugh-In* gave Robin his first big break, said, "I knew several Robin Williams. All were very eager to please, to make you smile.

"Robin is a born performer. He's always on. To the point, you wonder if he's ever 'off' . . . only when he's alone? Maybe?"

Williams occasionally referenced the laugh-clown-laugh syndrome of a comedian hiding unhappiness behind a jovial mask. After his death some colleagues explained that he'd been gratified by his success, only wishing that its height had lasted longer. Rather, he usually hid his anxieties about being liked, staying popular, pleasing family and close friends and, toward the end, about his health.

A *People* magazine editor revealed, "Mr. Williams was nervous and threatened to sue if his [having] herpes were made public. He said he couldn't tolerate becoming a pariah. . . . What impressed me was the lack of vanity about his photographs. His preference was for zany or funny shots where he didn't seem to be trying to be funny—he told me that."

A well-known actress who costarred with Robin said he was "very likeable and unspoiled" but "used humor as a barrier. He was so entertaining and inventive, but as soon as you started moving in, emotionally—I do not mean sexually—he'd be right into some new shtick, diverting you with laughter."

Like most actors, Williams enjoyed trying on a wide range of characters, from Popeye "the sailor man" and Peter Pan to Mrs. Doubtfire, Theodore Roosevelt, and TV's Mork from the planet Ork, in films as diverse as *Good Will Hunting* (a supporting Oscar), *The World According to Garp*, *The Fisher King*, *One-Hour Photo*, *Boulevard*, three *Night at the Museum* installments, and *Good Morning, Vietnam*.

Robin's makeup artist Cheri Minns explained, "It's like he didn't worry about anything when he worked all the time. Work was the true love of his life. Above his children, above everything. If he wasn't working he was a shell of himself. And when he worked it was like a light bulb was turned on."

Because Robin was likeable, ingratiating, even childlike, his competitiveness was seldom on general view. Fellow comedians, however, might experience it. Hispanic comedian Frank Maya recalled, "When I met him he was very supportive . . . gave me advice and sincerely, I think, wished me well.

"So it surprised me when briefly I talked about a few comedy stars, a few big names . . . I still remember his expression when I mentioned Seinfeld. . . . It was almost like I shouldn't dwell on a rival comedian. Yet I still liked him. He was competitive but not the kind that wants everyone else to fail."

A lesbian comedian remarked that Williams was "very friendly and respectful" and appreciated her humor, "which people don't always get." Later, she wondered if his ease and friendliness weren't due in part to "my not being a direct threat—being female, lesbian, almost unknown?"

With time the star's commercial status naturally diminished and he worked in "smaller" films and increasingly took smaller roles. He told the *Los Angeles Times*, "I love when I'm [a movie's] focal point, but you get older and sometimes have to be a satellite . . . perhaps an uncle kind of character."

He felt comic actors were at a disadvantage because "comedy is harder to write successfully. . . . It's not hard to rig up a dramatic situation and throw in a ton of conflict. Getting people to laugh is harder than making them feel sorry for someone. Good comedy needs a good plot. . . . Jokes aren't enough. You want comedy that comes out of situations and characters, not ha-ha funny lines."

Associates said one reason Robin did so many projects was a desire to have another hit, preferably a starring one. The more films, the more

The public was shocked as well as saddened by the 2014 suicide by hanging of brilliant stand-up comedian and movie star Robin Williams, sixty-three. His manic comic façade hid insecurity, desperation, and a workaholic ethic to which time added mounting mental and physical afflictions.

chances of a popular one. Eventually he began experiencing memory loss, paranoia, and occasional delusions. At one point he imagined his friend and fellow comic Mort Sahl was in grave danger. He kept telling third wife Susan he had to drive from their house in Tiburon, near San Francisco, to Mill Valley to Mort's apartment to make sure Sahl was safe. Susan kept talking Robin out of it, then he would start up again, until finally both fell asleep from exhaustion.

"Robin was losing his mind and he was aware of it," she admitted.

Yet he refused friends' and family members' advice to take time off from work. His children pleaded with him, but Dad wasn't that close. One biographer noted they had to "navigate past layer after layer of other people who also had access to him and wanted his attention—Susan, his assistant Rebecca, his managers. . . ."

Williams was taking supervised antipsychotic medications, but new prescriptions might improve one symptom while worsening another. On location in Vancouver he had a panic attack. Cheri Minns suggested he might feel better after slipping into a local comedy club and performing, to lift his spirits and remind him audiences still loved him. He broke down and cried. "I can't, Cheri. I don't know how anymore. I don't know how to be funny."

In May 2014 Robin Williams's situation was finally diagnosed: he had Parkinson's disease, "a degenerative disorder that attacks the central nervous system, impairing motor functions and cognition, eventually leading to death." Doctors told him that once they found the correct medication he could experience "another good ten years." Robin was unconvinced. (It was discovered posthumously that he was suffering from Lewy body dementia. Parkinson's disease in itself, without the associated dementia, does not cause the psychiatric problems he experienced.)

His focus was on the fact that with less and less memory, mobility, and general ability he would soon no longer be "Robin Williams."

Ironically, the brilliant comedian once enthused, "So much of show business is looks-oriented and when the looks go, so do the fans. But comedians, we can be funny till we drop."

For much of the public that didn't know the deed's medical background, Robin's 2014 suicide (hanging himself with a belt at his home) confirmed the stereotype of the tragic or angry (like Jerry Lewis) or maladjusted comedian. But several friends and associates stressed that until the illness's onset and complications from myriad medications, Robin was generally happy. Driven, yes, compelled to perform, perhaps needing to be the funniest, but delighted by his work. Or the fact of working.

No one denied that he worked too hard. After his death Williams was seen on the big screen in *Night at the Museum 3* and *Merry Friggin' Christmas*, and his voice was heard in a UK sci-fi comedy titled *Absolutely Anything* that opened in Britain in 2015 but not in the USA till 2017.

Comedian Marty Ingels asserted, "Those of us with a fraction of his gifts were envious. . . . His last big role was in a movie called *Boulevard*. I don't think it was Robin's first gay character, but he deserved at minimum a posthumous Oscar nomination. This was the grayest, most unflamboyant character, a downtrodden man resigned to a life of sheer boredom . . . and Robin was the most flamboyant straight guy ever. In this film it's him physically but the personality is totally someone else. Brilliant."

With the average star the final role tells something, a little or a lot, about that individual. In Robin Williams's case it wasn't any given role, it was the sheer amount and rate, the very necessity of work.

RUMORSTORM: NATALIE WOOD

Natalie Wood (1938–1981), born Natasha Gurdin, was the successful product of a fierce stage mother who supposedly replied, when the teenager told her a director had raped her, to keep quiet since he was giving Natalie a *lead*.

Marie Gurdin had a daughter named Olga by her first husband, who later left Russia for the United States. Two years after, Marie (also known as Maria) followed, only to find him living with another woman: end of marriage. Second husband Nikolai was said to look up to Marie and was rarely out of her sight. The couple had two daughters, Natasha and Lana (for Svetlana).

Natasha had large, expressive brown eyes. Though living in Northern California, Marie was determined to get her into movies. When a movie company went up to Santa Rosa and put out a call for extras, Marie and five-year-old Natasha were among the first to arrive. Olga, thirteen, would have loved to be an extra but was in school, where Marie intended her to stay. Olga went on to study drama, but in show business the breaks sometimes happen to those not seeking them.

The director of *Happy Land* (1943) was Irving Pichel. In 1945 Natasha did a screen test for him—no go. Marie talked him into a second one that did the trick. She moved the family to Los Angeles, where she arranged a job for Nikolai as a studio carpenter, and "Natalie Wood" made her official screen bow in *Tomorrow Is Forever* (1945) starring Claudette Colbert and Orson Welles.

Child stardom followed, including the holiday classic *Miracle on 34th Street* (1947) and a turn as Bette Davis's daughter in *The Star* (1952), wherein Davis took the girl's side when she pleaded with the director not to do a scene involving her jumping into the water. Natalie was afraid of drowning. Teen stardom was about to carry over into adult stardom when Wood costarred with James Dean and Sal Mineo in *Rebel Without a Cause* (1955), directed by Nicholas Ray, who apparently had an affair with the underaged actress.

The 1960s were Natalie's prime acting years with films like *Splendor in the Grass*, *West Side Story*, *Gypsy*, *Love with the Proper Stranger*, *Sex and the Single Girl*, *Inside Daisy Clover*, *This Property Is Condemned*, and *Bob and Carol and Ted and Alice*. The latter was Wood's last hit movie. In 1966 after co-producing her own unsuccessful vehicle *Penelope*, Natalie attempted suicide.

Meanwhile eight-years-younger Lana was half-heartedly pursuing a screen career, encouraged by Marie, who hoped to have, like Lilian Fontaine, two movie-star daughters (Olivia de Havilland and Joan Fontaine). But Lana had minimal luck, as with most aspiring younger sisters of female stars. Lana Wood is best known for the small but well-endowed role of Plenty O'Toole in the 1971 James Bond *Diamonds Are Forever* in which she greets Sean Connery, "Hi, I'm Plenty." He ogles her and assures her that she is. Oddly, the Hollywood rumor mill had created whispers that Lana was the illegitimate daughter of Olga.

Natalie Wood married and divorced Robert Wagner, then married an Englishman and had a daughter (Wagner had a daughter with his second wife), then Wood and Wagner remarried in 1972 and had a daughter together (sounds like a TV sitcom). Focusing on motherhood, Natalie worked less during the '70s. By decade's end her movie career had mostly turned to TV work, but she won a Golden Globe for the 1979 miniseries remake of *From Here to Eternity*.

Wagner remained a TV star with the series *Hart to Hart*, which he and Wood co-owned. Reportedly, the pair's biggest source of income was via their healthy slice of the TV megahit *Charlie's Angels*. Natalie and "R. J." often spent time on their fifty-five-foot yacht the *Splendour* [*sic*]. At Thanksgiving time in 1981, Lana, who was fond of "boats, fishing and diving," was not invited to join the three-person party aboard the *Splendour* at Catalina Island. The lone guest was Wood's costar in the then-filming sci-fi movie *Brainstorm* (1983), Christopher Walken.

Natalie kept her sister at arm's length, only partly because R. J. and Lana didn't get along. The intricate mechanics of the sisters' relationship are detailed in the chapter "The Princess and the Plebe" in this author's *Celebrity Feuds!* Lana Wood later stated that her sister might still be alive had Lana gone aboard with her.

On Saturday, November 28, at a Catalina restaurant Wood, Wagner, and Walken were seen and heard by staff and guests to be drinking copiously and at times arguing loudly. That night, back on the *Splendour*, the drinking and loud talk or quarreling continued. Close to midnight Natalie left the two men alone, presumably to get ready for bed. Some thirty minutes later Dennis Davern, the boat's captain, noticed the dinghy was missing.

On Sunday at 7:44 a.m. a police and Coast Guard search ended when Natalie Wood's body was found floating facedown, wearing a nightgown, socks, and a waterlogged down jacket, some two hundred yards away from the dinghy.

It was theorized that Wood, trying to untie the dinghy, slipped, hit her head, fell in the water and drowned. But why would she untie the dinghy? Going back to shore alone and at night and with her fear of being overwhelmed by water, made no sense. Besides, virtually everything ashore would be closed at that hour.

Another mystery is that a woman on a boat anchored about one hundred yards from the *Splendour* heard a woman yelling for help around midnight. The woman was dissuaded from seeking help when a male voice called out that he would come and get her (Natalie). Whose male voice was it?

The tabloid press speculated over and over that Natalie was flirting with or having an affair with her costar and that her husband was jealous. No other possibility between two of the trio was printed. Persistent rumors about either man didn't see print—not about ex–chorus boy Walken (one casting-director wife, no children) nor Wagner, who had myriad bisexual and gay actor friends. (Post-acting, Lana Wood sought a producing position on *Hart to Hart* but it went instead to gay secretary Mart Crowley, who penned the play *The Boys in the Band*.)

After Natalie's death her widower and sister cut relations and in 2004 Lana produced a TV biopic, *The Mystery of Natalie Wood*. Lana Wood has aired her suspicions about Wagner's involvement several times. A petition with several hundred signatures protesting the death's hasty and flawed police investigation led to a reopening of the case in 2011. Captain Davern came forward with allegations involving Robert Wagner, whose version of events changed over the years. Either way, "His version of events just didn't add up," according to Lieutenant John Corina of the Los Angeles County Sheriff's Department, and Detective Ralph Hernandez of the L.A.C.S.D. revealed that the corpse "looked like the victim of an assault."

Most shocking—but consider the source, for truth and tabloids are distant cousins—was a 2018 front-page banner headline: "Robert Wagner Killed Natalie Wood!" Whatever really happened, the death almost certainly wasn't intentional. Interestingly, an earlier suicide attempt by Wood went almost unnoticed in the tabloids. In any case the tragic result was the same.

MURDER-SUICIDE: GIG YOUNG AND PHIL HARTMAN

Murder-suicide where the husband kills his wife and then himself isn't common, but is less common in Hollywood (police often deem it a more working-class crime). Rarer is a case in which the wife is the killer, as with Phil Hartman.

Friends of Oscar-winner Gig Young insisted he didn't do it, that it was a frame-up. As it happens, Young was a friend of George "Superman" Reeves, whose supposed suicide turned out to be almost certainly murder.

Born Byron Barr (1913–1978), **Gig Young** was renamed after his character in *The Gay Sisters* (1942) starring Barbara Stanwyck. He was billed as Gig Young starting with *Old Acquaintance* (1943) starring Bette Davis.

"I heard Cary Grant got his first name from a character he'd played," enthused Young. "Naturally I was interested enough, when we worked together [in *That Touch of Mink*, 1962, with Doris Day], to ask him about it after I explained about my names. But Mr. Grant said, or reacted as if, he didn't remember."

Charming, good-looking, and a frequent smiler—smiles aren't a male-lead prerequisite—Young was typically cast as a second lead, the guy who doesn't get the girl. He was well liked by peers. Costar Jane Greer said, "Gig wasn't one of those dissatisfied actors.... He had no pretensions ... I did hear later that he hoped to prove himself in drama, but don't we all?"

By the late 1960s the actor had to descend a professional rung by doing a TV movie. He noted, "There are fewer female stars now for us actors to compete over on the screen." But in 1969 he played Rocky, the hard-bitten, devious entrepreneur emcee of the 1930s dance marathon that anchors *They Shoot*

Horses, Don't They? Jane Fonda and Michael Sarrazin starred, and Young won the Academy Award for Best Supporting Actor (his third nomination).

It was said in real life Gig "didn't get the girl" either. He married five times. Marriage number one ended in divorce. Wife number two died. Wife number three was twenty-years-younger Elizabeth Montgomery of *Bewitched* fame. Their seven-year marriage ended unamicably in 1963. Marriage number four ended in divorce and Young suing his wife over paternity of his only child, a daughter. Marriage number five reportedly went bad after three weeks.

Young's final wife was thirty-three years his junior. He met Kim Schmidt on the set of *Game of Death* starring Bruce Lee (the film was released in 1978) in 1973. A friend of Gig later stated, "She was sort of a mystery. With a past . . . and a not-great present. An actress . . . I'm not sure if she'd acted in Germany. . . . I heard some of her friends were hoodlums, not sure if that was a figure of speech.

"The three people I knew who knew Kim didn't like her. . . . I imagine she married Gig for his money or connections. Or both."

Friends said Young's and Schmidt's relationship was tempestuous, but they married anyway. Once married, his will became a bone of contention. The actor was leaving half his $200,000 estate to Kim but she wanted 100 percent.

At noon on October 19, 1978, Kim placed a phone order for groceries. She'd already phoned the doorman to ask about the weather; it was later speculated that she was expecting company that afternoon. Between 2:30 and 3:30 p.m. the Manhattan building's manager thought he heard two gunshots. He eventually located the source of the noise.

When police arrived they found the couple dead in their bedroom. The wife was on her back, a bullet having entered through her skull. The husband was facedown on the carpet, his hand around a .38-caliber snub-nosed Smith & Wesson pistol. A bullet had entered through his mouth.

Friends of Gig Young insisted that even if he were capable of suicide—some admitted he'd been drinking to excess—he wasn't capable of murder. Most insisted it was a setup, a double murder. A few said he didn't even own a gun. The case has not been definitively solved.

Interestingly, Gig Young and George Reeves, best known as TV's Superman, were friends. They'd been signed to Warner Bros. at the same time. When Reeves was found shot dead in his home, the authorities were quick to label it suicide. Subsequent facts indicate it was almost certainly murder, as Gig Young declared to mutual friends. Oscar-winner Red Buttons, who costarred in *They Shoot Horses*, told columnist Lee Graham, "We once discussed how often a murder is fixed to look like suicide, in real life and I guess even more in novels. Gig said there must be some cases where a suicide is made to look like murder. That, I couldn't figure out so we changed the subject."

In the 1980s the multitalented **Phil Hartman** (1948–1998) honed his comedic skills with the Los Angeles–based comedy troupe The Groundlings. There, he also polished his writing, working with Paul Reubens (aka Pee-wee Herman) as a writer and costar, including on the TV show *Pee-wee's Playhouse*.

"With Paul there was only room for one star," Phil later said. "It sounds presumptuous but I didn't want to keep hiding my bushel under his light, bright though he was. . . . I did hope to try some less limited roles."

Before acting, Hartman was a graphic designer and created the logo for the band Crosby, Stills and Nash. "I don't have to be the big cheese, but I do like to feel my creative juices flowing."

Hartman became famous thanks to eight seasons on *Saturday Night Live*. He wasn't the most bombastic or the most original cast member, but he also wasn't headed for hell in a drug basket and his type was such that even minus comedy he had leading man potential. Besides visuals and writing, he enjoyed voice work. He voiced Lionel Hutz and Troy McClure on *The Simpsons*. He also won a 1988 Emmy for Outstanding Writing for *SNL*.

Phil starred in the TV sitcom *NewsRadio* and the features *Three Amigos!* (1986), *Coneheads* (1993), *So I Married an Axe Murderer* (1993), *Sgt. Bilko* (1996), and *Jingle All the Way* (1996). "One of the things I'd ideally like to do is write, direct and star while my body's still good in a beach-and-surfing movie. I love beaches, I love surfing . . . it could be a cheesy beach-blanket-bingo type movie but with good writing, good music and no love handles I'd be really thrilled."

A modest and private man, Phil Hartman was married three times. Third wife Brynn, with whom he had two children, was known for public outbursts that distressed Phil. "He put up with her because he blamed the addictions, not her behavior," offered an associate in 1998. "On his money Brynn was able to indulge her [cocaine] and alcohol addictions." She was also on antidepressant medication but resisted all suggestions to attend a rehab clinic.

Phil Hartman began as a writer, then gained stardom on *Saturday Night Live*, and in movies and the sitcom *NewsRadio*. His third wife Brynn, addicted to cocaine and alcohol, was prone to public outbursts. An embarrassed Hartman defended her, stating she was a good mother. Until 1998, when Brynn Hartman shot Phil dead and then herself, thus orphaning their two small children.

Their arguments got louder and more bitter. Friends of the pair recommended couples counseling. Some friends of his recommended divorce. Referring to his wife's behavior, Hartman publicly declared that above all Brynn was a good mother. Yet she would soon make orphans of Sean, nine, and Birgen, six. It was later speculated that Hartman, increasingly fed up with his wife's habitual outbursts, had lately threatened to once and for all leave her.

The first deed occurred one night after a long alcohol session at a female friend's home. Brynn returned to the family house that Phil nicknamed The Ponderosa. While Phil slept she shot him in the head several times. She left the children behind and hurried out of the house.

Some time later, extremely agitated, she returned to the house with a friend, got hold of another gun, locked herself in the bedroom with her husband's corpse, then killed herself with a single shot to her head.